# Praise for
## *The Social Business Imperative*

"Whether you're a global brand, small local business, or individual who wants to turn your passion into a livelihood, this book simply and clearly articulates how to channel the power of social media to delight audiences and grow your business."

—Marne Levine, COO, Instagram

"Clara literally 'wrote the book' on social media with her first book, *The Facebook Era*. In this follow-up, she gives us a practical guide on how to drive social, mobile, and digital platforms to transform and elevate the customer and employee experience. This is a must-read for any business leader who wants to thrive in this time of disruptive change."

—Chip Bergh, President and CEO, Levi Strauss & Co.

"The combination of social media expansion and increasingly powerful data analysis capabilities is creating unmatched opportunities to fundamentally reorganize our businesses and ultimately better serve our customers. Clara Shih helps us understand how and why. This book is a milestone for all of those who want to successfully transform their traditional companies into a powerful and more customer-friendly social business—a business of the 21st century!"

—Henri de Castries, Chairman and CEO, AXA

"A book worth reading, a voice worth listening to, from a leader of real consequence. A clarion call on the promise and potential of social channels to transform business."

—Walter Robb, Co-CEO, Whole Foods Market

"Every company today must think of itself as a technology company and become customer-obsessed. *The Social Business Imperative* elegantly, succinctly, and powerfully describes why, how, and what to do."

—Kristin Lemkau, Chief Marketing Officer, JPMorgan Chase & Co.

"When it comes to mapping the brave new terrain of social technologies, Clara is miles ahead of the curve. *The Social Business Imperative* serves up a detailed and flexible plan of attack that will prove invaluable to forward-thinkers everywhere."

—Neil Blumenthal, Co-Founder and Co-CEO, Warby Parker

"In contrast to so many books about the promise and tactics of social media, Shih offers something much more valuable. *The Social Business Imperative* is a strategy and execution roadmap for everyone from boards and CEOs to front-line employees."

—Eric Ries, author of the *New York Times*-best-seller *The Lean Startup*

"Advancements in technology coupled with changing consumer preferences have ushered in a new, always-on era of the consumer. From understanding the needs of millennials to powerful marketing and customer strategies that drive sustained growth, *The Social Business Imperative* offers a comprehensive guide to implementing a social media platform and culture change to address the complex demands of today's social, mobile, digital, and in-charge customer."

—Dave McKay, President and CEO, Royal Bank of Canada

"From professional sports to media, entertainment, and retail, no aspect of business or consumer life has gone untransformed by social business. Clara's book is a clear and compelling guide for navigating and succeeding in this new era."

—Larry Baer, President and CEO, San Francisco Giants

"In her latest book, Clara explores an important reality we all face today: Consumers are socially connected, digitally minded, and have higher expectations than ever before. Read this and you will think differently about how to reach and serve your customers in this new digital environment."

—Helena Foulkes, President, CVS/pharmacy

"A must-read for today's business leaders, who must drive their organizations to embrace the growing opportunity on social media and stay relevant with customers."

—Ivan Chu, Chief Executive, Cathay Pacific Airlines

"Paraphrasing Maslow's hierarchy of human needs, after air, water, and food, what we all need and crave most is social connection—friendship, intimacy, and family. Maslow would have loved Clara Shih. Since her breakout book *The Facebook Era* in 2009, Clara has been showing us the way social media is changing our world. Clara's new book cuts through the tech-world jargon to deliver a message to business leaders everywhere: We are all social beings and in business, as in life, building relationships first is the key to success."

—Jim McCann, Founder and CEO, 1-800-FLOWERS.COM, Inc.

"*The Social Business Imperative* is a must-read for all client-facing business professionals, field leaders, and organizational leaders. Written by a master strategist, it will transform the way you conduct business."

—Robert R. Johnson, PhD, CFA, CAIA, President and CEO
of The American College of Financial Services

"Almost overnight, social media has transformed business and the way we as companies interact with our customers. In a way, social media has become part of everyone's job. Clara's book gets right to the heart of the matter and gets us thinking critically about what could be next on this roller coaster ride."

—Robin Hayes, President and CEO, JetBlue

"This book is a guide that connects social technologies to other critical technology-enabled trends that every business leader should understand: the Internet of Things, big data, mobile, and omnichannel. Clara peppers these insights with practical advice from her experience as CEO of a company taking advantage of these trends."

— Michael Chui, Partner, McKinsey Global Institute

# THE SOCIAL BUSINESS
IMPERATIVE

# THE SOCIAL BUSINESS IMPERATIVE

## ADAPTING YOUR BUSINESS MODEL TO THE

## ALWAYS-CONNECTED CUSTOMER

### Clara Shih

PRENTICE
HALL

Boston • Columbus • Indianapolis • New York • San Francisco • Amsterdam • Capetown
Dubai • London • Madrid • Milan • Munich • Paris • Montreal • Toronto • Delhi • Mexico City
São Paulo • Sidney • Hong Kong • Seoul • Singapore • Taipei • Tokyo

*Library of Congress Cataloging-in-Publication Data*

Names: Shih, Clara Chung-wai, author.

Title: The social business imperative : adapting your business model to the always-connected customer / Clara Shih.
Description: Boston : Prentice Hall, [2016] | Includes index.
Identifiers: LCCN 2016001412 | ISBN 9780134263434 (pbk. : alk. paper)
Subjects: LCSH: Information technology—Management. | Internet marketing. | Internet in public relations. | Strategic planning. | Social media. | Management—Social aspects.
Classification: LCC HD30.2 .S545 2016 | DDC 658.8/72—dc23
LC record available at http://lccn.loc.gov/2016001412

ISBN-13: 978-0-13-426343-4
ISBN-10: 0-13-426343-X
Text printed in the United States on recycled paper at RR Donnelley in Crawfordsville, Indiana.
2    16

**Editor-in-Chief**
Mark L. Taub

**Acquisitions Editor**
Trina MacDonald

**Development Editor**
Michael Thurston

**Managing Editor**
John Fuller

**Senior Project Editor**
Kesel Wilson

**Copy Editor**
Jill Hobbs

**Indexer**
Jack Lewis

**Proofreader**
Melissa Panagos

**Technical Reviewers**
Chris Rollyson
Jen Zimmerman
Nicole Pesce

**Cover Designer**
Chuti Prasertsith

**Compositor**
codeMantra, Inc.

*To Little Blake, who lights up my world.*


*In loving memory of Uncle Peter.*

# Contents

# Foreword

Innovation, I have long believed, is not only about rethinking products and processes, but also about rethinking the nature of relationships. This has never been truer than in the digital age.

For Starbucks, constant, relevant innovation around our relationship with our customers has always been a focal point. For more than 40 years, reimagining the way people connect—in our stores and in the communities we serve, and now online—has made Starbucks a brand that is about so much more than coffee. Our retail stores remain the Third Place, a welcome respite between work and home, because our partners (our employees) understand that human connection is as core to our business as crafting the perfect beverage.

Although my perspective on the role of digital innovation is seen through the lens of a consumer-facing brand rather than a traditional technology company, the truth is that no organization today is immune to the sweeping changes brought about by social, mobile, and digital. These technologies have forever changed how consumers experience the world and, as a result, how companies must interact with their customers. In our digital era, opportunities to connect with everyone, from customers to coworkers to community members, are greater than ever.

The question we must ask ourselves is no longer whether the ever-expanding assortment of digital tools poses a threat to the traditional ways we do business—that question has already been answered affirmatively. The question we should be asking, every day, is how our companies can maintain and enhance their relevancy in a world where digital and social media's effects will undoubtedly continue changing consumer and employee behavior at an accelerating pace.

We learned early in our company's digital and social journey that connecting with our customers online and in our stores should not be mutually exclusive experiences. Far from it: The potential for meaningful connections is what makes digital and social about much more than speed, convenience, and the cool factor. For any brand, digital and social have the potential to be about personalization, accountability, transparency, and authenticity. Used wisely, digital channels enhance loyalty and trust. That's why the digital domain truly is the Fourth Place.

Today, digital and social innovation is as critical to Starbucks as sourcing the highest-quality coffee beans. There is no doubt in my mind that any organization's growth, customer loyalty, reputation as an employer of choice, and long-term shareholder value are directly linked to a commitment to fully integrate digital and social into the foundational elements of the company.

When it comes to ongoing innovation, we must all put ourselves in the shoes of our customers by asking what they want, what they do every day, what they need, how they feel. Every business must ask these questions on behalf of its existing customers, whose behaviors change as technology evolves, as well as on behalf of its future customers—younger generations that leapfrogged over landlines, email, and cable, and grew up in the era of mobility, texting, and streaming.

Six years ago, putting ourselves in the shoes of our customers inspired Starbucks to create one of the first Facebook Pages for a consumer brand; today, Starbucks has 36 million followers on

Facebook as well as almost 6 million on Instagram. Three years ago, we built one of the most unique and powerful tools in the retail industry—our Starbucks card and mobile payment platform; today, that platform seamlessly integrates with our equally powerful loyalty program, and we process more than 9 million weekly mobile payment transactions in the United States. During the past year, we have created our own mobile apps so our customers can use their mobile devices to pay and order before they arrive at a store. Our partnerships with digital products, services, and media companies are helping us create a unique ecosystem of digital loyalty. Today, our customers can earn redeemable awards in the form of stars as they discover new music with Spotify, read stories that matter to them in *The New York Times*, and request a ride from Lyft drivers.

Each digital innovation, each new app, adds to the texture and relevancy of the overall Starbucks experience. Ultimately, the sum of the digital parts is greater than any one application.

Key to our efforts has been having members of the digital generation at the table, as part of our executive leadership team and in the boardroom. In 2011, Clara Shih, the CEO and founder of Hearsay Social and this book's author, joined Starbucks' board of directors. Clara's intelligence, her comprehensive understanding of technology and trends, and her proximity to the front lines of digital business in Silicon Valley give Starbucks necessary perspective. The fundamentals Clara shares in the following pages make *The Social Business Imperative* vital reading for any organization aspiring to be digitally smart. For existing companies, the book will elevate the role of digital throughout the enterprise. For entrepreneurs and startups, it will help ensure digital remains a priority.

For Starbucks, the same guiding principles that help steer our growth also inform our digital and social thinking:

- Only with *humility* can we remember that success is not an entitlement, but must be earned every day.

- Only with insatiable *curiosity* can we continue to explore the unknown.

- And only with *courage* can we constantly innovate.

In the Fourth Place, Clara continues to help Starbucks become even more humble, curious, and courageous.

Never before has it been so critical for companies to challenge the status quo. As seismic changes in consumer behavior continue unabated, businesses are both witness and participant. Those that commit to investing in digital and social in ways that surprise, delight, and matter to customers will not only enhance their relevancy in the marketplace, but also be seen as employers of choice.

We are all part of the inevitable digital future that is unfolding at our fingertips. That's why, today, digital is everybody's business.

**Howard Schultz**
**Chairman and CEO, Starbucks Coffee Company**

# List of Case Studies and Guest Author Sidebars

In my own experience, business books are most helpful when they include real-world examples and case studies. I have endeavored to include as many of these as possible in the pages that follow, including those listed here:

Chapter 2

- CASE STUDY: John Hancock Insurance Company and Fitbit

Chapter 3

- SIDEBAR: Millennial Attitudes and Ride Sharing by Logan Green, Co-founder and CEO, Lyft

Chapter 4

- CASE STUDY: Disney
- CASE STUDIES: CEOs at Virgin Group, American Family Mutual Insurance, General Electric, Medtronic, and Auto Nation on social media
- SIDEBAR: A Social CEO Leading by Example by Scott Ham, CEO, Transamerica Life & Protection

Chapter 5

- CASE STUDY: Misty Farukh, Raymond James Financial Advisor
- CASE STUDY: Florent Martin, Generali France Insurance Agent
- SIDEBAR: Perspective from a Field Leader by Marty Flewellen, Chief Distribution Officer, Transamerica Life & Protection

Chapter 6

- CASE STUDY: Karen Goodwin, Ameriprise
- CASE STUDY: Joel McKinnon, Farmers Insurance
- CASE STUDY: Warby Parker
- CASE STUDY: Penn Mutual Rugby

Chapter 7

- CASE STUDY: Operator
- CASE STUDY: Mave
- CASE STUDY: WeChat

Chapter 8

- • CASE STUDY: Wells Fargo
- • CASE STUDY: Ritz-Carlton

Chapter 9

- • CASE STUDY: L'Oréal
- • CASE STUDY: Unilever
- • CASE STUDY: Intuit

Chapter 10

- • CASE STUDY: Raymond James

# Acknowledgments

I'm indebted once again to my editor Trina MacDonald, who found me on Facebook (of all places) back in 2007 and took a big chance on me as an unknown author. Thanks for coaching me through *The Facebook Era* (Prentice Hall, first edition, 2009; second edition, 2010) and now this book.

Sincere thanks also to my writing partner Jessica Carew Kraft and book team Michael Thurston, Olivia Basegio, Marissa Lui, Nicole Johnson, Harry Go, Connie Sung Moyle, Gary Liu, Jill Hobbs, and Jack Cranston.

To the many tens of thousands of you from around the world who read my first book and encouraged me to write this sequel, *thank you*. Your comments, tweets, and letters inspire me.

I would also like to acknowledge:

- Steve Garrity, the co-founder of Hearsay Social and a close friend since college. We started our company in the summer of 2009 to bring to life many of the concepts from *The Facebook Era*. It is our company, our people, and our customers who inspired *The Social Business Imperative*.

- My reviewers Chris Rollyson, Jen Zimmerman, and Nicole Pesce, for their tireless efforts in keeping this manuscript honest, balanced, and readable.

- Adam Brotman, Wayne Bossert, Knut Olson, Brian Solis, Jen Grazel, and Ray Wang, for their early encouragement and input on the vision and direction of this book.

- Mike Agarwal, Daralee Barbera, Steve Bard, John Barkis, Carlo Besozzi, Annabelle Bexiga, Jaleh Bisharat, Bill Burke, Lisa Caputo, Tanguy Catlin, John Chandler, Steve D'Angelo, Iain Duke-Richardet, Tash Elwyn, Virginie Fauvel, Caroline Feeney, Emily Fink, Dan Finnigan, Jeff Fleischman, Marty Flewellen, Jade Fu, Mike Gamson, Victor Gaxiola, Ann Glover, Joanne Gordon, Joe Gross, Sanjay Gupta, Sam Guzman, Elyse Hackney, Scott Ham, Rand Harbert, Jackie Harmon, Denise Karkos, Pete Kazanjy, Paul LaPiana, Esther Lee, Kristin Lemkau, Mike Linton, Olivier Maire, Pam Marchant, Chris Maryanopolis, Ted Mathas, Eileen McDonnell, Theresa McLaughlin, Dennis Owen, Jeremiah Owyang, Sarah Pedersen, Penny Pennington, Trish Quan, Abhay Rajaram, Joe Roualdes, Kane Russell, Jon Sakoda, Sheryl Sandberg, Tim Schaefer, Elliot Schrage, Kim Sharan, Lisa Shalett, Sonny Shelke, Sean Shore, Amy Sochard, John Taft, Moshe Tamir, Kelly Thul, Erick Tseng, Dan Tucker, Xin Wang, Emily White, Mike White, Jenny Wiens, Doyle Williams, John Williams, Julia Winder, George Worley, Nick Wright, Karin Zabel, Yasmin Zarabi, and Weifang Zhu for their generous feedback, support, and contributions.

- My friends, colleagues, customers, investors, and partners at Hearsay, who push me every day to keep learning, inventing, and getting better.

- Als, Bex, Ev, Hayes, and Boots.

Above all, I appreciate the love and support of my family, especially my husband Dan, parents Sophia and James, brother Victor (who let me persuade him to join Twitter @vshih2, and now tweets more often and has more followers than me!), Aunt Susan, and grandmother Lau Kim Ping, who beat me to being our family's first published female author with her popular travel book published in Hong Kong in the 1980s.

# About the Author

 **Clara Shih** is a Silicon Valley tech entrepreneur and best-selling author. She is founder and CEO of Hearsay Social, an enterprise software company whose predictive omnichannel marketing platform helps financial advisors engage clients across social, text message, email, and websites while complying with industry regulations. A pioneer in the social media industry, Clara developed Faceforce, the first social business application, in 2007 and subsequently authored the *New York Times*–featured best-seller, *The Facebook Era* (Prentice Hall, first edition, 2009; second edition, 2010).

Clara has been named one of *Fortune*'s "Most Powerful Women Entrepreneurs," *Fast Company*'s "Most Influential People in Technology," *BusinessWeek*'s "Top Young Entrepreneurs," and both *Fortune*'s and *Ad Age*'s "40 Under 40." She was also named a "Young Global Leader" by the World Economic Forum.

Clara is a member of the Starbucks board of directors and previously served in a variety of technical, product, and marketing roles at Google, Microsoft, and Salesforce.com. She holds a B.S. and an M.S. in computer science from Stanford University, as well as an M.S. in Internet studies from Oxford University, where she studied as a U.S. Marshall Scholar.

Stay connected with Clara:

http://twitter.com/clarashih

http://facebook.com/clarashih

https://www.linkedin.com/influencer/clarashih

http://hearsaysocial.com/blog

http://socialbizimperative.com

# Introduction

*"A sequel is such a daunting thing, because you don't want to lose the magic and the charm of the first one."*
—Sandra Bullock

When I wrote my first book back in 2008, social networks were just getting off the ground. *The Facebook Era* articulated a radical vision for how social media would transform media, relationships, and influence, creating new opportunities for businesses in the process. Skeptics abounded. Even the title of the book was controversial at the time. People needed a lot of convincing that social media wasn't just a fad, so I drew on academic sociology research and drew parallels to the rise of the Internet 15 years earlier.

What a long way we have come. Today, you'd be hard-pressed to find someone who *doesn't* believe in social media's profound impact on every aspect of work, life, and society. As consumers, we live the social, mobile, and digital transformation every day—from the moment we wake up and scroll through Facebook to when we tweet the world good night just before falling asleep. Social media now drives more traffic to most websites than search engines do, and last year social media surpassed even email as the top Internet activity.

Businesses, too, have made great strides. Nine in 10 companies now use social media in some capacity. Yet tremendous untapped opportunity remains—$1.3 trillion in business value, to be exact, according to McKinsey Global Institute. Most organizations are still using social media only in superficial ways or only in select departments (generally brand marketing, recruiting, and customer service), but the rest of the organization has yet to catch up. And *very* few companies more than a decade old have built or adapted their entire business model for the Facebook era. Yet that's precisely where the biggest prizes await.

*Social Business Imperative* is the execution-oriented sequel to *The Facebook Era*'s vision. The pages that follow describe how social media has come of age for businesses (what I refer to as *Social Business*) in an increasingly mobile world, how organizations can take a strategic, proactive approach to operationalize Social Business in every major function and department, and how these currently siloed initiatives can be tied together cohesively to deliver efficient, consistent customer experiences and unlock transformational new business models.

There are two reasons why Social Business has become an imperative. First, social media is where customers spend their time and expect to engage. The continued dramatic rise in smartphone penetration and usage is driving up social engagement even further. Second, the so-called big data generated by customers on social, mobile, and digital platforms can be harnessed for predictive analytics—which in turn can be used to power new business models and practices that delight customers with personalized experiences, curation, and convenience.

## Customers—The Center of Social Business

Some organizations are still trying to force customers to endure frustrating, outdated communication methods such as never-ending customer service phone trees and impersonal web forms, but new and better alternatives are emerging every day for these customers. Across every industry and geography, today's customer has an entire universe of insight at her fingertips about millions of companies, products, and services. She also has an instant global platform through which to voice her opinions. The customer can tweet her questions, grievances, and suggestions, igniting a conversation with strangers and friends, and providing a great opportunity for companies to respond … if only they would listen.

In today's constantly connected world, where prospective buyers come to the table with opinions already formed, companies must first listen to what's being said about their products and services. (When's the last time you went to Twitter and searched for mentions of your company?) And in an age when buyers prefer to call the shots and research products rather than be sold to, companies desperately need to invest in content marketing that is authentic, easily readable and sharable, and able to teach the buyer something she does not already know. Companies ignore these needs at their peril, as laggards on the Social Business front risk becoming less relevant over time.

Today's customer demands a seamless experience across mobile, social, web, and in-store environments. To meet these demands, companies must re-architect their business processes and structures with customers at the center, breaking through what are often decades-old departmental barriers and technology silos. Leaders must enable and motivate cross-channel teams to work together for the common goal, instead of keeping mobile and online retail separate from in-store sales and print advertising. Each is a unique touchpoint in the customer journey. Treated as silos, they may cause customer confusion and even anger (just ask anyone who has ever been denied relief when trying to return an item purchased online to a retail store location). In the integrated Social Business venture, these spokes become a powerful wheel of customer interaction, a vehicle for establishing fierce loyalty and brand differentiation.

## An Organizational Transformation Imperative

In less than 10 years, social media has evolved from a fun website for college kids to write on each other's walls and 'poke' one another to become a robust series of networks defining a new set of relationships and interactions among people, brands, global causes, and political movements from the ALS Ice Bucket Challenge to ISIS.

Social Business has permeated every step of the buyer's journey and reshaped the rules of marketing, selling, customer service, product development, and much more. Take the sales function, for instance. Facebook, Twitter, and LinkedIn offer access to a wealth of personal and social context, providing reps with the right information to reach out through a warm introduction, tailor their outreach, and ultimately connect more meaningfully. Even prior to social media, consulting firm McKinsey had shown that salespeople such as insurance agents sell more when they know more about their customers. From new babies and new cars to job changes and relocations, social media has become one of the first places people go to share special news with the world. Social selling unlocks these insights in ways that are complementary and transformational to traditional relationship-building.

Social networks have also become *the* place where billions of consumers go to learn about and discuss new products and services, then to share their experience with friends and strangers. Until recently, social networks surrounded commerce transactions but didn't meaningfully enable transactions. The explosive growth of 'buy' buttons and payment-enabled mobile messaging apps (including WeChat and Facebook Messenger) is changing this. With their foundation of trusted-reputation networks, friend graphs, and social data, combined with these new transactional capabilities, social networks are fast becoming more than just a place to discover, validate, and review products. Indeed, they are poised to become robust commerce and service transaction platforms that will again reinvent how all of us live, work, and do business. Organizations have no choice but to mobilize and adapt accordingly.

## How This Book Is Organized

This book is divided into three parts. Part I discusses new business models that intersect with and are enabled by Social Business and millennials. Part II walks across the externally facing functions of an organization and examines how Social Business is applied in each case. Part III focuses on how to move from vision to execution and how cross-functional efforts can become aligned to create a whole that is greater than the sum of its parts.

## Part I: New Business Models

As we'll expand upon in Chapter 1, "The Social, Always-Connected Consumer," the ubiquity of smartphones and constantly updating stream of content, messages, and notifications have created a consumer that is connected 24/7. The unprecedented amount of engagement, enormous number of clicks, and sheer minutes and hours spent by consumers on a growing number of social media services translate into an enormous amount of data that, thanks to cheap cloud storage and processing, can now be fed into predictive algorithms across a variety of applications. The practice of predictive analytics—which is how we determine patterns and predict future outcomes and trends from this data—will play an increasingly important role in helping businesses serve and delight their customers.

Chapter 2, "The Internet of Everything and Big Data Explosion," explores how consumers now want to digitally connect and access not only virtual games, goods, and content, but also physical ones—such as their cars, homes, and personal health. In so doing, they are creating radically new streams of data. Companies will need to respond with new business models and customer engagement models optimized for frequent or even constant connectivity to the customer. One terrific example is what a South African insurance company, Discovery Limited, has done through its innovative Vitality Program, which issues wearable activity trackers to insurance customers.

The always-on connectivity of consumers has created simultaneously a sense of trust and community on the one hand, and a desire for instant gratification and convenience (some call it "laziness") on the other. Chapter 3, "Trust, Convenience, and Millennials: The Collaborative Economy," contemplates what these new norms will mean for traditional businesses.

## Part II: Business Functions Reimagined

Part II opens with Chapter 4, "The Management Team and Board Mandate," which makes the case that the game-changing potential of both totally new business models and totally new business practices call for management teams and boards of directors to become educated and directly involved in Social Business strategy and execution.

The five subsequent chapters walk through five respective major functional departments in a typical enterprise and consider how each should be capitalizing on Social Business: Social Sales, Social Marketing, Social Commerce, Social Customer Care, and Social Hiring. In the realm of social commerce in particular, a number of recent developments are giving rise to fascinating new use cases for transacting both on-demand services and product e-commerce.

Traditionally, functional leaders might read only the chapter describing their function, but in the new digital, customer-centric world order, everyone from boards of directors to front-line sales managers and chief marketing officers to recruiting, IT, and compliance directors must seek to understand the digital transformation taking place not only in their own department but in all departments. Only with this broader understanding can functional leaders collaborate on delivering a cohesive customer experience spanning previous organizational silos.

Although specific best practices differ by functional area, the common thread across all of these operations is the requirement for a new kind of leadership—one that encompasses both functional excellence and an innovation-oriented mindset.

## Part III: Enterprise Execution Playbook

The final section, beginning with Chapter 10, "How to Operationalize Social Business," looks at how enterprises can bring together multiple Social Business initiatives spanning different departments, product lines, and geographies to unlock synergies without unleashing bureaucracy.

Social Business presents enormous benefits for building brand trust, qualifying leads, communicating with customers, as well as recruiting and employee engagement. It's also brought to the forefront a set of complex issues involving legal, compliance, and cybersecurity. Chapter 11, "Legal, Governance, and Compliance Frameworks," discusses key risk areas introduced by Social Business and mitigation strategies, including those for highly regulated industries. Chapter 12, "The Changing IT and Information Security Landscape," weighs the role of traditional information technology organizations in today's age of disruptive innovation.

# My Personal Journey: From Engineer to Author to Entrepreneur

It's clear we are in a whole new age of innovation. Traditional firms will need to rethink their business models, organizational structures, and standard operating procedures. Entirely new firms will emerge that simply would not have been possible five years ago. My company, Hearsay Social, is one such firm.

Soon after *The Facebook Era* was published in 2009, my former Stanford classmate Steve Garrity and I quit our jobs (at Microsoft and Salesforce.com, respectively) to found Hearsay, an omnichannel marketing technology platform for financial advisors to connect with their clients on social media, websites, email marketing, and text messaging. Before "social business" and "big data" became part of the common vernacular, we founded Hearsay Labs (the original company name) out of my living room in San Francisco to take advantage of their intersection.

As part of a long list of regulatory requirements, financial services organizations need to retain records of all digital communications with clients. Most firms find this record-keeping incredibly onerous, but we decided to build Hearsay's entire value proposition around turning these retained records into big data opportunities!

When Steve and I first pitched our business plan, many venture capital firms dismissed our idea of building a Social Business platform. They thought social networking was a fad soon and sure to pass. Who would have guessed that five short years later, Facebook would be worth $300 billion and Hearsay would have 150,000 customers in 22 countries? We hope this is just the beginning, both for our company and yours.

Thanks to the countless many of you who read *The Facebook Era* and inspired me to found Hearsay. The book experience and startup experience have been life-changing, and I eagerly look forward to what the coming years and decades will bring.

See you on social media!
Clara
San Francisco, California

# PART I

## NEW BUSINESS MODELS

### The Rise of Millennials, Social Media, and Constant Connectivity

**1**

*"Overnight the digital age had changed the course
of history for our company. Everything that we
thought was in our control no longer was."*
—Howard Schultz, Chairman and CEO,
Starbucks Coffee Company

# The Social, Always-Connected Consumer

More than 2 billion people today around the world are active on social media—primarily Facebook, but also LinkedIn, Twitter, WeChat, Instagram, Line, Xing, Pinterest, Vine, and a dozen more forums of significant scale. For businesses, the imperative isn't merely to be where your customers are; it's re-architecting your business models and business practices around the new ways in which customers are discovering, researching, validating, and sharing constantly with friends, strangers, and influencers on social media.

Unlike in 2009, when I wrote *The Facebook Era*, social media today is no longer a place only for American college kids; it's a set of global channels spanning all demographics. According to Pew Research Center, even baby boomers have more than tripled their usage since 2010. Today, more than one-third use social media, with active users skewing toward those with higher educational levels and household incomes. According to a study conducted by nonprofit Common Sense Media, teens in the United States spend *nine hours a day* on social and digital channels for enjoyment (that is, excluding the time spent online for homework). In perhaps a sad commentary on their time-pressured lives, they spend more time connected than sleeping.

Across the board, today's consumers expect your business to be findable and ready to engage exactly when, where, and how they prefer. Even for what are ultimately offline transactions and consumption experiences such as vacation travel or dinner, the buyer's decision journey most of the time now begins on social media. Social networks are the new water cooler and town hall. Yelp has replaced Michelin as the restaurant curator. We are witnessing a seismic change in consumer power, behavior, and expectations—yet many businesses still lag far behind.

# Constant Connectivity

Today's always-connected consumers owe their rise to the concurrent explosion in smartphone penetration and social media over the last decade. Smartphones provided the *mechanism* for constant connectivity, whereas the never-ending, continuously refreshing streams of user-generated content from social media sites provide the *reasons* for consumers to continually connect (and in turn, share their own photos, tweets, and YouTube videos, further perpetuating the cycle).

A large part of why millennials and their successors, Generation Z, are seemingly unable to do anything without tweeting and texting their friends and family is simply that they've never experienced life disconnected. What's key is they similarly expect frequent digital touchpoints, digital responsiveness, and digital accessibility from the companies they do business with or are thinking of doing business with.

## The Age of the Empowered Customer

One implication of constant connectivity is that today's buyers can access information about your company, products, prices, competitors, and more, all on demand. Never in history have business-to-consumer (B2C) and business-to-business (B2B) buyers alike had as much power as they do today. They enjoy a dizzying array of product choices, ample access to product information and online reviews, and readily available public social media platforms to voice their opinions. Armed with their smartphones—79% of iPhone and Android users ages 18 to 44 have their mobile phones on them for all but two hours of their waking day—consumers are on social media sharing, researching, validating, and buying 24/7. Do your business practices acknowledge and honor their power?

It turns out the same patterns and behaviors of the socially savvy customer also apply to existing and prospective employees. With or without your approval, sanction, or knowledge, your employees are invariably talking about your company on social media with their friends, the public, and your customers. At its best, employee social engagement can serve as a wonderful means of brand ambassadorship, providing an authentic glimpse that is additive to your company's mission and influence. At its worst, disgruntled employees and careless employees can also tweet about their dissatisfaction and stir up all kinds of trouble, as organizations like the American Red Cross and British retailer HMV learned the hard way.[1]

---

1. HMV made the mistake of unceremoniously firing several employees before revoking their access to the brand's Twitter account. The unhappy employees took to Twitter, posting on the brand account @hmvtweets that the layoffs were a "mass execution." American Red Cross faced an embarrassing situation when its social media strategist Gloria Huang accidentally posted what she thought was a personal tweet about getting drunk with friends to the official @RedCross Twitter handle.

## The Social, Mobile, and Digital Last Mile

Evidence suggests that the always-connected consumer landscape favors always-connected businesses: Four of the top five companies on *Fortune*'s "World's Most Admired Companies" list this year—Apple, Google, Amazon.com, and Starbucks—are dominant digital players.

When it comes to digital, success begets success. The always-connected business enjoys three distinct advantages: consumer trust, convenience, and so-called big data. First, consumers tend to *trust* the companies with which they interact frequently digitally, and this is only becoming truer with time as average time spent on social, mobile, and digital channels continues to grow. Second, consumers generally find it more *convenient* to transact with businesses they already buy from frequently online, as these businesses are likely to have the consumer's preferences, address, and payment information stored and ready to go. Finally, the big data insights that can be harvested by always-connected businesses give them a leg up on their competition in personalizing customer experiences (think about Amazon's "Customers Who Bought This Item Also Bought" feature) as well as predicting moments of truth (e.g., LinkedIn knows you are probably looking for a new job if you suddenly make a bunch of enhancements to your profile).

The challenge for traditional, non-digital businesses is that the juggernauts that invented and own the "digital last mile" are crossing over into ever-evolving new categories. For example, Google has moved into travel and auto insurance, Facebook into payments, Netflix into original content, and Amazon into—well, everything. At greatest risk in the new world order are businesses that (1) lack digital touchpoints and/or (2) have infrequent or indirect customer interaction. If either—or worse yet, both—of these scenarios describes your organization, you need to act now, because time is running out.

A big part of social media sites' appeal and ability to scale is that each is, in its own way, a curator and marketplace of sorts for other people's content, products, and services. Traditional firms should consider how they, too, might reimagine themselves playing the role of conductor rather than command-and-control producer. Any business of significant size and scale should strive to own a piece of the digital last mile—that is, to have a portal, website, mobile app, wearable, or other digital destination that consumers frequent to engage or transact with the company. This is extremely difficult to do well, as you are then essentially competing against Google, Amazon, Facebook, and Instagram for coveted consumer mindshare and scarce real estate on smartphone home screens. Very few companies that are not Google, Amazon, Facebook, or their peers will win this battle, but it's important to nonetheless try and think big.

Now you might wonder whether it's even possible for a business to go from having few digital touchpoints and infrequent customer interactions to owning a meaningful segment of the digital last mile, but this is precisely what John Hancock Insurance has done. Partnering with the South African financial company Vitality, John Hancock has begun issuing wearable Fitbit trackers to customers, all of a sudden creating daily digital interaction moments. As we'll explore in the next chapters, the rise of connected devices and the sharing economy is opening new frontiers in the form of digital-last-mile opportunities that are yet to be claimed and could be incredibly valuable.

Starbucks offers another instructive example. In less than a decade, it has gone from being a frequently trafficked but essentially non-digital company to launching a successful, highly complementary digital ecosystem spanning everything from mobile orders and payments (Starbucks processes more than 8 million mobile transactions *every week*) to e-commerce coffee subscriptions and premium content that's made available via in-store WiFi.

## The Social Business Imperative

Today, every company has to become a Social Business. Consumers are constantly connected, and social media is where they spend the majority of their time while connected. As social networking sites broaden their functionality, consumers will be able to do far more than 'like' and retweet. Already, consumers spend a staggering 1.7 hours on average per day on social media, representing 28% of total online activity, according to GlobalWebIndex. Facebook, Twitter, Instagram, Snapchat, and LinkedIn now own vast pieces of the digital last mile. As these sites and apps expand into everything from mobile messaging and payments to 'buy' buttons, wearables (as evidenced by Facebook's acquisition of Oculus VR), and even the on-demand economy (such as LinkedIn's ProFinder), they are becoming powerful platforms that deeply intersect every phase of the buyer's journey—from discovery and research to validation, customer service, ratings and reviews, and increasingly commerce and transactions.

Signs point to this being exactly what consumer want. Millennials, who now represent the largest generation in the American workforce and the most rapidly growing demographic segment in terms of purchasing power, especially seek constant reassurance from friends and family when it comes to buying decisions—and they turn to social media to obtain this validation. Across all generations, consumers expect to research companies and individual salespeople and practitioners on social media, as well as consult friends on social media for everything from where to go out to dinner and which book to read to which dentist, wedding planner, or financial advisor to work with. Increasingly, only through these vast social media pipes can many businesses meaningfully access the hearts, minds, and wallets (in that order) of the social and always-connected consumers.

You must master the Social Business Imperative *even if* you have already succeeded in owning a piece of the last mile and have direct digital channels to your customer such as a mobile app, web portal, email list, or wearable device. The reason is that as much time as your customers spend logged in to your dedicated channel, they spend *far more time* not logged in (and instead logged into a social media site or app). Also, while many customers may have signed up for your dedicated channel, *far more* customers and prospective customers have not and may never sign up. Finally, your customers expect to research and validate their purchase decisions on social media, even if they ultimately come back and transact on your site or in your store. This reality explains why companies like Starbucks have invested significant time, resources, and executive attention in amassing and engaging with more than 50 million social media fans and followers through sharing and facilitating incredibly rich content, community, and conversations.

The Social Business Imperative encompasses much, much more than just creating a Facebook Page or claiming a Twitter handle. Constant connectivity and social media's growing role across the buyer's journey represent a sea-change and step-change in how companies have operated up to this point. For many firms, Social Business requires a shift in cultural mindset as well as defining and embracing a totally new customer engagement model.

## We've Always Been Social

To be social is to be human. Long before the digital age, all business was local and social, and good customer service wasn't hard to find. Shopkeepers knew their customers by name, knew their preferences, and even knew their schedules. Shopkeepers understood that building longstanding relationships with customers would result in repeat visits and loyalty; to that end, they used their personal networks to enable sales and conversely incorporated customers into their social networks. Good business has always been about trust, relationships, and personal accountability.

If anything, earlier forms of technology and media made us behave in bizarre ways that deviate from our authentic social nature. Companies in search of expanding their market reach at ever-lower costs began embracing mass-marketing techniques, so-called direct marketing, in the form of unsolicited cold calls, mailings, and (later) promotional emails. Of course, there's a reason we now refer to these techniques as "junk" and "spam." Mass marketing stripped away the human connection, eroding trust and longstanding relationships between businesses and customers. Buyers have learned to combat cold calls with caller ID and "do not call" lists, just as they combat unwanted email marketing with spam filters and direct mail with their recycling bins. In pursuit of efficiency, many businesses instead became commoditized, losing what was special and valued by their customer in the first place.

How do businesses reestablish true relationships with their customers? Surely an always-connected business that spams its customers will not succeed. First and foremost, businesses must be authentic and play by the rules of *permission marketing*. They must go back to the earlier emphasis on building long-term trust rather than optimizing for the one-time click or transaction. They must also build a sense of community and double-down on loyal customers, with the understanding that one happy customer today means dozens more tomorrow thanks to testimonials, ratings, reviews, and sharing on social media. An email I received from my friend Jessi Hempel, writer at *Wired*, sums it up nicely:

> Visiting Tupelo, Mississippi, this week makes me think of the future of business on the Internet. Here's why: Few people come to Tupelo and few people leave. It's a small town.

Business gets done because people have relationships. You get a mortgage because the bank president goes to your church and has known you since you were knee-high. You go into the department store downtown and pick out what you want and the woman behind the desk marks it down in her credit book, and sends you a bill at the end of the month. You do your business with her because you know her and like her and when your baby was born last month, she brought you over lasagna. As someone who grew up in cities, I have a misplaced nostalgia for this experience, and this dense social fabric. There are awful things about it, too, of course. (God help you if you are new to town.) But it strikes me that this is what the modern-day business aspires to create through best practices in social and best use of big data, and that maybe the product of those tools could make me feel as good about consuming goods and services as I do when I'm in Tupelo.

The Social Business Era is both a by-product and an enabler of our desire to connect with one another and with the brands, businesses, interests, and icons that define, influence, and serve us. Every organization today faces a golden opportunity—indeed, an *imperative*—to once again truly connect with its customers, to listen, to get personal, and to do all of this with the scale and efficiency made possible by technology. Data and convenience do not have to mean commoditization—quite the opposite.

## Social Media State of the Union

When *The Facebook Era* was published, there were just a handful of social networks. Today, there are a multitude. Facebook alone has more than 1.5 billion users, and a dozen social networks have hundreds of millions of active users each, including Twitter, LinkedIn, Instagram, WhatsApp, WeChat, and Line (Figure 1.1).

Fledgling, little-known startups a decade ago, the "big three" generalist social networks Facebook, Twitter, and LinkedIn are now all publicly traded companies representing hundreds of billions of dollars in combined market capitalization. Mobile messaging apps (e.g., WeChat, Facebook Messenger, WhatsApp, and Snapchat) have also taken off in a big way and have quickly become powerful clearinghouses for commerce and transactions.

Although the lines are blurring as each social network or app seeks to expand its audience and functionality, here is a rough generalization of how each major social media site is being used by businesses:

- **Facebook** is the top global social network, making it an absolute necessity for any retail business. For businesses ranging from local mom-and-pop shops to mega-corporations, Facebook can help them find customers, build brand reputation, and stay connected through organic and paid posts.

- **Twitter** stands out as the premier short-form (limited to 140 characters), real-time social network, where tweets can go viral in a flash. With hundreds of millions of active users, the site offers businesses opportunities to spot trends, respond to customer complaints in real time, and start movements.

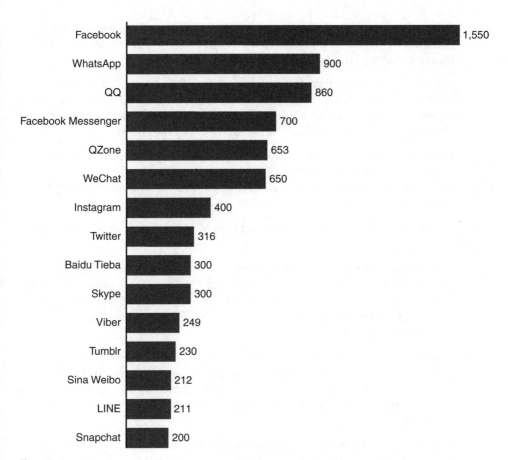

**Figure 1.1**
*Most popular global social networking sites* (Source: Statista, November 2015)

- **Instagram** (acquired by Facebook in 2012, but remains a stand-alone app) is a popular, mobile-only app for stunning, eye-catching photos. It has quickly been adopted by visually oriented brands as a means to get front and center in the consumer's daily stream.

- **Vine** (acquired by Twitter in 2012, but remains a stand-alone app) is a social network for recording and posting six-second videos. It started out like an Instagram for video (though Instagram now also has video capability). For businesses, Vine is ideal for product teasers and "micro" action videos, used to great effect by companies such as GoPro, Urban Outfitters, and The Gap.

- **Tumblr** (acquired by Yahoo in 2013, but remains a stand-alone site) is a blogging platform that is popular with younger, digitally active consumers. It's self-described as "really, really simple for people to make a blog and put whatever they want on it. Stories, photos, GIFs, TV shows, links, quips, dumb jokes, smart jokes, Spotify tracks, mp3s, videos, fashion, art, deep stuff." Businesses like this platform because of its easy-to-use user interface and ability to reach arguably the most influential group of Internet users. Sephora, for example, posts products and video how-to's on its Tumblr account, often featuring celebrities to boost viewership.

- **Pinterest** is about collecting ideas and designing products, homes, fashion, and more, so it's a similarly ideal fit for visual brands and occasions. A good example of its commercial potential can be seen in Home Depot's Pinterest account, which currently has more than 300,000 profile followers across several dozen boards.

- **LinkedIn** is a professional social network, which is especially popular with recruiters and B2B sales and marketers. It's ideal for generating B2B leads, searching for and connecting with potential new recruits, finding your next job, and networking and sharing across specialized discussion groups.

In addition, here are the top mobile messaging apps (Chapter 7 explores them in greater detail):

- **Facebook Messenger** is Facebook's own mobile messaging app, which benefits from being fully integrated with its parent social network. Users can make phone and video calls; send money, virtual stickers, and animated GIFs to friends; and, in a fairly recent twist, transact with retailers including Everlane and Zulily and on-demand service providers including Uber.

- **WhatsApp** (acquired by Facebook in 2014, but remains a stand-alone app) has half a billion monthly users who engage with the app's mobile messaging service as a free alternative to texting. Global businesses have adopted the technology for the same reason—for $1 per year, they can instantly communicate with motivated millennials.

- **Snapchat** (which famously rejected Facebook's offer to be acquired for $3 billion in 2013) is an ephemeral instant messaging social network with more than 100 million users. There is no unending feed here—visual messages called "snaps" disappear after they're read by the recipient. Businesses have found Snapchat can be a great way to motivate audiences to take immediate action. For example, fast-food brands Taco Bell and GrubHub have "snapped" limited-time discounts on their menu items.

- **WeChat**, developed by Chinese Internet giant Tencent, is a fascinating case study of what a social, mobile messaging app can become. What began as a simple mobile text and voice-messaging app now boasts more than 1 billion users (including 70 million active users outside of China) and has become the one-stop shop of choice in China for everything from accessing public accounts (similar to Twitter) and making payments (both peer-to-peer transfers as well as bill payment) to hailing taxis, booking doctor's appointments, checking real-time traffic and air quality, and reporting incidents to the police. WeChat embodies the power of owning the digital last mile and the hearts and minds of today's always-connected consumer.

Each of these channels provides unique opportunities for your sales team, customer service agents, recruiters, and brand marketers to meaningfully connect to and, increasingly, transact with consumers.

## Social Business Comes of Age

The good news is that most companies no longer need convincing of the imperative to be on social media. Seventy-seven percent of *Fortune* 500 organizations now have an official social media team and presence. More than ever, businesses are getting on social media. But simply being on social isn't enough. Putting up a Facebook Page or @replying customers on Twitter is a start, but it won't transform the organization by itself.

One obstacle may be organizational knowledge and readiness. The research firm Altimeter found that only 27% of employees of the supposedly top "socially engaged" companies are actually engaged with social media and feel they know how to use it—mostly, these individuals are confined to marketing and customer service. In reality, the Social Business Imperative requires mobilizing your entire organization to embrace the always-connected consumer. To be both proactive (to stay relevant) and responsive (to meet the expectations of the always-connected consumer), everyone in your organization—from your salespeople, customer service agents, and marketers to your recruiters and executive team—must be ever-present on the virtual town halls of Facebook, Twitter, and LinkedIn.

To fully capitalize on these opportunities, division and department leaders must personally own the Social Business strategy for their respective groups. Tactics can yield interesting use cases and insights, but strategic opportunities involving new business models and business processes must be considered at the very top. In other words, don't delegate social media to the new college grad and then think you have it covered. The combination of grassroots enthusiasm from millennial employees combined with an executive strategic mandate can be very powerful. Once you establish your initial presence, charge your organization's leaders with periodically reviewing new capabilities and consider testing new ways to leverage social networks. This is exactly what the ride-sharing service Uber did recently, resulting in an integration that now allows consumers to hail a ride from within Facebook Messenger.

To become truly effective, Social Business must be integrated into the company's standard operating procedures. It cannot be a one-off team or program. Want to institutionalize social selling? Don't make it optional. Change the curriculum for new-hire onboarding, train your sales managers to coach their reps on social media, and start measuring and managing to social performance metrics such as new connection growth and 'likes' generated from published posts. Want to enable commerce transactions through Facebook Messenger? You may need to re-architect how your organization approaches order fulfillment and customer support.

## The Omnichannel Mandate

Today, e-commerce represents 9% of total US retail and continues to grow rapidly thanks to mobile commerce (Figure 1.2). But even traditionally or inherently offline purchases are heavily influenced by social media—both what friends and the public are saying about specific businesses and how those businesses and their brand representatives are themselves engaging with consumers. The Corporate Executive Board found that, on average, 57% of a purchase decision has *already been made* via social media and other online sources before the prospect even engages with a sales representative.

**E-Commerce as % of Total Retail Sales, USA, 1998–2014**

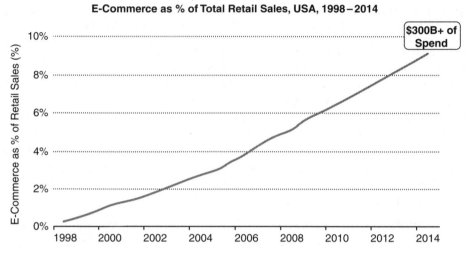

**Figure 1.2**

*US e-commerce retail sales have grown from less than 1% of total retail sales in 1998 to 9% today* (Source: Kleiner Perkins, Forrester 2015)

The purchase of your product may occur online or offline, but one thing is for certain: The buyer's journey increasingly begins online, and specifically on social media. You need to meet that buyer wherever she begins her journey. What's become apparent is that social networks are key to maximizing customer lifetime value both online and offline, encompassing research, browsing, buying, return visits, and loyalty before and after the sale.

A common buzzword these days is "omnichannel." When most companies describe this term, they are referring to either setting up an e-commerce sales channel or resolving channel conflict between e-commerce and brick-and-mortar stores.

A more thorough and nuanced definition for omnichannel is needed. First, we must clarify whether we are talking about a customer engagement (for marketing and/or support) channel or a sales transaction channel. For some companies, it may not make sense or even be possible to sell their products through an owned e-commerce channel, but almost all companies should be *engaging with* customers in an omnichannel fashion (including on social media). Second, many companies make the mistake of focusing all of their digital attention and resources on a digital transaction channel, *but fail to introduce digital basics to their salespeople and brick-and-mortar stores.* Not only do these organizations miss out on the easy leverage that can be realized from modernizing already-successful channels, but they also inadvertently create a confusing and inferior customer experience.

A comprehensive omnichannel strategy considers the entirety of the customer journey, from discovery and research before a purchase to the purchase itself and post-sale period, creating a seamless experience across brick-and-mortar stores, online stores, mobile stores, mobile app stores, telephone sales, in-person sales, content marketing, and review sites, whether paid, owned, or earned (Figure 1.3). Omnichannel done right means your salespeople are findable and responsive on Facebook and LinkedIn, your customer service teams are monitoring and replying on Twitter, your outdoor billboard branding complements your Facebook ads, and your gorgeous in-store display provides a hashtag for customers to use when posting a selfie they've taken in front of it. It means that you delight customers when they're with you face-to-face, connect seamlessly with them between visits via social media posts and mobile messages, and can immediately reference both store and web interaction history when they call into your phone support center. Being skilled at omnichannel contact means that the customer has a consistent experience with your brand across all touchpoints, even as each experience is tailored and optimized to the specific channel.

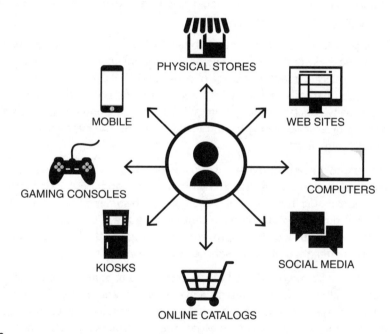

**Figure 1.3**
*The customer at the center of your omnichannel strategy* (Source: Hearsay Social)

Maintaining a consistent experience across all of these various channels is one key to success. Another is the successful capture, analysis, and application of data. Organizations must track and measure customer behavior across every channel and reconcile clicks, interactions, and transactions to craft personalized experiences—what many are calling the "segment of one." The omnichannel challenge is much bigger than social media alone, but it's critical to keep social media in mind when architecting a cohesive omnichannel customer experience.

Finally, functional leaders will need to become educated on the digital transformation taking place not only in their own department, but in all departments, so that they can collaborate more closely than ever before to create the cohesive omnichannel journey that today's customers expect. This unprecedented need for cross-functional understanding is what motivated Part II of this book, which systematically walks through sales, marketing, commerce, customer service, and recruiting.

## New Business Models, New Business Practices

Social Business is no longer optional. Today's social, always-connected consumers spend most of their waking hours sharing and being influenced on social media. Their expectations for how businesses should interact and transact have been forever transformed, and there is no looking back.

Companies, especially those that have traditionally lacked digital touchpoints or have low interaction frequency with their customers, need to rethink their business practices and even business models to adapt to this age of constant digital connectivity and influence. As we'll discuss in Chapter 4, senior management teams and boards must own and drive their company's Social Business strategy. It is inadequate and unwise to shunt this responsibility to lower-level managers, entry-level positions, and interns, as is currently the case in some organizations.

The future is bright, the opportunities vast. Customers are sharing more than ever before about themselves, their preferences, and their honest opinions about your company in real time on social media. There is an unprecedented rich stream of data flowing from social media that businesses can access to capture the pulse of consumer sentiment, identify moments of truth, look in the proverbial mirror, use as the basis for continual improvement, and delight their customer like never before.

There has never been a more exciting time for companies to again become truly customer-centric, albeit now at great scale and efficiency thanks to big data and predictive technologies. But these opportunities will be available only to those Social Businesses that know how to own and navigate the social, mobile, and digital last mile. Read on and see how!

# 2

*"Hiding within those mounds of data is knowledge that could change the life of a patient, or change the world."*
—Atul Butte, Stanford School of Medicine

# The Internet of Everything and Big Data Explosion

Twenty-five years ago, a young computer scientist by the name of Tim Berners-Lee presented a paper on the World Wide Web, outlining an easy way to access files on connected computers. Little did he know that his idea would pave the way for a global phenomenon that would touch billions of people and transform every aspect of our lives. Berners-Lee's vision transformed the way the world communicates, discovers, and transacts. But web pages were just the beginning—they were the first wave. The second wave of the Internet was about connecting people. Social networking sites like Facebook and Twitter are the Internet of People, a crowdsourced directory of sorts identifying and connecting more than 2 billion people—nearly one in four people worldwide.

Before us now is the third wave of connectedness—the Internet of Things, or IoT for short. The Internet of Things goes beyond the digital realm, enabling communication with and among physical objects not totally unlike what was predicted by *The Jetsons* animated sitcom decades ago (Figure 2.1). From connected cars and smart homes to wearable wristbands and delivery drones, a never-ending global system of inter-connected devices and big data is emerging that will completely transform how we live, work, and get around. We are at only the beginning stages of this revolution. Cisco estimates there will be more than 50 billion devices connected to the Internet by 2020, 10 times the number of people online.

IoT is essentially a network of physical objects that can sense the environment (or other objects) and then, based on certain configurable thresholds, take an autonomous action and communicate this action to users (generally through a smartphone app).

**Figure 2.1**
*The 'crazy' ideas in The Jetsons, a popular futuristic animated sitcom that ran from the 1960s through late 1980s, are not so far off after all* (Source: Moviestore Collection/REX)

The "Things" are anything that can have a sensor attached to it, such as everyday consumer devices and even cars, machines, and buildings. IoT is useful for gathering and using information to increase productivity and efficiency (often by partial or full automation of a task that previously required human intervention), enable new services, or achieve some other health, safety, or environmental benefit.

There are a several reasons why I felt it was important to include a chapter on IoT in this book. First, business leaders should understand that the always-connected customer is about to connect in ever more ways, creating new segments of the digital last mile that need to be built and claimed. Second, there are rich opportunities to marry IoT data about the offline world with social data about online behavior and preferences. This being said, entire books can be (and have been) written about IoT. We cannot hope to provide an in-depth analysis of the full set of use cases, business models, and especially the privacy and security concerns that a comprehensive discussion would warrant within the confines of a single short chapter. So we will instead endeavor to provide a quick state of the union.

## What IoT Means for Businesses

The business implications of IoT cannot be overstated. A new software and service layer needs to be established, maintained, and monetized—the question is, who will build and own these new digital roads that lead directly into the home, into the car, and to the consumer? Forward-thinking product manufacturers will seize the opportunity to transform customer relationships from one-time or infrequent purchase transactions to an always-connected relationship. In turn, in many categories, consumers' perception of quality is increasingly evolving to incorporate digital accessibility and convenience.

For many organizations, this revolution will likely involve a new business model focused on the long term, generally in the form of a recurring revenue stream. The closest analogies I can think of are how printer companies lose money on the hardware and make it up on ink, and how makers of blood sugar monitors give away the devices to people with diabetes and make it up on the testing strips. But now multiply that outcome times a thousand—the opportunity is no longer just refills but software applications and potentially mobility services, insurance, transportation and logistics, health care, media, entertainment, and more, depending on the device being connected. The firms that get this right have an opportunity not only to deepen customer relationships and loyalty, but also to capture entirely new categories of consumer spend, mindshare, and utility. These firms will own the future and literally run the physical world.

Today's product makers will need to reinvent themselves as service providers. Doing so will require a new mindset and even corporate culture. The shift won't be easy, but the alternative is to risk being intermediated and commoditized by whoever does own the software and service layers. All around us, new and uncharted digital-last-mile opportunities are being created. To capitalize on them, business leaders must deeply embrace the notion that the Internet and "the real world" are not separate, but rather increasingly and irreversibly intertwined.

## IoT Realities and Possibilities

For consumers, IoT turns our mobile phones into smart remote controls where we can simply tap an icon to control, summon services from, or otherwise interact with or be notified by everyday objects and appliances. The already-always-connected consumer is connecting to an ever-increasing array of new devices.

IoT is finally taking shape thanks to several technological and market developments. First, the always-connected consumer's tendency to have her smartphone at her side at all times makes it an ideal "universal remote" for IoT. Connecting even hundreds of devices is a cinch with smartphone apps.

Second, the confluence of cheap and easy prototyping, manufacturing, funding, and go-to-market ecosystems is giving rise to a hardware renaissance resulting in thousands of innovative new smart "Things." 3-D printing and low-cost programmable circuit boards, such as the Arduino and Raspberry Pi, have drastically brought down the costs of prototyping, design, and development. Global product supply chain firms such as San Francisco–based PCH have democratized access to outsourced manufacturing in China. Financing and product distribution aren't the significant hurdles that they once were thanks to crowdfunding platforms like Kickstarter and Indiegogo.

The final building block for ubiquitous IoT is connectivity. From Bluetooth and 4G to WiFi, the connectivity infrastructure has undergone a phenomenal expansion in recent years. WiFi is pretty much everywhere these days and available at a very low cost because it operates on an unlicensed spectrum. The price of bandwidth has also gone way down, by a factor of nearly 40 times over the past 10 years.

By now, we've all heard about the proverbial "cloud" where data is stored on servers in large data centers, sometimes located far away from the data's origin. With IoT, there will be more distribution of network intelligence that is located near the data source. This model is becoming known as the network edge, or "fog." Using fog instead of the cloud for data storage also has the advantage of being cheaper and speeding up the process of storing and retrieving data. Finally, most network hardware now supports the most recent version of the Internet Protocol (IP) standard, which allows 128-bit addresses, instead of the predecessor 32-bit addresses, creating exponentially more capacity to register IoT devices (this had been a previous hindrance).

Today, three categories of IoT are already well developed and currently in use: wearables, the connected car, and the connected home (including both examples in the preceding paragraph). Two additional categories, the connected city and the industrial Internet, are on the horizon, and will be important final developments in creating a truly global network of people and objects (Figure 2.2).

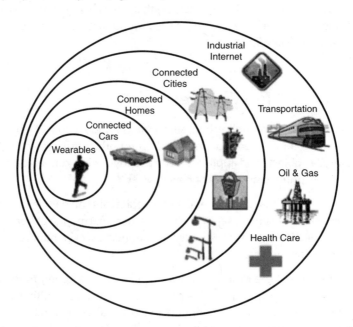

**Figure 2.2**
*The Internet of Things landscape highlighting five key verticals where the IoT are currently under way: wearable devices, cars, homes, cities, and the industrial Internet* (Source: Goldman Sachs Global Research in an article published by Harvard Business Review)

# Wearable Devices

Whether strapped to your wrist, clipped to your eyewear, or hidden under your clothes, wearables are the fastest-growing sector of IoT, with 35 million connected devices currently in use. According to the Acquity Group, 22% of consumers already own or are planning to purchase a wearable device within the next year. By 2018, the wearable technology market is projected to be worth more than $8 billion.

Wearables include all of the popular fitness trackers, such as Fitbit and Jawbone UP, that monitor and collect data on physiological activity including heart rate, perspiration, breathing rate, sleep cycles, and blood oxygen levels. Wearables also include cameras, motion trackers, headsets that can project data and images onto the real world (known as augmented reality), smart breast pumps, and security devices like workplace ID badges.

The most popular wearable to date has been the Apple Watch, which has amped up the competition on the wristwear scene. This is an area poised for explosive growth: Strategy Analytics reported that global smart watch shipments are growing at an exponential rate. By 2020, we will likely see annual production at 400 million devices, excluding the associated phones, tablets, and PCs.

While some of the most highly touted new wearables have not gained widespread adoption (like Oculus Rift) or have not proved successful in the market (like Google Glass), dozens of well-established products are already in use and hundreds more are on the horizon. At this early stage of their development, it's easy to dismiss wearable devices as amusing gadgets and passing fads, but they actually have the potential to become massive disruptors of the modern world.

Wearables seamlessly integrate our daily routines with helpful technological utilities. We don't need to boot up a computer, unlock a mobile phone, or swipe and tap into an app—wearables provide constant, more frictionless connectivity. In addition, the "exhaust stream" of big data from these devices provides unprecedented new ways for businesses to claim their piece of the digital last mile and deeply understand their customers.

Perhaps the greatest advances in wearable technology to date have been in the realm of health, wellness, and athletics. Athletic coaches and trainers are already analyzing data from smart shoes and smart clothing (such as Nike+ E-Kit and NuMetrex Heart Sensing Racer Tank Top)—for example, vertical leap, heart rate, quickness, and number of times jumped during a game or workout—to help athletes continually improve.

But wearables are not merely limited to measurement. There is an emerging class of wearable therapeutics, such as Chrono (administers a precise amount of nicotine based on real-time nicotine levels in your bloodstream), Snug Vest (inflates to provide a hug-like squeeze to relieve anxiety associated with autism), and Halo Neuroscience (founded by my husband Dan; delivers precise neurostimulation to improve brain performance).

## Connected Cars

First, consider what the *un*connected car is doing technologically today. Most contemporary models have 20 times the computing power of a desktop computer and require 100 million lines of software code, churning through as much as 25 gigabytes of data per hour of operation. To date, most of this digital technology has focused on the vehicle's internal functions, such as antilock brakes and power steering, or navigation, but advancements in IoT will bring attention to the car's ability to go much farther, connecting to drivers, roads, and more in ever-greater ways.

New IoT technologies are already revolutionizing the automotive business and offering totally new revenue streams from new business models. General Motors' subsidiary OnStar was an early pioneer in this space. More recently, Audi, Tesla, and Volvo have introduced a Connected Car service in partnership with AT&T. Their cars offer high-speed 3G or 4G connections for a monthly subscription fee. GM is also phasing in LTE support, which allows vehicles to become WiFi hotspots with connectivity for several devices.

By 2025, the majority of vehicles on the road in industrialized countries will likely be connected to the Internet. These cars will be constantly capturing data about fuel consumption, pollutants, wear and tear, speed, and location when in use. Such a shift will be transformational not only for the auto industry, but also for all adjacent and digital industries. Today, a handful of forward-thinking insurers are already utilizing data from actual driving patterns to much more accurately calculate risk and adjust premiums. Traditionally, most insurance companies have placed customers into broad categories of risk based on proxy metrics such as age, marital status, and type of car. But new telematics devices allow insurers to go from proxy risk to actual risk based on how much people actually drive, where they drive, how fast, and how they react to road conditions. For example, State Farm's Drive Safe & Save Program allows drivers to qualify for lower premiums by installing a telematics device in their vehicle and proving they are safe drivers. Basic analysis of driving patterns provides a way to verify who is driving and drastically minimize the risk of fraud. Metromile, a Silicon Valley startup company, similarly utilizes in-car telematics to offer pay-as-you-go insurance based on miles driven.

Of course, the ultimate connected car is the autonomous vehicle, exemplified by Google's Self-Driving Car. Over the last few years, Google's autonomous cars have driven 1 million miles without a human driver. There have been some accidents, though none serious and none where the autonomous car was at fault. Google's cars are already smart enough to navigate through busy urban streets full of pedestrians, cyclists, and all sorts of other complications, and development continues at a furious pace. The company expects to have a finished product ready to sell on the market in the next several years. In the meantime, Apple, Uber, Tesla, NextEV, and a slew of traditional auto manufacturers are all rushing to develop their own proprietary autonomous driving technologies.

Companies like Ford, Toyota, and BMW, which traditionally focused on physical supply chains and manufacturing, have been thrust into entirely new businesses, including software, mobility services, insurance, transportation and logistics, media, and commerce. Who bears the risk and cost of an auto accident if there's no human driver? What will people do during their long commutes when they no longer have to drive because cars drive themselves? Perhaps they will want to stream a movie or join a videoconference meeting.

## Connected Homes

The concept of a connected home has been around since the 1960s, yet the home is one of the few domains in our lives still operating primarily with analog solutions. According to Gartner, only 16% of US households currently use some form of smart home technology, and most often that technology is a security alarm system.

The home, therefore, is an area ripe for growth. Home automation devices such as smart thermostats (e.g., Nest), smart entry, smart locks, and WiFi-enabled light switches allow for comfort and convenience, while security monitoring devices capture trespassers and immediately alert the appropriate authorities.

Naturally, all of these connected devices in the home present fantastic customer engagement opportunities. Imagine an interactive digital mirror that advises you on which hair products, makeup, clothing, shoes, and accessories would work best for you on any given day, based on the temperature and humidity outside or meetings on your calendar. Looking into the mirror, you could see image projections of each suggested option and make a selection either from your own closet or from an on-demand shopping service such as Poshmark. Now who's the fairest of them all?

Think this is mere fantasy? Actually, the technology now exists to make Cher's futuristic closet in the 1995 movie *Clueless* a reality. Metail, a London-based technology company, has already developed software that builds a 3-D model of you, including hairstyles and skin tone. Someone just needs to combine this technology with a smart mirror and closet to bring the fashionista's dream to fruition.

Turning to the kitchen, Samsung has made a splash with its smart, camera-enabled refrigerator that can beam photos of what's inside to your phone so you can see what you need to pick up at the store. The refrigerator also analyzes images of its contents and sends alerts when a particular food item is likely past its expiration date. Amazon.com's Dash Replenishment Service (DRS) takes this further up the supply chain by enabling connected devices to order refills of physical goods when supplies run low, such as a coffee maker that orders more beans.

Elsewhere in the home, Whirlpool Brand's new smart washing machine can detect when you are about to run out of laundry detergent and provide automatic ordering through DRS. Brother smart printers, which for years have provided notifications when ink and toner are low, can now take the next step and order replacement cartridges. These scenarios may sound crazy but are now reality.

# The Big Data Explosion and Predictive Applications

The billions of people (on social networks) and billions of Things (on IoT) using, clicking, sharing, and sensing every second of every day are creating enormous mountains of data and metadata. Increasingly, forward-thinking companies are analyzing this "big data" to reveal statistical patterns and associations, often unexpected, to deliver greater efficiency, convenience, and delight to customers.

Big data analytics is now consistently identified as one of the top economic growth, competitiveness, and productivity drivers for businesses. According to McKinsey Global Institute, the application of big data analytics to retail and manufacturing could yield $300 billion in savings and value creation, while offering an additional $300 billion in productivity gains in the healthcare and government realms within the next five years.

All the data in the world, however, is useless without analysis yielding actionable insights. This is where predictive analytics comes in. How does it work? How do companies analyze empirical behaviors and habits of people so as to predict or influence future scenarios?

First, you take an initial set of data (called a "training set") to discover potentially predictive relationships using some combination of hypotheses (for example, a retailer might hypothesize that someone interested in buying a new iPhone is also likely to buy a new iPhone case) and Bayesian or Frequentist statistical regressions. From there, you can apply "machine learning" algorithms to continuously fine-tune the prediction based on feedback.

A well-known example of predictive analytics, known as collaborative filtering in this case, is Amazon.com's "Customers Who Bought This Item Also Bought" feature (by company estimates, it drives more than one-third of product sales). If large numbers of people consistently ignore all of the suggested products listed on the first page of the "Customers Who Bought This Item Also Bought" section, then a good machine-learning algorithm would show different items in that space in the future. Otherwise, if lots of people click on and ultimately purchase a product listed on the second page of the section, the algorithm ought to move it to the first page for future visits.

Many of these IoT examples incorporate predictive analytics, but they just scratch the surface of what's possible. Predictive insights have potential applications in almost every industry—from political campaigns and motivating people to get flu shots to driving retail store visits, preventing crime, and reducing waste.

### Target's Pregnancy Predictor

Many people are familiar with the well-reported predictive strategy that Target successfully employed and that drew a lot of press a few years ago. Target developed an algorithm to tag each shopper with a "pregnancy prediction" score so that it could promote baby products to the right customers at the right time. Target's algorithm was based on years of data, which suggested that consumers who suddenly start buying scent-free soap and extra-large bags of cotton balls, hand sanitizer, and washcloths may be signaling they are getting close to their delivery date, since they subsequently tend to buy diapers and wipes.

Though clever, this marketing strategy had unintended consequences. Sometimes parents found out that their teenage daughter was pregnant, though she hadn't told them yet. The targeted print mailer sent to their house outed her secret and caused some family drama. As this example illustrates, predictive analytics are not without controversy and risks. But this example also shows just how accurate these measures can be.

Other industries have also been able to draw on data from millions of consumers to create targeted promotions and cross-sell offers. The travel industry, which has always produced voluminous transactional data, routinely employs big data analytics to predict patterns in consumer behavior to instantly modify flight prices and cross-sell hotel or rental car offers on the fly. Orbitz, an online booking company, wondered if Apple users might be drawn to higher-end hotels. Its predictive analytics efforts confirmed this suspicion, indicating that visitors who accessed the Orbitz website or mobile app from an iPhone, iPad, or Mac tend to spend as much as 30% more per night on hotel stays. As a result, Orbitz modified the landing page and featured promotions shown to Apple users compared to Windows users.

Beyond the realm of sales and marketing, predictive analytics can help companies stay ahead of breakdowns and other problems. ATMs, self-checkout machines, and ticket kiosks can relay data about their performance, or even local weather and foot traffic patterns, allowing technicians to be summoned quickly to prevent or minimize costly downtime.

Finally, predictive analytics from IoT data could completely shake up the insurance industry, as illustrated by the earlier examples of State Farm's Drive Safe & Save Program and Metromile, as well as the following case study of John Hancock Insurance Company.

### Variable, Fitness-Based Pricing for Life Insurance

Last year, John Hancock, the US division of Canada-based global insurance company Manulife, became the first insurer to offer customers discounts for sharing ongoing personal activity data from a wearable device and attaining certain fitness milestones. As part of the Vitality Program, individuals who opt to share their data are given a free Fitbit monitor, which they can authorize to automatically send their fitness data to the insurer. Customers are encouraged to maintain active lifestyles, earning up to double-digit percent discounts on their insurance premiums, as well as gift cards, discounted hotel stays, and other perks for achieving various fitness activity levels.

*continues…*

In the past, buying a life insurance policy required customers to share detailed medical information upfront to lock in their insurance premium schedule for the duration of the policy—in essence, data collected during a snapshot in time was used to predict risk in the future. John Hancock is reinventing the risk calculation by using real-time data to continually update and reprice risk. By exposing the underlying risk data and desired milestones (namely, longer and more frequent workouts) to customers, the insurer is changing its role from passive financial risk company to proactive coach for a healthier lifestyle.

Historically, insurance customers have had little reason to be in regular communication with their insurance company unless there was a claim, but Vitality has turned this pattern on its head. Vitality capitalizes on constant connectivity to encourage customers to exercise more, thereby increasing profitability for John Hancock, because healthier customers live longer and delay the death benefit payout associated with life insurance policies.

In an industry that for decades has not innovated much and had infrequent, analog-only interactions with customers, Vitality represents an entirely new engagement paradigm, transforming and deepening the relationship John Hancock can now have with its customers while transforming its actuarial table and core business model. This trend is not limited to the United States. European insurer Generali and Asian insurer AIA have launched similar Vitality programs in their core markets.

Vitality is a terrific example of how IoT has opened new opportunities for traditional, non-digital firms to claim key pieces of the digital last mile and reorient themselves around today's always-connected consumer. There are interesting lessons companies from all industries can draw from the success with wearables realized by John Hancock, Generali, and AIA.

## Predictive Insights from Social Business

Thanks to all of those clicks, comments, tweets, views, and shares, social media has become an incredibly rich and powerful source of big data for companies to analyze and use along a multitude of dimensions.

In fact, my own interest in Social Business started with the idea of applying predictive analytics to help sales reps reach out to the right customer at the right time with the right message. After writing my first book, *The Facebook Era,* I founded and am currently CEO of Hearsay Social, a Silicon Valley technology company that does just this. Hearsay's platform helps relationship managers "hear" what customers are sharing on social and other digital channels (using natural-language processing and machine-learning algorithms) and, based on what's shared, select what to "say" to these contacts that is likely to resonate with them.

For example, Hearsay's predictive algorithms look for clues indicating someone has had a baby, notifies financial advisors of this prediction, and suggests content suitable for new parents (such as information about setting up a trust or 529 college savings plan). Social media sites such as Twitter and Facebook have become one of the first places people go to share special moments with their friends and the world, and the majority of consumers now expect to be able to find, research, and communicate with their advisors and other service providers through social, email, web, and text messaging.

## Summary

Every connected room, home, car, and device represents a brand-new segment of the digital last mile. We are still in the early innings of connected devices, so much is still up for grabs. From Facebook's smart device app development platform Parse and the company's acquisition of Oculus VR, the developer of virtual reality wearable goggles, to Chinese social media giant Tencent's TOS+ operating system for smart devices such as TVs, watches, and smart home appliances, it's no wonder the current masters of the digital screen are eager to stake their claims in this territory. The consumer mindshare, data, and utility generated from managing our physical lives (via IoT) will eclipse even those associated with our digital lives. Traditional firms should take note and take action, for a great prize awaits.

The promise of IoT is that devices will be able to communicate with us, with each other, and with other people, generating gigantic amounts of data that can be crunched with advanced analytics for better decision making, along with greater efficiency, higher convenience, and a more delightful consumer experience. In just a few short years, IoT will become integral to our lives in the form of wearables, connected cars, connected homes, and much more. Soon, we will see connected offices, cities, and industries. IoT will be the biggest disruptive technology movement yet, connecting every aspect of our physical space and lives to our digital devices, identity, and activities. Social network companies are already racing to see which aspects of the IoT last mile they can lay claim to.

Much as the first two waves of the Internet's development led to sea-changes in the economy, IoT will revolutionize business, designating clear leaders and laggards in technology and nontechnology industries alike. Who will be the Google, Facebook, and Netflix of IoT? Perhaps it will be your company.

**3**

*"Give me what I want, when I want it."*
—Consumers everywhere

# Trust, Convenience, and Millennials: The Collaborative Economy

Drivers for hire. House rental this weekend. Valet service from anywhere. Ingredients for tonight's dinner recipe delivered to your doorstep. Someone to clean your house, mow your lawn, help you move, cater your party, walk your dog, or babysit your kid RIGHT NOW. The collaborative economy is all around us, accessible via mobile apps on our smartphones through which we can hire underutilized assets (such as empty houses, idle cars, and labor) from other community members via Lyft, Uber, Airbnb, Luxe, Instacart, Thumbtack, TaskRabbit, and other real-time service marketplaces.

While *collaborative economy*—also known as the sharing economy (though this is somewhat of a misnomer, given that people are really "renting" rather than "sharing"), gig economy, on-demand economy, or peer-to-peer commerce—is a relatively new and trendy term, the idea of sharing or renting is nothing new. As defined by my friend Jeremiah Owyang, founder of Crowd Companies and key thought leader in this space, the collaborative economy is "an economic model where commonly available technologies enable people to get what they need from each other." Certainly Vacation Rentals By Owner (VRBO), Craigslist, eBay, and even used clothing stores and carpools fit this description, and all of them have been around for decades.

What *is* new and unprecedented is the expected instant gratification and high participation rate, which have been fueled by nearly ubiquitous smartphone penetration and increased levels of online trust thanks to social networks. Mobile devices that are location aware and able to process real-time transactions have enabled widespread adoption of the collaborative economy by instantly connecting workers and consumers. There are now more than 2 billion smartphone subscribers worldwide, which means 2 billion people who can more easily than ever connect to the supply or demand side (often both) of the collaborative economy. As noted in Chapter 2, smartphones have become the remote control by which consumers can order almost anything with a tap and swipe. For on-demand workers, smartphones are the dispatcher and gig supervisor, continually collecting data on everything from GPS location to customer ratings.

Just as the Internet of Things digitally connects all physical objects, so the collaborative economy digitally connects on-demand labor with consumers. From transportation and hospitality to home improvement, dining, and child care, the collaborative economy is extending the digital last mile to traditionally offline services. The opportunities in this realm are enormous. PwC estimates the movement from traditional employment and services to collaborative, on-demand consumption is driving upward of $15 billion in annual revenues today, with this revenue stream expected to exceed $300 billion in the coming decade. Table 3.1 summarizes the top players in this market.

**Table 3.1    Major Collaborative Service Categories and Providers**

| Category | Marketplace Companies |
| --- | --- |
| Transportation | Uber and Lyft are the largest and best-known ride-sharing services. Consumers can select from a traditional car service (town car or SUV), taxi, or community driver (least expensive option), and within minutes their ride will show up. |
| | Luxe is an on-demand valet parking service, targeting urban consumers who are frustrated with having to keep circling the block in search of a parking spot. |
| Food and food delivery | DoorDash, Postmates, and Caviar (acquired by Square) are mobile-first delivery services that enable consumers to order from popular local restaurants and have those orders delivered typically within an hour. |
| | Sprig, SpoonRocket, and Munchery actually make, sell, and deliver all of their own food; thus they are more like virtual restaurants. |
| | For consumers who appreciate the convenience of delivery but want to cook themselves, Instacart and Postmates provide on-demand grocery delivery and Blue Apron delivers preportioned ingredients for seasonal recipes it formulates. |
| Delivery | Shyp will send an on-demand courier to pick up packages that consumers wish to send, then take care of all the packaging and shipping, including comparing rates across FedEx, UPS, and USPS. |
| | In addition to food delivery, Postmates also provides general courier services for "anything." Uber has also expanded into delivery and logistics. |
| Tasks/gigs | Thumbtack, TaskRabbit, and Handybook help connect consumers with professional services delivered in the home, such as housecleaning, home repair, painting, and dog-walking. |

| Category | Marketplace Companies |
|---|---|
| Hospitality | Airbnb is the leader in allowing consumers to list, discover, and book apartments, rooms, entire houses, and all kinds of unique spaces, such as castles, yerts, and treehouses. HomeAway and VRBO are more traditional listing services and do not currently handle payments. |
|  | Hotel Tonight provides consumers with great deals on last-minute hotel inventory. |
| Professional services | Priori, Upcounsel, and Lawdingo connect mostly small and medium business (SMB) clients looking to trim costs with experienced business lawyers for both one-off projects and ongoing legal services. |
|  | Scripted is a marketplace for businesses to find writers who will draft blog posts, email campaigns, whitepapers, and other collateral. |
|  | Upwork, Freelancer, and LinkedIn ProFinder are more generalist business professional marketplaces for everything from web and mobile development, design, and translation to accounting, legal services, and copywriting. |
|  | Doctor On Demand, MDLive, American Well, and Teladoc offer quick virtual consultations with licensed physicians. |

For traditional companies, the greatest risk is losing control of the customer as the last mile goes digital and onto someone else's mobile app. The threat isn't disintermediation (as was a common fear with the Internet), but rather *intermediation* by a collaborative economy platform such as Postmates or Uber. Perhaps that is the reason why GM invested $500 million in Lyft in 2016. As we'll discuss later in this chapter, the challenge for many product and service companies today is finding a way to stay relevant to a customer who increasingly seeks services over products and service marketplaces over service providers.

## Social Networks Meet the Collaborative Economy

Social networks have provided an important foundation of online trust, which has in turn enabled the emergence of the collaborative economy. It's easy to take for granted now, but this online trust is relatively new. In the early days of the web, users didn't use their real names, and forums and chats were populated with fake identities prone to spamming and scamming. A *New Yorker* cartoon published in 1993 illustrates the state of online trust prior to Facebook, popularizing the saying, "On the Internet, nobody knows you're a dog" (Figure 3.1).

"Real identity" on the web, popularized by Facebook and LinkedIn's respective real-name policies, is actually relatively new. When you deal with a Facebook-verified person on the web whom you may not know personally, you are able to (usually) rule out that you're interacting with a fake bot or a scammer. All of the major social networks have invested tremendous resources in this area, and it has created a new level of trust online. The collaborative economy platforms are doing their part, too.

**Figure 3.1**
*A 1993 New Yorker cartoon underscoring the lack of trust on the Internet* (Source: The New Yorker)

### Building Trust in the Collaborative Economy

Today, numerous collaborative economy sites, from Airbnb to Lyft, encourage customers to log in with their Facebook credentials to foster trust through use of real names, real user photos (Lyft drivers are shown the Facebook profile picture of whoever has ordered a pickup to help them identify the right passenger), and mutual connections.

Lyft and Uber conduct background checks and driving record checks on drivers, and Airbnb created a special Verified ID badge, which many hosts and guests look for when deciding whether to host or stay with someone. To earn the badge, users must submit a government-issued form of identification, connect a social profile (such as LinkedIn, Facebook, or Google) to their Airbnb account, upload an Airbnb profile photo, and provide a verified phone number and email address.

Generous guarantees and refund policies are also important for convincing skeptical consumers to transact digitally, as eBay demonstrated with its Money Back Guarantee for buyers and Seller Protection program for sellers. Airbnb has a similar Guest Refund Policy (say, if the amenities or number of bedrooms does not match what was in the listing) and Host Guarantee (protection against property damage up to $1 million).

But for Facebook and LinkedIn, providing trusted online identity is just the beginning. In very different ways, both of these organizations are seeking to play an even greater role in collaborative economy transactions. As we'll explore in greater detail in Chapter 7, Facebook Messenger's recently introduced payment capabilities will unlock many new areas of social commerce, including on-demand transactions. I would bet that in relatively short order, Facebook will become a major clearinghouse for consumer products and on-demand services between or involving its members. Facebook Messenger has already been integrated with on-demand service companies like Uber to allow consumers to transact within the Messenger app. In the Uber case, consumers can order rides in the context of making plans with friends (Figure 3.2). The integration automatically provides an estimated wait time and arrival time to all parties involved. In China, WeChat users have been able to hail a Didi Dache taxi from within the app since 2014, though it functions more as an "app-within-an-app" rather than in context with messages.

**Figure 3.2**
*Consumers can order a ride from Uber from within Facebook Messenger* (Source: Facebook)

Professional services, by comparison, are typically not on-demand services. Instead, they often involve extensive vetting, and the services are provided over a period of weeks, months, or years rather than instantly. Upwork (formerly Elance-oDesk) and Freelancer are the leading professional services marketplaces, but LinkedIn has recently entered into the space with its new ProFinder service, which connects businesses and individuals with freelance accountants, bookkeepers, content strategists, copywriters, editors, graphic designers, and more.

LinkedIn brings important elements of trusted online reputation, such as profiles, connections in common, experience, education, endorsed skills, and recommendations, to the equation and will likely be a formidable player. ProFinder is a logical extension to LinkedIn's existing Talent Solutions business, which enables recruiters to connect with qualified candidates generally for full-time positions. Both professional service marketplaces and transactional service marketplaces will dramatically change our economy and society.

## Millennial Attitudes Transforming Business

Like social media, the collaborative economy has gone mainstream but hails from a millennial upbringing. Lyft, Uber, Airbnb, Thumbtack, TaskRabbit, and more were created by millennials for millennials. Generation Y attitudes and expectations continue to be a key driving force behind the growth of the collaborative economy. Therefore, we will begin with a short discussion of this fascinating generation.

Having grown up amidst the tech boom-and-bust of the late 1990s and housing boom-and-bust and Great Recession of 2008, and often mired by student loans, the millennial generation is skittish about consumption and employment. Unlike their parents, millennials are not as interested in owning a car or home. Instead, the most prized possession for millennials is their smartphone, which most say never leaves their side.

Millennials now constitute the largest population cohort the United States has ever seen and are the largest civilian labor force, accounting for more than one-third of all US workers. Millennials value flexible work hours and want jobs that enable them to be constantly connected, according to research by Internet analyst Mary Meeker. Consulting firm Archpoint found that one-third of millennials would actually forgo a higher salary to work at a company that did not limit their technology access, and more than half wouldn't accept a job at a company where social media sites are blocked. Nearly half use personal smartphones for work purposes (compared to 18% of older generations), and more than 40% of millennials are likely to download and pay out of pocket for apps to use for work purposes in the next 12 months.[1] It's no surprise that 2.7 million (44%) of the on-demand workers in the United States are millennials, according to findings from MBO Partners and Emergent Research.

---

1. "Freelancing in America," survey of 5000 working Americans commissioned by Freelancer's Union and Upwork (formerly Elance-oDesk), September 2014; "Generation Y: Understanding the Work Habits of Millennials," Halogen Software blog, September 2014; "The State of Workplace Productivity Report," Cornerstone OnDemand, August 2013, survey of 1029 employed Americans age 18 and older; "Millennials at Work: Reshaping the Workplace," PWC, 2011.

On the consumption side of the equation, Barron's has calculated millennials' purchasing power to be $200 billion annually. Here are six additional millennial behaviors and attitudes worth noting. As you will see, many of these have crossed the chasm, so to speak, and are now true of the broader consumer population.

- **Prefer convenience, experiences, and access over ownership.** The Great Recession changed consumer attitudes toward possessions and social status. According to BAV Consulting, 66% of all consumers (and nearly 80% of millennials) now say they aspire to a more minimal lifestyle with fewer things. These individuals find more satisfaction and status in experiences (widely trumpeted through social media, no doubt), than in pricy material possessions. The sustainability movement, popular among millennials, has further aligned attitudes against a material culture. Finally, far more millennials than non-millennials report a desire to "visit every continent and travel abroad as much as possible," according to a survey by Boston Consulting Group.

- **Insist on access to information and transparency.** While millennials are highly skeptical of "corporate mouthpieces" and advertising, they trust and rely on online ratings and reviews. More than half reported accessing user reviews and researching products from multiple information sources while shopping. Cumulative ratings and reviews posted by previous customers have become incredible validators and drivers of purchase, influencing more than 80% of millennial buying decisions.[2] Would you buy a humidifier with a two-star rating on Amazon? Would you dine at a restaurant rated negatively by your friend on Yelp? Most millennials wouldn't.

- **Want to consult friends and family.** Although millennials self-identify as being independent, their behavior indicates a desire to constantly seek reassurance from friends and family on major purchase decisions from consumer electronics to financial advice. Often, they turn to social media to do so. More than 50% of millennials explore brands via trusted friend groups on social networks, and they tend to favor brands that have company Facebook Pages and mobile websites. A majority also use social media to talk about products and brands they are proud to support.

- **Expect constant mobile connectivity.** Nearly 90% of millennials have their phone on them at all times, and roughly half say they would sooner give up their sense of smell than give up their access to technology.[3] Technology firm Mitek found that more than 80% of millennials believe it's important for retailers to have high-quality mobile apps, while 86% say there are still many websites that lack good mobile functionality. In addition, 36% have made a decision on where to buy or switched providers based on mobile functionality, and 14% say they would not do business with a company that doesn't have a mobile site or app.

- **Demand instant gratification.** When millennial consumers tweet to complain about poor customer service, they expect an immediate response. When they order a Lyft or Uber ride, they expect the car to show up immediately. Many cancel the order if the

2. Archpoint, http://www.archpointconsulting.com/articles/8-truths-about-millennials-can-change-way-you-do-business

3. Archpoint, http://www.archpointconsulting.com/articles/8-truths-about-millennials-can-change-way-you-do-business

estimated arrival time is more than 10 minutes. Millennials carry these expectations of instant gratification with them into every arena of their work and home lives—and hence the explosive rise of the collaborative, on-demand economy.

• **Drawn to urban (and urban-like) environments.** In her book *The End of the Suburbs*, *Fortune* editor Leigh Gallagher follows the path of rapid urbanization in America. Consistent with millennials' preference for access and experiences over ownership, she found that many millennials are choosing to live in urban areas with a higher population density, which typically offer convenient access to shops, cafes, and restaurants, and cut down on commute times. This has been an important enabler for local on-demand service marketplaces, which depend on proximity of people and economies of scale.

## Millennial Attitudes and Ride Sharing

Logan Green, Co-founder and CEO, Lyft

The culture of ownership is changing. A generation of millennials came of age against a backdrop of economic uncertainty, social change, and a shift in power dynamics away from institutions and back to individuals. My generation questions the status quo, invents new ways of doing things, and focuses on social impact in everything we do. This is the "we" generation, not the "me" generation. A generation that favors experiences over material possessions. A generation that trusts a recommendation from a friend more than an expert.

So it's not surprising that all of these dynamics intersect to create a shift away from individual ownership and to an economy that is based around goods and services when, and only when, they are needed.

At Lyft, we see these trends manifest themselves in people's everyday lives. Ride sharing is expanding rapidly because millennials don't value car ownership—they value time and convenience more. The cost of car ownership is real. It is still the second highest household expense in the United States, higher even than food. And it is utilized just 4% of the time.

For millennials, it doesn't make sense to own a car. The percentage of 16- to 24-year-olds with a driver's license is less than 70% for the first time since 1963. In 1984, young adults were almost 40% of new-car buyers in America—a record high. Today, that percentage is just 27% and declining. When we surveyed people, about a third said they don't need to own a car.

These ownership and attitudinal patterns will have major ramifications for our economy and our cities. When we move from individual car ownership to transportation as a service—a car when you need it, in minutes—we profoundly improve our cities and our communities. A city with less congestion isn't just a more pleasant place to live—though it certainly is. It's also an opportunity to rethink the way we build our cities. We can have parks instead of parking lots. Walkways, not freeways. A city built around people, not cars.

When we move away from individual ownership to shared services, we can redesign the physical infrastructure in a way that brings people and communities back together. We can spend less time in traffic and more time making an impact on our communities and the world. This will be the lasting impact of the collaborative economy.

## Not Just Millennials

As much as people love to dissect Generation Y, the truth is that many of these attitudes have actually permeated the mainstream population. A lot of consumers these days—not just millennials—want to do their own product research, validate purchases with family and friends, and find convenience and instant gratification. These expectations are the natural result of constant connectivity. While millennials may have been the first generation to be digitally savvy, a lot more people across every generation fit this description.

Take the topic of trust in big banks and big corporations, for example. This level of trust has been on the decline for decades (Figure 3.3).[4] Occupy Wall Street—a protest against the lack of trustworthiness—was seeded by millennials but spread to a broad cross-section of society.

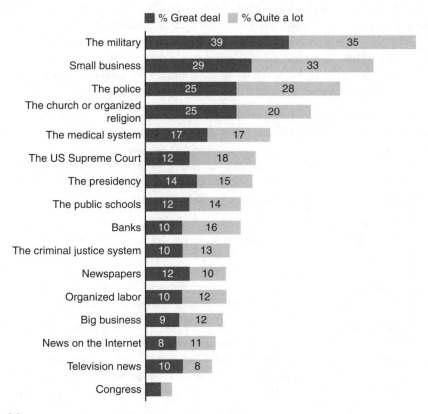

**Figure 3.3**

*Of all US institutions, American consumers are most skeptical of Congress, big business, and big media—both television news and Internet news* (Source: ©2015 Gallup, Inc. All rights reserved. The content is used with permission; however, Gallup retains all rights of republication.)

4. Millennial Disruption Index, a three-year study of roughly 10,000 millennials, conducted by Scratch/Viacom Media Networks. http://www.miteksystems.com/about/news-releases/millennial-study-one-in-three-want-to-communicate-by-snapping-a-mobile-photo

As trust in too-big-to-fail corporations and their advertising campaigns has eroded, there has been a simultaneous rise in trust of friends and peers to fill the gap. Through social media and online ratings and reviews, friends' and peers' opinions are now more accessible than ever before, creating and reinforcing this behavior of consulting the community.

## Lessons from Collaborative Marketplaces

In ever-expanding categories, consumers have demonstrated they want instant access to products and services without the ownership and commitment. Today, there are at least a dozen unicorn (valued at $1 billion or more) collaborative companies, including Uber and Airbnb (both valued at double-digit billions), Lyft, Didi Kuaidi (China), Ele.me (China), Delivery Hero (Germany), Hellofresh (Germany), Instacart, Blue Apron, BlaBlaCar (France), Ucar Group (China), and GrabTaxi (Singapore). Incredibly, none of these companies existed a decade ago. To be fair, some may not exist a decade from now. Many of their business models are expensive and hard to scale, and it's not clear in all cases what the path to profitability looks like.

Even with these caveats, traditional businesses can glean important lessons from the early success of these collaborative services. Elements of their practices, such as branding and humanizing service professionals or offering online ratings and reviews, could be applied to any business. First and foremost, collaborative companies have adapted to the expectations of today's always-connected consumer (and worker), recognizing that convenience and a delightfully easy-to-use mobile app have become table stakes:

- **Create a dead-simple mobile app.** All successful collaborative companies start with a simple-to-use mobile app or build an integration into one of the top mobile messaging apps such as WeChat or Facebook Messenger. No matter how much complexity there is behind the scenes in matching drivers with riders or coordinating who cooks or picks up a meal, all of it is abstracted from both consumer and worker, and the end result is the consumer is able to order what she wants in seconds, with just a few taps.

- **Humanize service providers.** The Lyft driver who comes to pick you up isn't some anonymous cog. You are shown her name, photo, hometown, and hobbies. The etiquette is to sit in the front seat and fist bump: It is a truly human interaction. On Airbnb, people renting out their homes aren't called "landlords." They are "hosts" who share their photos and interests on their profiles. More broadly, the more skilled the professional, the more consumers expect to be able to research *that specific individual* online before they decide to go with him or her, even if they trust the company overall.

- **Provide community ratings and reviews.** After every Lyft or Uber ride, Airbnb stay, or Postmates delivery, both consumer and service provider rate each other and can leave detailed reviews. Consumers value transparency and have come to expect peer ratings and reviews. These days, many consumers, especially millennials, won't set foot in a restaurant without first consulting Yelp, a dedicated community review site for local businesses. Online reputation has become so essential that LinkedIn has recently launched its own freelance marketplace, called ProFinder.

- **Offer speed and convenience.** Today's consumers expect things to happen instantly. They do not want to be put on hold or made to wait. Consumers routinely cancel on Uber drivers who are too far away, and they hang up when the hold music has been playing for too long. Consumers also value convenience. They do not want to walk to a taxi stand or even have to pick up their own groceries—they want everything to come to them. This is why Starbucks is testing delivery service as an extension to its Mobile Order and Pay app and why Amazon Prime has become so popular. Recently, Uber launched a new delivery service, UberRUSH, which allows customers ranging in size from 1-800-FLOWERS to local small businesses to tap into its local transportation network. The challenge is that last-mile delivery is extremely expensive.

- **Proactively share status updates.** Consumers also expect real-time status updates, such as how the ride-sharing apps display a map of where the driver is at precisely that moment. Consumers want to know how far away the driver is so they can come out and meet the driver just as he is pulling up. Online apparel retailer Everlane has started sharing order status updates via Facebook Messages so customers know when their order has been shipped and what the ETA is.

- **Store payments and preferences.** The beauty of mobile apps is it's generally secure to keep users logged in to your app. Lyft, Instacart, and Postmates all do just this. They also store payment information and preferences, such as recent orders and last pick-up/drop-off points, making it extremely easy and frictionless to place a new order.

- **Democratize access to luxury.** Private car service used to be reserved for busy executives, the wealthy, and special occasions such as prom or weddings. The same was true for courier service, private chefs, valet service, and on-location hair and makeup services. By mobilizing community labor and allowing for fractional ownership, collaborative marketplace companies have been able to drive down costs, increase demand, and democratize access to these once-luxury products and services.

- **Activate idle resources and find buyers in local regions.** A big aspect of the collaborative economy's cost advantage comes from tapping into unutilized or underutilized local assets, such as an idle town car, an empty house, or an unemployed person.

Collaborative companies are also fascinating from a business-model and supply-chain perspective.

- **Extremely lean supply chains.** Uber and Lyft are the world's largest taxi companies but own no vehicles. Airbnb is the world's largest hotel, but owns and leases no real estate. By claiming the digital last mile *for both workers and consumers*, these companies have been able to build multibillion-dollar businesses off of mobilizing and managing *other people's* underutilized time and assets.

- **Demand-based pricing.** Although demand-based pricing has been around for years, such as for plane tickets and even bridge tolls, it has not traditionally been applied to most arenas. Uber's surge pricing and Postmates' blitz pricing have brought this practice into car service and deliveries, respectively, partly to help temper demand when it far exceeds the supply of workers at that moment.

- **Big data and machine learning.** Uber learns from every pickup, every ride, every rating. It collects data on which driving speeds were achievable on which roads, where there was gridlock traffic, and which routes drivers tended to take despite the driving directions suggesting otherwise. All of this data feeds into its self-driving car project. In a head-spinning twist, Uber is using its drivers to learn how to someday replace all or most of those drivers with an autonomous vehicle.

Once they solve the initial chicken-and-egg problem (generally by offering free trials to new customers and guaranteeing minimum earnings per hour worked for workers), collaborative marketplaces can get very large very quickly. They exhibit inherent network effects and, therefore, tend to be winner-take-all, monopoly-like markets. Ever heard of Summon, Hailo, Curb, or Sidecar? Neither have most people. Uber and Lyft dominate the ride-sharing space.

Often, collaborative companies claim to be removing the middleman. In reality, they are the new middleman, albeit a more efficient and tech-savvy one. As essentially monopolies, they have tremendous power in both setting prices for consumers and determining how to split revenues with workers.

The conventional view of the relationship between the customer and the company is like a one-way conveyer belt. The consumer sits at the end, waiting for products and services to roll off the line, so to speak. The company hopes it has produced or staffed for what the customer demands, and it is all very straightforward. This view has become outdated. In today's on-demand economy, companies must build a conveyer belt that goes in multiple directions. It is no longer one-way to consumers, but rather goes back and forth and around, involving consumers who also sometimes double as drivers and workers, and a whole new cast of characters who bring new value to the supply chain and customer experience.

In this new world, as Jeremiah Owyang has pointed out, product makers are being reinvented as service providers (think of the IoT business models described in Chapter 2 or Blue Apron delivering fresh ingredients and recipes), service providers are becoming marketplaces (Lyft, Uber, Luxe, Postmates, and Instacart are all great examples), and marketplaces are giving rise to products. For example, in "participatory commerce," community members get involved in the funding, design, or creation of products. Kickstarter and Indiegogo do this for crowdfunding. Threadless, Minted, and Local Motors do this for T-shirts, wall art/cards, and auto vehicles, respectively.

Retailers and product makers that fail to participate in serving or at least transacting with the customer risk becoming commoditized. As Silicon Valley tech executive Andy Raskin has pointed out, most people don't notice, care, or remember the manufacturer of the last plane, bus, or train they rode on. They don't choose to fly on United Airlines versus Virgin based on who made the plane or choose to have their laundry done by Laundry Locker versus Rinse based on which brand of detergent each uses (beyond, say, specifying they want detergent that is natural and eco-friendly) or where the detergent was purchased from.

For existing companies with a well-defined mission and organization, it can be hard to grasp—much less test and implement—this fundamental shift in the relationship with the customer. But it's not impossible, as furniture and housewares retailer West Elm has shown with its LOCAL program, in which the company essentially functions as a marketplace for the wares of local artisans. West Elm customers are asked to vote on their favorite small business makers from the local community. West Elm then provides the winners, such as Brooklyn-based jewelry designer Re Jin Lee, with a monetary grant and a platform both digitally and in West Elm stores to generate awareness and sell their goods.

## Challenges and Criticisms of the Collaborative Economy

The collaborative economy has been under attack on several fronts. First, many of these marketplace companies are still fundamentally unprofitable and will require very large sums of capital to reach profitability. One reputable venture capitalist who invests in this space said he would be surprised if most of these companies survived over the long term, as they are very far from a sustainable business model. For some, the challenge is being able to raise enough money to reach profitability and have a shot at becoming self-sustaining.

Second, regulatory battles are still being fought over whether rules that apply to traditional industries such as taxi companies and hotels ought to apply to marketplaces such as Lyft, Uber, and Airbnb. Critics accuse collaborative companies of playing regulatory arbitrage, operating in gray areas just beneath the rule of law and maximizing user acquisition and profit until the laws can catch up.

Related to this is the ongoing debate about whether on-demand workers should be treated as contractors or employees. No one can deny marketplace companies have benefited immensely from the lower cost of hiring on-demand workers as contractors, but the tide seems to be turning on this point: Certain cities and jurisdictions, including Seattle, are allowing certain types of workers to unionize. In 2015, several marketplaces, including Sprig, Luxe, and Instacart, voluntarily began to transition some of their independent contractors to employees, complete with benefits such as unemployment insurance, worker's compensation, Social Security and Medicare contributions, and, depending on the number of hours worked, health insurance. Although this practice raised their labor costs by 30% or so, these companies say they are benefiting from being able to train employees, hold them to certain quality standards, and maintain a consistent schedule, which will ideally increase predictability and reduce turnover.

A third criticism leveled at collaborative companies is that they try to present a more social and community-oriented face to consumers than is actually the case. Critics argue that Zipcar, Capital Bikeshare, and Airbnb are just glorified renting and leasing. Even the words "sharing" and "collaborative" can seem like propaganda. As much as millennials self-report themselves as being mission driven, they and other consumers more broadly cite affordability and convenience—not a sense of community—as the top drivers of their decision to consume on-demand services. The truth is that most people don't want to befriend their Uber driver, get to know the previous owner of their designer dress, or spend a lot of (or any) time with their Airbnb host!

Ride-sharing marketplaces work because rides are relatively transactional, and it's more efficient to not have to rely on the same driver each time you need a ride. Airbnb works because most people don't want to rent the same place in the same city over and over again. For certain jobs, however, customers actually want to keep working with the same individual professional because of the trust and context that have been established. Home services, professional services, salons, and child care all fall into this category. This was the challenge for Homejoy, which was founded in 2010 as a marketplace for in-home cleaning services. Customers used the site to find and book a professional cleaner—but once they found someone they liked, many went off Homejoy, working directly with the cleaner. The company shut down after five years and raising nearly $40 million of venture capital.

A final challenge is what the future will look like for drivers in the ride-sharing economy given that Uber is developing its own autonomous vehicle and competitors like Lyft will just as easily be able to deploy autonomous vehicles being developed by Google, Tesla, Apple, and a handful of other companies. The automation of many job categories beyond professional driving is a much larger issue confronting society that is discussed at length in two of my favorite recent books, *Rise of the Robots* by Martin Ford and *Second Machine Age* by Erik Brynjolfsson and Andrew McAfee.

## Summary

Although Airbnb, Lyft, and Uber are the standouts, the on-demand model that these companies helped to pioneer now extends far beyond extra space and shared rides. Almost anything can be shared, rented, and ordered.

Millennials may have started the collaborative consumption trend, but many other consumers have now followed in their footsteps. Our relationship with goods and services has fundamentally shifted because of our smartphones and social media. Large social network companies including WeChat, Facebook, and LinkedIn see the opportunities this trend has opened up and are rapidly moving to become facilitators of the collaborative economy.

For a small but growing segment of the population, access to goods and services now trumps ownership, and the idea of peer-to-peer transactions seems a more convenient, affordable, and trustworthy alternative to buying from big companies. Collaborative models are now firmly established within the transportation, hospitality, and food sectors, and will likely be applied to far more sectors in the future. Even where they are not directly applicable, traditional businesses stand to glean valuable lessons from the success of these marketplaces. In the new world order, customer expectations are higher than ever. Businesses will need to embrace speed, convenience, transparency, and mobile transactability while becoming much leaner and more agile in their operations and supply chains. Companies that empower individuals—be they employees, brand ambassadors, or customer evangelists—with information, flexibility, and convenience will win their hearts, minds, wallets, and hours, while companies that fail to do so will have a tough time staying relevant and staying in business for long.

# PART II
## BUSINESS FUNCTIONS REIMAGINED

### Social Business Across the Organization

# 4

*"The riskiest thing we can do is just maintain
the status quo."*
—Roger Iger, CEO of Walt Disney

# The Management Team and Board Mandate

As venture capitalist Marc Andreessen has said, "Software is eating the world." In an age when every aspect of our lives from physical devices to offline services is being digitized, every company needs to think of itself as a technology company.

But that's not enough. Every business today must also think of itself as a Social Business. Social media and the new business models it enables are changing the relationship that it's possible for companies to have with their customers. For many companies, a successful transition into Social Business will require a change not only in their customer engagement model, but also in their mindset, culture, and organizational structure. The decision to fully digitize, make some risky bets to see what sticks, and enter fundamentally new businesses can be made only by company leadership.

Unfortunately, it's all too easy to delegate the responsibility for social media, often to an entry-level person who has grown up on Instagram. Or maybe the customer support rep who discovers customers are tweeting about the brand is suddenly promoted to run the social media operation. In many companies, social media responsibility is owned by siloed, low-level teams in marketing and customer service. When asked whether they are on social media, the senior executives at these companies say yes, but don't really understand what the big deal is, as these efforts are far removed from their core business initiatives. In such a case, what they have is not Social Business.

Social Business starts with being responsive on Twitter and amassing a large following on Facebook, but it doesn't end there. Management teams and boards need to drive and guide Social Business strategy and execution in several main areas:

- **New business models.** Leaders must study and honestly assess how the Internet of Things, collaborative economy, and mobile messaging could be disruptive to their core business models. Might there be an opportunity to "disrupt yourself" and test a new idea, such as what John Hancock, AIA, and Generali are doing with wearable fitness monitors? Does demand-based pricing make sense for your business, and is it feasible to move toward a leaner supply chain? Product companies shifting into a new role as service companies will have to take a longer-term view of the customer and develop new business models.

- **New distribution channels.** Just as they weigh the pros and cons of various offline sales distribution channels, today's business leaders need to consider whether and to what extent they will participate in someone else's online store, mobile messaging app, or 'buy button' program (more on this in Chapter 7) versus trying to launch their own. Does your organization have the brand equity, frequency, and digital chops to own the digital last mile? Will you own and invest in the digital last mile for marketing and customer support only or also for distribution? Will you offer delivery to the customer's doorstep?

- **New marketing channels, participants, cadence.** Traditionally, a relatively small number of people on the marketing team were responsible for marketing. Today, thanks to social media, far more people are involved from both inside and outside the company: customer service representatives, salespeople, recruiters, current customers, disgruntled former customers, and influencers, to name a few. In addition, the always-connected consumer expects your company to be in touch frequently but noninvasively. This can be hard to get right if your organization isn't used to being in touch on a regular basis. How will you re-architect not just your marketing department but your entire company and mobilize external brand ambassadors to deliver against this new reality?

- **Execution speed.** As discussed in Chapter 3, one secret to the success of on-demand marketplaces like Lyft and Instacart has been the ability to provide instant gratification to today's highly impatient consumer. Leaders of traditional businesses need to think about how long their customers are being made to wait and whether there are ways to more aggressively streamline supply chains, speed to market, and in-store checkout—really, the entire process from demand generation to payment to order fulfillment.

- **Organization structure and knowledge.** CEOs and functional leaders need to become educated on the social, mobile, and digital changes taking place in every department. Customer expectations of a unified experience—from e-commerce checkout to store visit to Twitter exchange with your customer support rep—requires previously siloed departments to work together and break down barriers like never before. The danger of over-delegating or having your sales team understand only social selling without an appreciation for social marketing and social customer service is missing the big-picture opportunity to stitch together a powerfully cohesive customer journey.

- **Big data.** An important by-product of digitizing more of your business is the data you can now more easily glean on everything from customer buying habits and the most efficient segments of your supply chain to which cross-sell offers are most enticing and what the return on investment is from responsive customer service. All of the social network companies, including Facebook, LinkedIn, and Twitter, as well as other digitally dominant players like Google and Amazon make the vast majority, if not all, of their revenues from monetizing the immense amounts of data they collect from owning vast sections of the digital last mile. How should you pay them for access to their data while amassing and deploying your own?

- **Agile, risk-taking culture.** All of the strategy and ideas in the world will be meaningless if your organization cannot execute. Social Business execution requires the right mindset and culture, where the occasional failure is acceptable in the name of testing new ideas and delivering at the speed of today's customer. Especially for more traditional organizations, this is far easier said than done. The desired behavior must be modeled, consistently communicated and recommunicated, and celebrated, all while keeping the core business that made your organization great in the first place afloat and humming.

- **Cohesive customer experience.** How will all of these new business models, distribution and marketing channels and stakeholders, and data fit together and be presented to the customer in a consistent, cohesive manner?

# A Lesson from History

True business transformation needs to be embraced by and driven from the top. History is littered with examples of failure by management teams and boards to embrace disruptive change. Successful companies in particular can get drunk on their own success and start to believe their current business models will last forever, whereas struggling companies can easily fall into the trap of becoming totally consumed by stopping the bleeding and forgetting to play offense.

Blockbuster is one example. Throughout the 1990s and the early 2000s, Blockbuster seemed unstoppable in its quest to provide home movie and video game rentals. At its peak, the company employed nearly 60,000 people and had more than 9000 stores worldwide. In 2000, Blockbuster CEO John Antioco even had the opportunity to acquire then-fledgling Netflix for a mere $50 million (at its peak, Blockbuster was worth $5 billion). Today, Netflix has a market capitalization of $40 billion. Blockbuster filed for bankruptcy in 2011 and a year later was sold to Dish Network for $233 million. Blockbuster was blinded by its own success and, in the end, got "eaten" by software—just like RadioShack, Motorola, and Circuit City. It's all too easy for even very smart and capable leaders to be continually consumed by the here and now, or to assume the future will be a linear continuation of the past when, in fact, a step-change lies on the horizon.

# A CEO's Vision for Social Business

Netflix is a very different story. It has profited enormously from recognizing and acting on convenience, community, and technology trends. In the early days of streaming, Netflix was still solely a DVD mailing service, and it too could have been disrupted. Instead, the company bet big and launched its own streaming service.

Netflix is a Social Business. Its management team has embraced social media and community across a multitude of business functions. CEO and founder Reed Hastings personally champions social media. He leads by example and has cultivated an impressive following on his Facebook profile, numbering 350,000 employees, customers, partners, and fans at the time of this book's writing. He so deeply understands and lives Social Business that he was invited to join Facebook's board of directors in 2011.

Thanks to Hastings's leadership, the Social Business mandate extends across the entire Netflix organization. Netflix harnesses the power of predictive analytics with its personalized recommendation engine, "Other Movies You Might Enjoy," based on community behavior. The company has cultivated huge social media followings for its hit series, such as *Orange Is the New Black* (more than 5 million Twitter followers and Facebook fans) and *House of Cards* (2.5 million Twitter followers and Facebook fans), offering a new level of engagement and community for viewers. Netflix has even enlisted a community of bloggers called the #StreamTeam, specifically targeting passionate moms, to blog about Netflix shows and content.

Because of the real-time connection to customers, Social Business can help company leaders stay more relevant and innovative. Adopting a Social Business mentality means constantly listening to customers and allowing (even encouraging) them to keep your business on its proverbial toes.

But Social Business is not without its risks. In 2012, one of Hastings's posts on Facebook, "Netflix monthly viewing exceeded 1 billion hours for the first time ever in June," prompted a Securities and Exchange Commission (SEC) review of whether this was considered a violation of Regulation Fair Disclosure ("Reg FD") (Figure 4.1). Ultimately, the SEC ruled in Netflix's favor, acknowledging the importance of social media as a communication channel with the public. Companies can now use social media to disseminate investor information in compliance with Reg FD, provided the chosen social

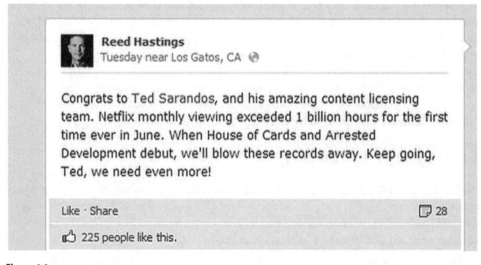

**Figure 4.1**
*The Facebook status update by Netflix CEO Reed Hastings that prompted an SEC investigation*
(Source: Facebook)

platform is open for anyone to access and investors are given prior notice about which social platforms will be used to disseminate information. At other companies where management teams don't personally understand the strategic importance of social media, an incident like the one triggered by Hastings's post would have likely resulted in a social media ban, causing the company to miss out on perhaps the most important customer engagement channel of our time.

You might wonder if Netflix's agility stems from its status as a still relatively young company (it was founded in 1997). Perhaps—but even 100-year-old companies have no excuse and really no choice but to embrace the undeniable and seismic changes resulting from today's social, always-connected consumer. Disney has been around for much longer than Netflix but is another company that has gotten Social Business right, as the following case study explores.

### Disney: The 100-Year-Old Social Business

Disney has remained relevant throughout its nearly 100-year history through constant reinvention, innovation, and, more recently, its brilliant mastery of social media.

Disney's biggest innovation wins have occurred both organically and through visionary acquisitions, such as Pixar, the YouTube channel network Maker Studios, and social games maker Playdom. Disney has gone far beyond movies and theme parks to become the leader in digital publishing and apps for kids.

Within its flagship theme parks, Disney harnesses the power of big data analytics to predict visitor activity, making its operations more efficient and the visitor experience easier to navigate. Just recently, the company rolled out MyMagic+, a smart wristband that allows guests to seamlessly check into their hotel, enter rides, and pay for goods on site. In turn, Disney's operations team can see in real time which rides have the longest lines, which food stands are most popular, and where bottlenecks may warrant intervention.

Disney's "happiest social media strategy on the planet" includes hundreds of social accounts on every popular network from Facebook and Twitter to Vine, YouTube, Pinterest, and Instagram, which are used to connect authentically with fans and thrill them with a level of spectacle that they won't find anywhere else. Disney's efforts deepen emotional ties to the brand, offering engaging content that sparks curiosity and further engagement, like videos about how *Toy Story* characters are developed or behind-the-scenes tours of popular Disney World rides.

Today, all levels of the company utilize social media in different ways, but the initial decision to invest big in social, wearables, and other forms of innovation was driven by CEO Bob Iger and his management team with the full support of the board of directors. They recognized Disney's need to be out front in terms of adopting and deploying the latest technology, and their bold bets have paid off.

At most companies, the C-Suite and board of directors are not the ones leading social and digital innovation. At all too many companies, management teams and boards of directors are too consumed with maintaining the status quo to think about how the business can adapt and remain successful in a radically different future.

## Social CEOs Leading by Example

As with any change, the best way to drive Social Business transformation is to model the desired behavior. Social Business transformation is not quite as easy as signing up CEOs with a Twitter handle, but leading by example is a good start. Today, 68% of CEOs have no social media presence, and most of those who are on social media have only a LinkedIn profile. This has to change.

Despite CEO skepticism (Figure 4.2), there is actually huge, leadership-transforming upside for CEOs who take the plunge and get on social media. For example, social media participation allows CEOs to go directly to the source and get an unfiltered pulse on what and how customers are thinking, rather than waiting months for results of expensive "voice of the customer" focus groups to be massaged and formally presented. Social media represents the modern-day versions of mystery shopping and walking

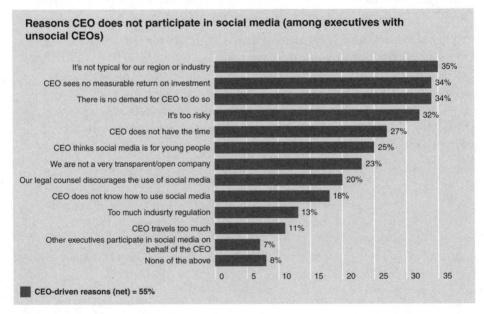

**Figure 4.2**
*Top reasons CEOs give for not participating in social media* (Source: "The Social CEO: Executives Tell All," Weber Shandwick and KRC Research, 2013)

the halls. That company letter that CEOs used to write to staff once a year? Now it's a quarterly Periscope chat and more frequent updates on social media. Many of those social, always-connected consumers work at your company and expect the same frequent, authentic touchpoints from you that they expect from other brands they love. Your customers and employees alike want to feel constantly connected to your authentic leadership.

A friend who is a *Fortune 100* CEO in financial services recently told me he has resisted joining social media because "It's not my personality." He doesn't like to constantly talk about himself, yet that's what he sees people doing on social media. I told him both of his observations are spot-on. Many people on social media are true narcissists, but it doesn't have to be that way (and such behavior usually isn't well received). Effective CEOs listen first and use social media to celebrate and promote their people, their customers, and their communities.

My friend was also concerned that if you don't know what you're doing on social media, you might come across as inauthentic. He's right about this, too. Effective social media communication requires learning a new way to speak and write. Many executives are used to authoring long, formal memos. Such missives don't work on social media (and generally don't resonate with millennials and members of Generation Z, who tend to have short attention spans and tune out corporate-speak). Social media posts need to feel authentic (casual language, like you would use to speak with friends or family, free of slogans and jargon) and follow a convention of shortcuts, abbreviations, and hashtags instead of full and complete sentences. The easiest way to learn is first to observe, practice, rinse, and repeat (you could sign up under a pseudonym to test it out).

Another obstacle holding CEOs back from "going social" is the risk of criticism or backlash. "Why stir the pot?", these skeptics say. Yet the reality these days is that people will complain and criticize even if a CEO does not have a social media account. On social media, everyone has a voice and an audience. Participating on these networks and inviting comments is a way to gather intelligence on customers and catch potential public relations landmines, ideally before they blow up. Not being on social media at all runs the even bigger risk of not making your values and mission known—a dangerous proposition in an era where customers and employees demand transparency and want to know what companies and company leaders stand for.

Not every CEO can be a Richard Branson (Figure 4.3) or Marissa Mayer on social media; each of those leaders has millions of social media followers. But that's the beauty of social media—there are as many different channels and ways of engaging as there are individuals. Social CEOs are strategically important not only for lifestyle brands and media companies like Virgin and Yahoo, but for almost all companies. As Figure 4.4 illustrates, Jack Salzwedel (CEO of American Family), Jeff Immelt (CEO of GE), and Omar Ishrak (CEO of Medtronic) are three leaders from very different industries who actively engage customers, employees, media, and other stakeholders on Twitter.

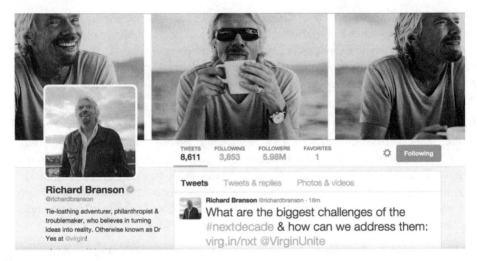

**Figure 4.3**
*Richard Branson (@richardbranson), CEO of Virgin Group, has approximately 6 million Twitter followers and is active on every social network* (Source: Twitter)

**Figure 4.4**
*Example tweets from three Fortune 500 CEOs: Jack Salzwedel (CEO of American Family Mutual Insurance), Jeff Immelt (CEO of General Electric), and Omar Ishrak (CEO of Medtronic)* (Source: Twitter)

Mike Jackson, CEO of Auto Nation, is another great example (Figure 4.5). Social CEOs like Jackson boost the reputations of their organizations, and they can also help to humanize a company. Public relations firm Weber Shandwick found that CEOs who engage with social media are more likely to be rated as good communicators. Social CEOs foster a corporate culture of openness and transparency that ultimately empowers both employees and customers. And when CEOs are active on social media, it sends the message to all employees that social media is important and strategic. Finally, if there is ever a social media crisis, social CEOs help resolve the issue better and faster because they are already on the scene and have built up credibility and following.

**Figure 4.5**
*Mike Jackson (@CEOMikeJackson), CEO of Auto Nation, tweets daily* (Source: Twitter)

The following sidebar offers guidelines for how CEOs and management team members can get started and engage.

### Guidelines for CEO Social Engagement

- Listen and explore. Social media isn't a one-way broadcast; it's a multiway opportunity for dialogue.

- Write content yourself whenever possible. If you are overwhelmed with people tweeting at you, consider training a few people from your social customer service team to learn your voice and respond on your behalf.

*continues…*

- Don't talk at your audience; engage them with questions and new insights.

- Respond as quickly as possible, with courtesy.

- Social proficiency develops over time, so give it a year or two to hit your stride.

- Recognize that the customers, employees, investors, and media representatives you are talking to are all just people. Cultivate your personal voice and be authentic. Ask yourself how your best customer, angriest customer, entry-level employee, and teenage daughter would respond before posting your message.

There are only three instances I can think of when CEOs need not be social: (1) if you have just one or very few customers (to whom you can directly reach out, and vice versa), (2) if you are dealing with confidential or national-security related information and products, and (3) if you have a monopoly (when customers have no choice, nothing is really an imperative).

In a bygone era, it was common and acceptable for denizens of the C-Suite to sit in a command-and-control ivory tower, disconnected from employees, customers, and other stakeholders. Today, similar to how an open office layout democratizes the physical space of a company, social media connects everyone in a 24/7 virtual discussion. Listening in on these interactions can provide company leadership with unparalleled insight into what is happening with customers and employees. Are they dissatisfied? If so, why? Social media offers the incredible opportunity to hear and then take action on what people are feeling about a brand.

With more than 2 billion people on social media today, it has never been more important for senior leaders to experience the world as their customers, employees, partners, and investors do—that is, through the lens of social, mobile, and digital. In the following sidebar, Scott Ham, CEO of financial firm Transamerica Life and Protection, shares his personal experience in signing up for social media and describes what he has learned.

## A Social CEO Leading by Example

Scott Ham (@ScottHamTA)

CEO, Transamerica Life & Protection

Like any busy CEO, I was initially hesitant to get on social media due to the time commitment and compliance concerns. And while there was no question that the brand as well as my client-facing employees should be on social media, I wondered whether I as CEO also needed to have a presence.

My conversations with leaders inside and outside the company persuaded me that there is unquestionable value for organizational leaders to be present and to engage. In 2012, I joined

Twitter and also really began investing in my LinkedIn presence. My experience has validated that there is immeasurable value to the brand, employees, customers, and partners when leaders personally engage that far outweighs the time and compliance investment.

I do all of my own tweets and am connected to thousands of my employees, customers, and partners. I have learned that people are constantly "listening" to social and engaging through social media—social media is an important part of how many of our customers and employees experience the world and, as such, represents a highly efficient channel for messaging leadership, success stories, and company vision and direction.

In particular, the real-time insights, direct feedback, and conversational nature of social media have been priceless. Leaders of large organizations never want to be far removed from their front-line employees and their customers. Social media can be a powerful and direct channel to both.

Above all, CEOs should be on social media because it's on us to lead by example. We can ask our people to embrace innovation and the social customer journey, but the greatest credibility comes when we ourselves do so through our actions in addition to our words. I have encouraged my senior management team to do the same, as I have seen no greater, more effective, or dynamic means of communicating our company's vision and mission. Social media allows my management team and me to interact with our people and our customers in an informal and authentic way. When done well and truly invested in, social media can be a priceless marketing, public relations, and relationship-building tool.

Your existing customers, and more broadly, the vast majority of consumers today, are using social media to discover, educate themselves, and aid their purchase decisions. Prospective employees and partners are doing the same. Part of this investigation entails researching the organizations with which they are considering doing business. A CEO who is active and authentically sharing on social media can help "seal the deal" by conveying the message that the business is a progressive, transparent, customer-focused organization.

I truly believe that social CEOs are viewed as more forward-looking, effective, accessible, and inspiring. This perception helps build brand loyalty, supports employee acquisition and retention, and contributes to a virtuous circle of customer engagement and connection, making social media well worth the couple hours a week on average I spend on this effort. It may sound like a lot of time, but in my experience, it has been easy to engage whenever I have a few extra moments— waiting in line, in transit, after reading the morning news. Social media has become an important part of any business's strategy and deserves our focus.

# The Social Business Agenda for Boards of Directors

A majority of board directors and C-Suite executives say they use social media in their personal lives but aren't ready to make their corporate life social in the same way. When boardrooms are polled about the importance of social media, only half are convinced of the value of engaging with this channel, even when presented with clear financial evidence of its benefits. So what is really at the core of management's resistance?

One challenge is that the vast majority of directors are not digital natives, nor are they even digital immigrants. A recent Deloitte survey of board practices found almost none of the 100 top large-cap companies had a director younger than age 40. Social media represents a foreign, uncomfortable zone for most directors, and one in which they haven't spent enough time to understand really what it is about. Approximately 44% say that the information they glean from social networks is mediocre or poor, while only 1% say that the information offered is excellent. This parallels many of the same concerns listed in Figure 4.2 that hold back CEOs from getting on social media. We're at the beginning of a pretty steep learning curve for these folks who continue to take a wait-and-see approach.

Another reason for board-level resistance to social media could be the nature of corporate governance structures, which are designed to maintain stability (and for good reason!) rather than address disruptive change.

Often when social media participation is brought up for consideration in the top tiers, the case made fails to be compelling because the use cases and measurements are not yet fully linked to traditional business key performance indicators such as revenue growth, profitability, and shareholder return. Sentiment analysis and number of follows, mentions, and likes don't yet easily translate into comparable-store sales and earnings per share. There certainly is a process of educating business leaders about the entirely new system of value that social media presents. At the same time, it is incumbent upon members of the C-Suite to make the link and show how social media engagement provides advantages in terms of return on investment, employee engagement, inventory costs, and brand equity.

---

## Note

A handful of public companies have recruited millennial directors as another means of injecting native social, mobile, and digital thinking into the boardroom. I am an example of this, having joined the Starbucks board in 2011. Other examples include Emily White, who was recruited to Lululemon's board when she was Business Lead of Instagram at Facebook, and former Google Analytics VP Amy Chang, who serves on the boards of both Informatica and Splunk.

---

# Viewing Social Media Offensively Versus Defensively

There are two ways that boards and management teams need to think about social media: defense and offense. Defensively, companies must anticipate the new threats posed by social media, such as reputational risk, employee productivity, legal and compliance concerns, and security breaches. Offensively, companies must invest ahead of the curve to adapt their marketing and distribution strategies as well as product offerings and business models to the Social Business era.

## Addressing Social Media Risk

First, let's discuss reputational risk. Before the days of the Internet, PR crises typically stemmed from a bad headline or a disparaging news report. These incidents were few and far between, and generally rooted in truth, as most journalists could be relied on to do a fair amount of due diligence before breaking a story. Today's world is very different. A select group of professional journalists no longer monopolizes the news-making industry; rather, 2 billion members of the public have the power to potentially make or hurt a brand in seconds.

Sometimes what gets shared and goes viral is not substantiated in fact or is an exaggeration of the truth, yet it may be equally damaging as a real incident. North American fruit spread company Smucker's experienced this phenomenon first-hand when a consumer-led campaign, #BoycottSmuckers, went viral on Twitter and Facebook. Consumers upset with Smucker's stance against labeling GMOs (genetically modified organisms) initially took to social media to complain, hoping their efforts would result in a change in the company's policy. When Smucker's tried to take control of the situation by deleting these comments on Facebook, consumers got angry and shifted from complaining to calling for a boycott of all Smucker's products.

The lesson here is threefold. First, consumers want and demand to be heard. If you try to shut them down, they will shout even more loudly and escalate the situation. In general, companies shouldn't delete comments unless they are clear violations of service, illegal, threatening, or profane. Second, not being active on social media is not the answer. Consumers can and will still complain, and they'll be angry that you aren't there to at least listen. Third, boards and management teams should anticipate that any controversial news or decisions they make will quickly make their way to social media and should create a contingency plan, such as temporarily staffing up the social media team and providing special crisis management training and talking points.

The role of today's boards and management teams is to be informed of and anticipate these risks, and then to ensure that the right teams and structures are in place to prevent, mitigate, or otherwise deal with them after the fact when these situations invariably arise.

On the regulatory front, government agencies have not issued many guidelines for social media, but there are some sticky areas, particularly in relation to investor communication and in industries that have strict regulations guiding what they can and cannot claim about their products. The Federal Trade Commission's (FTC) blog disclosure rules, the Financial Industry Regulatory Authority's (FINRA) social media guidance, and SEC Reg FD (as described earlier) are all examples.

Staying on top of the evolving landscape of rules and regulations is crucial to avoiding or minimizing expensive and distracting repercussions. Some companies, such as Dell, make sure that all employees who could potentially speak externally about material information receive extensive training so that they stay SEC compliant. We'll dive into major risk areas such as employment law, false advertising, privacy, intellectual property, and security in Chapters 11 and 12.

For now, here are the top defense-oriented questions that directors (especially those serving on audit committees) should be asking management teams:

- What is our policy for employees on social media? What are they allowed to say about the company? How do we train them on how to protect the security of their accounts and what they are allowed to discuss with regard to proprietary, sensitive, or material information?

- What are the full set of corporate and employee social media activities taking place today, and do they comply with current and future potential regulations, such as Reg FD, FTC rules on endorsements, and FINRA's social media guidelines?

- How do we monitor popular social platforms for potential negative sentiment regarding our company and products?

- Do we have a social media crisis management plan in place to address situations such as a false rumor "going viral" in the middle of the night? How quickly would we be able to act in such a situation, who is authorized to represent the company, and through which channels would we be prepared to respond?

- How does our share of voice on social media compare to that of competitors, and how is this trending over time?

- How is social media used in the recruiting of new employees? Which information is acceptable for recruiters and managers to consider in hiring decisions, and where do they source it?

## Unlocking Social Business Opportunities

As great as the social media risks may be, the greatest risk of all is doing nothing and missing out on the seismic digital changes sweeping the consumer landscape and customer journey. When I wrote *The Facebook Era*, investing in social media initiatives could provide a company with a competitive advantage. But more and more, a social strategy has become table stakes, and not taking advantage of it means falling way behind.

Boards and senior leadership teams are equally beholden to understanding the plethora of opportunities to unlock the value in Social Business. We have already discussed this relationship in terms of the IoT and collaborative economy, and will further explore it in the following chapters on social sales, marketing, customer service, and e-commerce.

Offense-oriented questions board directors ought to be asking include the following:

- What are the official and unofficial ways our company, executives, and employees currently use social media to engage current and prospective customers and employees?

- How are we training and onboarding new employees in terms of the business use of social media?

- Are we cultivating a brand following on social media? How are we measuring the effectiveness of our social media efforts?

- How do we monitor social media to understand developing trends? How do we operationalize these insights and transform them into business growth initiatives?

- What is our strategy for engaging social media influencers in our space?

- How do we capture and use competitive intelligence on social media?

- How do we capture and use customer data while respecting customers' privacy and without losing authenticity?

- Are we equipping our senior leaders with the training and tools to incorporate Social Business into their respective functions and disciplines in a way that enables business transformation?

- Do we fully understand the latest Social Business developments around Facebook Messenger payments and commerce? What is our point of view on whether this makes sense for our retail business?

## Summary

Although social media failures are fodder for many news reports, the real story should be about the everyday successes of companies building their brands with online networks—one tweet, one message, one positive customer interaction at a time. In reality, truly disastrous tweets are no more common than shark attacks, and forgoing a social media presence is no defense against a social media publicity attack. Firms should always be cultivating customer relationships and building third-party advocates who will rise to their defense when needed—what Howard Schultz calls investing in the reservoir of trust.

It's becoming clear that the biggest risk in social media is not being on social media at all or only participating superficially. Although social media responsibility is part of everyone's job, the true prize for companies is to be engaged with and informed in Social Business at the highest levels, and that starts with CEOs and boards of directors. Only then can companies seize the full opportunities presented by Social Business for everything from improving brand reputation and transforming employee engagement to attracting top recruits, harnessing big data, and ultimately driving business growth in this exciting new era.

# 5

*"Buyers are engaging differently today and expect
salespeople to engage on their terms. Because buyers
have become omnichannel, modern sales teams must too
become omnichannel."*
—Stephen D'Angelo, Vice President of Global Sales,
Hearsay Social

# From Transactional to Trusted Advisor: The Social Sales Professional

Let's begin our walk across the enterprise, examining how its traditional departments need to transform to adapt to the social, always-connected customer and stake their claim of the digital last mile. We'll start with sales, because in most organizations, it is the least technologically forward external-facing department and at grave risk of irrelevance.

So far, we've discussed at length the incredible degree to which today's buyer is social, mobile, digital, and totally in charge of the buying process. Yet many sales organizations are still dialing for dollars and operating in the Dark Ages as far as customers are concerned. Despite clear evidence that cold, one-size-fits-all tactics no longer work, companies continue to invest large sums of money in sales training programs that perpetuate outdated push tactics—tactics that are increasingly obsolete for the new generation of digitally savvy customers and prospective recruits.

Once upon a time—and not all that long ago—the world was led by salespeople and the majority of products were sold, not bought. Companies continually added features and new products. Complexity was accepted and even considered desirable, because then consumers would have to go to a sales rep to have things explained.

But now it's a new world for sales professionals, in several respects. First, today's consumers do not want to feel as if they are being "sold to," but rather want to call the shots and drive the buying process. To meet this demand, companies need to focus on simplicity—both product simplicity and a simple customer experience. Second, consumers discover, add, and drop brands based on what friends, strangers, and influencers say on social media. Salespeople won't get to the plate, much less get to bat, if they and their marketing teams don't get this right and fail to properly cultivate customer and influencer relationships on social media (the topic of Chapter 6). For this reason, today's salespeople depend on their marketing teams more heavily than ever. Finally, the role of and value added by sales reps are changing. In many sectors, demand generation can now happen without a salesperson's involvement, and to an ever greater extent post-sales servicing is being centralized into efficient call centers. This means sales professionals need to focus on the activities that customers uniquely value from them—trusted, highly tailored advice.

As consumers, we live this new reality every day, but for most sales organizations, Social Business represents a sea-change. Not since telephones were invented has there been a more important time for field leaders and sales professionals to embrace new technology. It's now a matter of survival—the onslaught of disruptive consumer technologies is only increasing and accelerating, and there's no going back. The only way to succeed is to adapt to today's omnichannel customer, who sometimes wants to meet in person, at other times wants to call, but more and more primarily wants to email, text, and connect on social media.

Many well-intentioned organizations make the mistake of investing all of their digital efforts in cultivating digital direct transaction channels but forget to modernize their sales organizations in tandem. Unfortunately, these organizations are both missing the low-hanging fruit and creating a confusing and inconsistent customer experience.

"Omnichannel" is not just about setting up e-commerce capability. It's also about connecting all of your existing customer channels to the social, mobile, and digital last mile, including and especially your sales organization. In today's interconnected environment, all B2B and B2C sales professionals must individually become omnichannel—become findable, accessible, responsive via social media, website, email, and text message just as they are in a face-to-face context or on the phone. The organizations that employ these reps must play a proactive role in enabling this digital field transformation or else risk losing their best people, not being able to attract the next generation of reps, and ultimately risk losing relevance with customers.

### The Modern-Day Buyer's Journey

The buyer's experience has changed from linear and representative driven to customer driven, nonlinear, and highly influenced by social media and other digital sources (Figure 5.1). Consumers have developed new habits as the result of interacting with new apps and new technologies. Today, consumers look up restaurants and hair stylists on Yelp before booking. They watch YouTube trailers before committing to watch a movie. They look up teachers on Rate My Professors, doctors on Healthgrades, and business professionals such as lawyers, accountants, and bankers on Google and social media before they set foot in the classroom, clinic, or office.

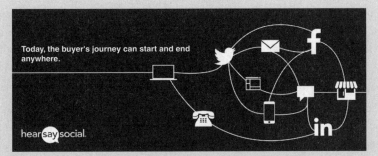

**Figure 5.1**
*Today's customer journey crisscrosses multiple channels, online and offline, and is primarily customer driven rather than sales or marketing led* (Source: Hearsay Social)

Today's sales reps need to adapt to these new realities:

- **Customers have complete access to information.** In a bygone era, many reps assumed that their customer knew very little, so they spent a lot of time touting their products' features. Sometimes reps withheld key details (like pricing) and weren't always motivated to tell the customer the whole truth. These selling tactics certainly didn't enhance the public's perception of sales professionals. Customers became wary of interacting with reps because they didn't receive any added value from being sold to. Today, comprehensive information about your products and services is freely available to your customers 24/7 across multiple channels and devices. Customers expect to be able to digitally and anonymously "window shop" before they are willing to speak with a rep. To add value to this process, reps have to do more than just parrot back the information that customers can find themselves. Instead, reps must interpret, customize, and apply information for the customer's benefit. Of course, there's plenty of misinformation on the web, so reps should be prepared for some customers to be misinformed.

- **Customers want to research the individual salesperson or service provider with whom they are working.** As part of their online research, most customers want to validate the service provider through online sources before proceeding. These sources typically include third-party review sites (such as Yelp, Rate My Professors, and Healthgrades), social media profiles, and local websites. It's not enough that a service professional is employed by Deloitte, Regis Salon, Northwest Community Hospital, or Allstate—more and more customers want to know about the specific individual with whom they will be working. Does my accountant have both tax and audit experience? Does this hair stylist know how to work with Asian hair? Where did my surgeon attend medical school? How long has this financial advisor been in

*continues...*

the business and is she connected with anyone I know? For anything that matters, customers want to know who the individual provider is and verify that she will provide high-quality service. For anything that doesn't matter, they generally prefer to transact online more cheaply, quickly, and efficiently.

- **Customers drive the buying process, rather than the reverse.** Customers dictate the buying process and time frame. Rather than sales reps initiating a linear purchase decision via a cold call, customers now call the shots, often seeking data from multiple sources including trusted connections on social media. The result is a messy, nonlinear process, as illustrated in Figure 5.1. Traditionally, buyers were forced to navigate cumbersome multistep buying processes. Today, sales reps are the ones who must navigate and conform to the customer's buying process as it traverses diverse digital and analog paths.

- **Customers expect speed, status updates, and omnichannel accessibility.** Amazon and Uber have spoiled your customers. Today's customer holds companies and salespeople to the same expectations of being available digitally and on demand (social, mobile, digital, phone, in person). If the customer has to wait for something, she at least expects to receive regular updates on the status of her order or request.

- **The sale is the beginning rather than the end.** Social media gives every buyer a voice to share his or her experience. Both positive and negative experiences get amplified. The buyer's journey used to end once you closed the deal, but today the sale is just the beginning: The buyer could go on to become either a loyal evangelist or a detractor for the salesperson and company.

Even with inherently "offline" purchase decisions such as selecting a wealth manager or a latte, the buyer's journey increasingly begins online on social, mobile, and digital channels. CEB found that on average, 57% of a buyer's decision occurs online *before* he or she is even willing to engage with a sales rep. Although many consumers choose to "showroom"—that is, browse in brick-and-mortar locations and then buy online from a different retailer—even more are doing the reverse—researching online and then visiting a retail location. Companies and reps must meet their buyer wherever he or she begins the buyer's journey and be available and responsive *without being creepy or annoying*.

## Do We Need Salespeople?

The digital age has shaken up how customers interact with businesses. As we just discussed, buyers now want to direct their own buying decision journeys, gathering information from their social networks and other online sources. Increasingly, buyers are not only starting their journeys online, but also are completing these journeys with "frictionless" online transactions that bypass a salesperson altogether. Indeed, according to Forrester Research, e-commerce has been rising steadily, growing from a base of less than 1% of US retail sales in 1998 to 9% as of 2014.

From the company's perspective, investing in building out an e-commerce channel can also be very attractive. Feet on the street are expensive to hire, train, manage, motivate, and compensate.

So, why have sales reps at all? Will the selling profession become obsolete now that companies like Amazon have shown us how personalized, powerful, and delightful e-commerce can be? The answer is "It depends."

## The Obsolete Sales Rep

When eBay began selling used cars in 2000, skeptics abounded. Four short years later, eBay Motors had sold its 1 millionth car. More recently, Tesla Motors has shown that customers are willing to buy even high-end automobiles online. Tesla invites drivers to purchase its new and used luxury electric vehicles (boasting a $70,000-plus price tag) through its website. With a few clicks, the deal can be financed instantly. Customers never need to talk to a salesperson. This was unthinkable in the car business, especially in the luxury market, even 5 or 10 years ago.

As the e-commerce customer experience continues to improve and people's comfort level with transacting online increases in parallel, a growing number of industries are seeing their distribution channel mix shift away from sales professionals. Traditional travel agents, stockbrokers, and auto salespeople are just a few examples of recent casualties.

More broadly, the data seem to suggest that technology is not only eating the world but also eating jobs. In their landmark book *The Second Machine Age* (2014), MIT professors Erik Brynjolfsson and Andy McAfee lay out compelling research showing that automation specifically is destroying more jobs than it creates and making even traditional white-collar professions obsolete across a growing number of fields, ranging from education and medicine to law and financial services (Figure 5.2).

In a *New York Times* op-ed piece, Brynjolfsson and Andy McAfee summarized this trend:

> As digital devices like computers and robots get more capable thanks to Moore's Law (the proposition that the number of transistors on a semiconductor can be inexpensively doubled about every two years), they can do more of the work that people used to do. Digital labor, in short, substitutes for human labor. This happens first with more routine tasks, which is a big part of the reason why less-educated workers have seen their wages fall the most as we moved deeper into the computer age …
>
> [And yet] technologies are going to continue to become more powerful, and to acquire more advanced skills and abilities. They can already drive cars, understand and produce natural human speech, write clean prose, and beat the best human *Jeopardy!* players. Digital progress has surprised a lot of people, and we ain't seen nothing yet. Brawny computers, brainy programmers, and big data are a potent combination, and they're nowhere near finished.

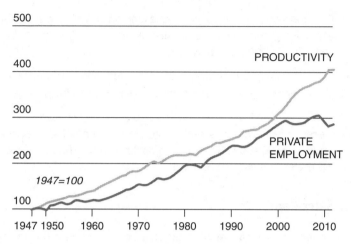

**Figure 5.2**
*For much of history, including the Industrial Revolution, new technologies resulted in job growth. In the late 1990s, however, a "Great Decoupling" occurred* (Source: U.S. Department of Labor)

There's no question that the sales profession is evolving and that some reps will be left behind. Whether a rep will become obsolete or thrive comes down to these factors: the value that the rep can add, the customer experience, and productivity (What productivity level does the industry structure and margins require?). In other words, obsolete sales reps are those who (1) spend time doing things that computer algorithms can do better and faster, (2) haven't adapted to engage how and where today's buyers want (i.e., digitally and on the buyer's terms), and/or (3) sell products that don't require human coaching and explanation (often but not always, these are highly commoditized, low-margin products).

### Many Sales Reps Are Plagued by Low Productivity

Many reps are still spending too much time on the wrong activities. A survey of more than 800 sales executives across the Americas, Asia, and Europe conducted by The Conference Board and Alexander Proudfoot Consulting found that sales reps, on average, spend a mere 11% of their time actively selling. The rest of their time is consumed by administrative tasks, problem solving, travel, and downtime (Figure 5.3).

Traditionally, companies have helped mitigate the administrative burden on field reps by hiring inside reps or office support staff to take care of this work. Increasingly, however, companies cannot afford the extra personnel or the stakes are too high to delegate a high-value prospect to a less-skilled assistant. Without the right tools, reps are finding it harder and harder to stay productive and hit

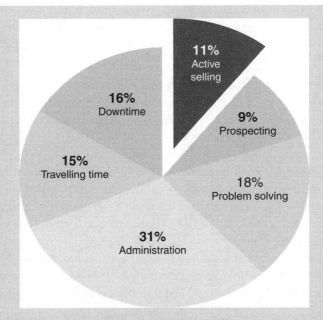

**Figure 5.3**
*On average, field reps spend nearly half their day on administrative and problem-solving tasks and just 11% of their time actively selling* (Source: Alexander Proudfoot Company, Sales Effectiveness Study, 2009)

their numbers. To avoid becoming obsolete, sales organizations should consider investing in these four areas of productivity technology:

- **Streamlined transactions.** The likely lowest-hanging fruit for most organizations is to go paperless with online forms and e-signatures. Much of the administrative burden previously cited involves dealing with forms, contracts, and other unwieldy paperwork that must be faxed or scanned back and forth between reps, customers, and legal departments. DocuSign, EchoSign (acquired by Adobe in 2011), and RightSignature are all popular solutions.

- **Team coordination (B2B).** Especially in B2B situations where multiple individuals in a vendor organization work together to sell to multiple decision makers and influencers in the buyer organization, having a single view of customer and interaction data, as well as an ability to coordinate tasks and activities across various individuals, saves on time, redundancy, and costly errors. No wonder that customer relationship management (CRM) database software is a $20 billion-plus market, led by Salesforce.com, Microsoft, Oracle, and SAP. B2B reps are also turning to LinkedIn Sales Navigator, a premium-subscription enhancement of the popular free social networking

*continues…*

site, to help them prospect for customers more productively. Sales Navigator's TeamLink feature allows reps to see who within their company is connected to leads and contacts so they can request a warm introduction.

- **Customer collaboration.** In the age of customer participation, providing digital platforms for sales reps to actively collaborate with customers can be a powerful way to build trust and accelerate customer learning while cutting down on travel time and costs. The most popular category of sales collaboration technology is web presentation and videoconference software, such as Citrix GoToMeeting, Cisco WebEx, and ClearSlide. Depending on the product and customer, reps may also find success with creating and moderating private Facebook Groups or LinkedIn Groups either to serve a single customer with multiple points of contact or multiple customers who might have similar questions and enjoy a sense of community with one another. Specific to the financial advice industry, eMoney Advisor (acquired by Fidelity) provides an online portal for financial advisors and clients to jointly view account information and walk through what-if scenario planning in real time.

- **Predictive analytics.** Perhaps the greatest prize can be found in the area of predictive analytics. In every organization, sales leaders aspire to get every rep performing at the level of their best reps. Analytics allow them to pinpoint the specific behaviors that result in closing the biggest deals in the shortest amount of time. Analytics can be as simplistic as basic lead scoring or as advanced as recommending "next best actions" for reps.

I was so fascinated by this last point that I was motivated to quit my job at Salesforce.com six years ago and found Hearsay Social, a company focused on driving predictive analytics for financial advisors. Indeed, the "hear" part of "Hearsay" is a set of predictive algorithms that scan digital customer data, from social media posts and website visits to email opens and clicks, to pinpoint buying signs and then prompt sales reps to reach out to the right client with the right message at the right time through the right channel. The result has been double-digit lifts in new client acquisition, growth in existing client wallet share (assets under management), and Net Promoter Score (NPS).

In the broader market, companies like Yesware, Infer, SalesGenius, and Lattice Engines are driving innovation in this area. The technology from Lattice Engines, for example, helps Dell's small business sales teams find newly incorporated businesses that may need to purchase computers and tablets.

Without technology tools and know-how, reps will be increasingly hard-pressed to exceed quotas and justify the high costs of recruiting, training, and compensating field organizations. Those organizations that fail to master the technology and data driving this evolution will fall further and further behind.

## Customer Experience Is the Product

With today's buyer wielding all the power, the customer experience reigns supreme. Reps are an important part of that customer experience, and those who are unwilling or unable to engage how (customer driven) and where (omnichannel) today's buyers want them to will become obsolete. *Harvard Business Review* found that more than 90% of decision makers refuse to engage, much less buy, based on cold outreach. Clearly, reps need to become savvy about going through their social networks.

In the Facebook era, customers are voting with their 'unfollows,' and the verdict is that there's no place for old-school cold callers and product pushers. To meet the new "standards," organizations must stop viewing customers as one-size-fits-all and must stop teaching reps to talk "at" customers using generic scripts. Brute-force reps who make 100 calls in a day hoping to yield one qualified prospect are being outcompeted by thoughtful reps who leverage technology. A joint study by LinkedIn and C9 Inc. of 9000 sales professionals across three dozen companies found that social sellers achieved 7 times more pipeline growth and 11 times greater revenue growth.

As important as face-to-face meetings, phone calls, and certain direct mail initiatives continue to be, the reality is that growing numbers of customers now refuse to do business with reps who are not easily findable and reachable through social media, mobile, and web. Their demands are based both on convenience and on the fact that they cannot validate the trustworthiness of reps who lack an online footprint.

Customer experience has become so paramount that it is now a core pillar of the value proposition customers are buying. According to CEB, the sales experience accounts for more than half of B2B customer loyalty.[1] Incredibly, this implies that the sales experience is even more important than the underlying product or service being sold! Customer experience has become (a big part of) the product, and it must be customer-centric and omnichannel.

### Optimal Channel Depends on Product Complexity

Despite the best efforts by reps and managers, certain industries over the long term may be destined to have much smaller sales organizations or to not have any reps altogether. Low-margin, well-understood products requiring minimal explanation and customization, such as flights, books, and standardized parts, truly seem better suited for e-commerce. (I wish this weren't the case for books, as I loved frequenting my neighborhood bookstore. Alas, consumers voted with their wallets and it closed a few years ago.)

*continues…*

---

1. http://www.executiveboard.com/exbd/sales-service/challenger/b2b-loyalty-drivers/index.page

Seat 8B on United Airlines flight #862 is identical whether you buy it from Expedia or pay a premium to purchase it through a travel agent. For most people, it does not make sense to pay a premium for the flight. But travel agents have not completely disappeared. There are far fewer today than in the 1990s (roughly 13,000 in the United States compared to the peak of 34,000), but the number is not zero. The industry has evolved into two models: high-volume, lower margin, self-service (such as Expedia) and niche (such as corporate travel, luxury travel, cruises, and complex itineraries). There are big winners in both models. All have embraced social media. However, the agencies that failed to move in either direction are no longer with us—they got stuck offering an undifferentiated service at a premium, which is no-man's land.

In contrast, industries that are high-margin, high-stakes, highly customized, complex areas, or that require sign-offs by multiple parties (e.g., enterprise software, major advertising creative services, and investment banking), will depend on professional selling for some time to come. For these products and services, there is no easy price-comparison site, and customers would rather pay more to get the best possible service provider.

Of course, every company wants its products to be highly differentiated rather than commoditized. Companies must innovate relentlessly. At the same time, lower-margin products can be viewed as loss leaders used to generate leads for a more profitable customer relationship over the long term. The best companies make themselves available across multiple channels, provide differentiated offerings, and, above all, *make it easy to do business*.

## The Age of the Social Sales Professional

Signing up with a Twitter, LinkedIn, or Facebook account isn't enough. The age of the Social Sales Professional will be marked by field transformation, which requires a shift in mindset, approach, and daily practices.

The expectations for reps in the Facebook era are extremely high. Those who can deliver value above and beyond that offered by an e-commerce site, mobile app, or call center represent a new elite class of professionals; they comprise a powerful combination of product expert and trusted advisor. These men and women are "social" in several ways. First, they have mastered the digital last mile and are equally comfortable engaging customers in person, on the phone, or via social, mobile, or web. Second, they leverage predictive analytics and other technologies to minimize the amount of time they spend on administrative tasks and to elevate the customer experience they are able to deliver. Social Sales Professionals also make a habit of connecting with and maintaining quality relationships using social networking sites so that they can be personable on digital channels and build up trusted reviews and referrals. Most importantly, they collaborate with and are viewed by colleagues, partners, and customers as trusted advisors who are masters of their craft. They are the opposite of obsolete.

Customers will benefit from working with these Social Sales Professionals. One of my favorite digital thinkers is John Hagel, founder and co-chairman for Deloitte's Center for the Edge. He recently blogged about how technology-enabled professionals will democratize access to high-quality, personalized advice:

> The very wealthy have had trusted advisors for ages, in the form of wealth managers, concierge doctors, or personal shoppers. This business model worked for them because the very wealthy could spend enough to justify the significant time and effort it required to get to know those people deeply enough to become trusted advisors. The rest of us simply could not access this kind of expertise and advice.

> But that's all changing now. With the advent of Big Data, sophisticated analytics, social software, the Internet of Things, and cloud computing, just to name a few of the enabling technologies, the "trusted advisor" business model now has the potential to expand from the niche of the very wealthy to become a mass-market event. These technologies make it feasible to compile a detailed understanding of the social and economic context of the individual at much lower cost than previously imaginable. We don't have to submit to detailed interviews or fill out endless questionnaires to provide this information. The trusted advisor, with our permission, can simply watch and analyze the "digital exhaust" from our activities to develop deep insight into who we are and what is important to us.[2]

Throughout the 1980s and 1990s, cold calling and email blast technology sacrificed quality for quantity of sales interactions. Social selling returns us to a more personalized era of customer interaction, but with greater efficiency and productivity. Instead of treating every lead as if she has the same generic concerns, Social Sales Professionals do their homework first so they can personalize their pitches and spend time getting to know customers as *people with individualized needs*. They take the long-term view, building rapport over time, instead of trying to maximize the value of a single transaction. The free availability of information means that salespeople can no longer withhold information or tell half-truths, as these would surely be uncovered with a quick Google search.

## A New Class of Elite Professionals

Computer algorithms like IBM Watson and roboadvice websites are besting the best of human actors in all sorts of fields—from medicine and day trading to *Jeopardy!* and chess. How are those of us in sales going to up-level and keep ahead of automation?

The truth is that for Social Sales Professionals, there's nothing to worry about. After laying out their compelling and frightening case for net job destruction due to predictive technologies, Erik Brynjolfsson and Andy McAfee discussed areas that will likely not be

---

2. https://www.linkedin.com/pulse/disruption-trusted-advisors-john-hagel

replaced by machines anytime soon. As Brynjolfsson noted in 2015 on PBS's *Newshour*, "There's an explosion of opportunities ... where you need to know how to relate to other people, and that's something that we can cultivate and encourage to a greater extent, and where humans still have a huge edge over machines." *New York Times* editor Quentin Hardy put it nicely: "In a world rich in digital information ... the personal trust and relationship that still comes by spending time with someone, has become even more valuable."

Yes, digitization is happening to every industry and algorithms are swallowing jobs. Even so, explosive growth is occurring in areas where relationships matter, where the Social Sales Professional rules, and where the personal—*human*, if you will— element brings benefits that roboadvisors and other computer algorithms can't mimic.

There is room—indeed, there is an *imperative*—for a new elite sales approach that embraces technology to drive both rep productivity and relevance and allow trusted advisors to be high touch at scale. In truth, the world has never more needed smart, informed salespeople. Our world is flush with data and choices such that buyers can't efficiently wade through every topic that is important. Social Sales Professionals who can cut through the data stream and guide customers toward what is best, with their best interests in mind, are and will continue to be at a premium.

Sales in the age of the skeptical and informed online buyer requires a new approach to customer engagement. CEB's Challenger Sale methodology has done much to characterize this new approach. The most successful reps come up with new ideas for their customers and challenge the assumptions that customers hold going into the conversation. They offer innovative solutions for increasing revenues, saving on costs, avoiding risk, engaging employees, and defending against competitors. Today's busy buyers demand that reps offer something in exchange for their time and consideration of the rep's product. What those customers need are new insights. They need to know what their peers and competitors are thinking and doing. You, as the Social Sales Professional, are in a unique position to tell them. You regularly meet with many more of their peers than they do, so you can give them a playbook for their position that they can't get anywhere else.

## Becoming a Social Sales Professional

Today's savvy customers want to work with a Social Sales Professional who will teach them something they can't Google for themselves and who will help them decide to buy rather than asking for the sale. To meet this need, sales reps must create and maintain a professional, but authentic, branded presence online and on social media, and share excellent content that people want to read. At the same time, sales professionals must be careful not to invade these channels and bombard customers with information—for customers will just as quickly unfollow, unfriend, and unsubscribe.

Social selling is not a replacement for calls and in-person meetings; it is an important on-ramp and way to stay in touch between meetings. San Francisco–based wealth advisor Misty Farukh is a terrific example of someone who knows how to engage with today's always-connected client, as detailed in the following case study.

### Social Professional in Practice

Misty Farukh, CFP, is a financial advisor in San Francisco, California. She actively maintains a Facebook Page, Twitter account, LinkedIn profile, and website for the wealth management practice she co-leads with her father, Abu Farukh.

When Abu started in the business 35 years ago at Morgan Stanley Dean Witter, wealth managers did much of their prospecting face-to-face or by scanning the local paper for news about prominent local business owners and executives, then sending them a letter of congratulations (the best practice was to include the newspaper clipping with a handwritten note) and introducing themselves and their services. Most of the time, advisors would not hear back from the vast majority of these people. If somehow they got lucky and heard back and then were able to convert the prospect into a client, the standard client engagement model was to check in once a year, cycling through the same list of questions: Are you still in the same job? Has your income changed? Has your marital status changed? Did you have any more children? And so on.

Fast-forward to today. Misty is a millennial and serves millennials—both the next generations of wealth in the families her father has served and the scores of tech workers and entrepreneurs in San Francisco in need of financial planning and advice. To Misty and her clients, the old way of prospecting and engaging seems outdated and inefficient. Even just a few years ago, she recalls, it was a challenge to get information out to clients quickly enough. Sending a letter took days to get compliance approval, not to mention mailing time.

Today, a far better and more modern system is in place for both Misty and her clients. For one, Misty is easily findable. Interested prospective clients who Google Misty find her social media profile and website in the top search results. Clicking into these sites, it's easy to get a sense for her educational background, values, experience, and personality.

Misty periodically shares timely and relevant content that she believes her clients will find interesting, helpful, or entertaining. For example, she posted a video about "5 Career Lessons from Han Solo" to coincide with the release of the new *Star Wars* movie. Earlier in the week, she shared a point of view on what the Fed's decision to raise interest rates meant for investors. When clients 'like' or share her posts, this information appears in the social feeds of those clients' friends, helping spread the word about Misty and her practice.

When Misty identifies an opportunity to work with someone new, she checks on social media first to see who they know in common so she can request a warm introduction. Her clients think highly of her and are often more than willing to provide

*continues…*

these referrals. Among her existing clients, a tweet about expecting a first child might prompt her to send a congratulatory message or card. She might also casually suggest that the client ought to start thinking about college planning. Often, this starts the dialogue, rather than waiting until the annual review and cycling through the same list of generic questions. Misty is careful to act authentically and not make the client feel uncomfortable about having shared this information on social media.

Social media has changed the depth of relationship, frequency of interaction, and degree of personalized advice possible for relationship managers like Misty. Misty still meets with her clients face-to-face and routinely speaks to clients on the phone, but in between those meetings and calls, she and her clients use social, mobile, and web channels to stay in touch easily and often.

At this point, you may be thinking, "I want to become a Social Sales Professional, but how do I make the leap?" Certainly, this is the question many of my customers at Hearsay Social posed to us, especially after they had taken the initial step of signing up for social media accounts. Working with more than 100,000 sales professionals, including Misty Farukh, we developed a framework encompassing four steps to help you get started.

## STEP #1. Be Findable

The first step is for reps to be findable on the channels that their prospects and customers expect to engage. This is akin to being listed in the Yellow Pages or Rotary Club directory 20 years ago. Just as you want to research your prospect (see Step #3), so your prospects will want to research you online before engaging with you in person or on the phone. They will Google you and expect to find your social media profiles and website. And your website better be responsive, since more and more customers are using their mobile devices to look you up.

A decade ago, being listed in the Yellow Pages was not optional for business. In fact, many companies and reps paid more for a premium listing to stand out from the competition. The same is true today for establishing a presence on social networking sites. When most millennials are saying things like "If you aren't on social media, then you don't exist," reps can't afford to be absent from these channels and lose credibility. But it's not just millennials: In the wealth management realm, for instance, a study conducted by FPA and LinkedIn found that 77% of prospective clients expect the financial advisor with whom they are considering working with to be findable on the web or on a social networking site. More than half research the advisor online before making or accepting any direct contact.

An effective business social network presence needs to be branded and consistent, yet personal and authentic. Facebook Business Pages are ideal for retail salespeople and offer a way to separate their professional and personal identities (the latter is best served through a Facebook Personal Profile). Twitter is great for sharing news, curated articles, and retweeting customers.

LinkedIn profiles in particular have become an important place for professional branding (many people view it as their online résumé) and are how potential clients are evaluating whether you are someone they would like to do business with. Knowing how to present yourself most effectively on each social network is key, as each network has its own culture and expectations and plays a different role. If an insurance agent sponsors a local kids' baseball team, a snapshot of her posing with the players is an ideal post for Facebook or Instagram, but perhaps less appropriate for LinkedIn, where people expect more business-oriented updates. Figure 5.4 illustrates how one insurance agent in France has created presences across LinkedIn, Twitter, and Facebook.

**Figure 5.4**
*LinkedIn profile, Twitter account, and Facebook Business Page for Florent Martin, a "findable" Generali insurance agent based in Lamastre, France* (Source: LinkedIn, Twitter, Facebook)

Consider the relevance of any other network for your current customers as well as your ideal future market. Google+ Pages may be a no-brainer because it ranks high in Google search results. Snapchat could be ideal if you're selling to teens. Instagram is great for any industry that brands and sells using visual images. All of these social networks are free to join; the true cost is the time it will require to maintain your profiles. Whichever networks you choose to join, it's important to keep a consistent brand image across all of them, and to fill out all relevant fields, such as information about your education, experience, qualifications, business hours, and address. Above all, remain active. While a consistent presence across all of these sites will help you get found, a competitor who has done the same *and* is also consistently posting and responsive will come across as more helpful and qualified.

In certain sectors, such as health care or financial services, regulatory agencies dictate what can be posted and how reps portray themselves online. In these cases, a supervisor or principal—someone trained in compliance—must approve content. In Chapter 11, we'll get into the details of how to address these regulatory concerns.

### Dos and Don'ts for Being Findable

**DO**

- Fill out profile sections completely, including address, phone, hours, business description, educational background, and experience.

- Upload a professional headshot and cover photo.

- Use the same name and try to claim the same handle on all sites. For example, my social media URLs are facebook.com/clarashih, twitter.com/clarashih, and linkedin.com/in/clarashih.

- Keep your profile and contact information up-to-date.

- Depending on your brand and industry, try to be as authentic as possible while remaining professional. Authenticity is the etiquette and expectation on social media.

- Make sure your website is search-engine optimized by covering these four bases: (1) social (website links to your social profiles, and social posts link back to your website), (2) mobile (responsive), (3) local (not just a generic corporate site but one specifically branded around the sales rep), and (4) dynamic (periodically refreshed with fresh content).

- Have a plan for how you will respond when someone finds you and reaches out. Map out a sales process.

**DON'T**

- Don't make your social profile or website look like an ad. There is no greater turn-off.

- Be authentic, but don't use an inappropriate (overly casual) profile photo or cover photo.

- Don't make any spelling or grammatical errors, which reflect poorly on your professionalism. It's worth double-checking.

# STEP #2. Grow Your Network

The reps who got listed in the Yellow Pages 20 years ago didn't just sit back and wait for the phone to ring. Similarly, establishing a digital and social business presence is necessary but not sufficient. Being findable is just the beginning. To succeed in today's competitive marketplace, reps need to be proactive, and networking is the name of the game.

Networking used to take place entirely in person. Coaching or sponsoring a Little League team, joining the Rotary or Kiwanis Club or the Elks Lodge, joining the board of the local symphony, chairing the local chapter of a college alumni association, and serving as an active member of a church congregation were and remain effective ways for reps to establish themselves as trustworthy figures and to meet lots of prospects.

Social networking sites, however, enable networking on steroids. As I wrote in *The Facebook Era*:

> Behind the scenes, social networking sites like Facebook, Twitter, and LinkedIn have lowered the cost of staying in touch, so we are all staying in touch with more people. It's like when we went from in-person meetings to phone calls, and from phone calls to email. Each time, the cost of staying in touch went down, so our capacity to maintain relationships went up. We can call or telemarket to more people than we can see face-to-face on a regular basis. We can email or email-market to far more people than we can call on a regular basis. Today, we can become Facebook friends, LinkedIn connections, follow or be followed on Twitter by far more people than we could visit, call, or email. Over time, thanks to new technologies, the average number of relationships each of us is able to have is increasing.

Reps can and should keep coaching Little League teams and joining Kiwanis—but now, social media lets them exponentially reap the benefits of staying in touch with clients and prospects between meetings. In addition, you can network online, either by browsing your connections' connections or by searching for keywords, job title, location, alma mater, and more. LinkedIn's premium subscriptions, including Sales Navigator, offer advanced search filters that allow sales professionals to get highly targeted in finding customers. If you share school affiliations, interests, or professional groups with a contact, that makes reaching out much easier and increases the likelihood of successfully engaging a prospect.

Social networking sites also help boost referrals. Customers can leave reviews on Facebook and Yelp, as well as offer endorsements and testimonials on LinkedIn. Like Misty Farukh, you can search for prospects on each social networking site to see if you have friends in common, then ask one of those friends for a warm introduction. Sometimes, those referrals come from current customers. Just as often, they may come from personal connections and centers of influence. In fact, one large home mortgage sales organization that works with Hearsay Social instructs its loan officers to focus their social media efforts on connecting with real estate agents, as they are the biggest source of new business for this particular firm. In the Facebook era, cultivating a loyal community of both customers and influencers is critical for success.

Finally, hypertargeted advertising on Facebook, LinkedIn, and Twitter can be a very powerful tool for prospecting and upselling your customers. If you are a B2B sales rep, you are generally not responsible for your own advertising and lead generation (so ask your marketing team to read Chapter 6). In contrast, if you are a B2C rep, most likely you are a contractor, franchisee, or sole proprietor and could likely benefit from social media ads.

Perhaps in the past, you bought Yellow Page ads; invested in branded fridge magnets, signage on park benches, or billboards; or took out an ad in the local high school musical playbill. Now imagine taking these funds and instead using them to reach very specific audience profiles—such as those delineated by age, gender, ZIP code, employer, or job title, or people who just started a new job, began a new relationship, or became a new parent—with highly targeted messages tailored for that specific group. Or imagine being able to run a campaign just for prospects who have visited your website, even if you don't know their names or have their email addresses. Facebook Ads allow you to do both and more (Figure 5.5), helping businesses reach more people with content marketing, drive website traffic, reach people nearby, drive attendance to events, and get people to claim special offers.

**Figure 5.5**
*(Left) An example of a Facebook advertising campaign being set up to target women aged 28–40 with children. (Right) How a Facebook Event Ad appears to consumers* (Source: Facebook)

To get started, visit facebook.com/ads, linkedin.com/ads, or ads.twitter.com. You can play around with different ad configurations for free and test for as little as $2 to $10. For local advertisers that are part of larger national franchises, Hearsay Social's Facebook Ads Module can be used to manage corporate-to-local campaigns (Figure 5.6). Brands can suggest or mandate specific copy and creative content, preset certain campaign attributes, and allow local entities to run their own campaigns based on these templates.

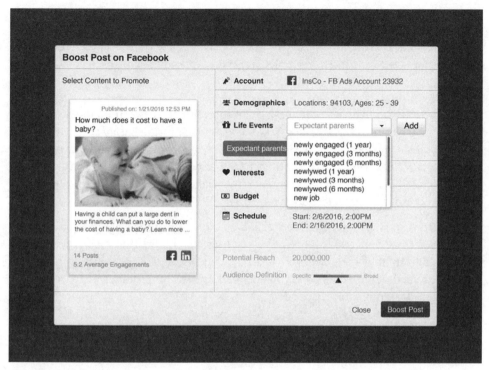

**Figure 5.6**
*Hearsay Social's Facebook Ads Module allows local agents that belong to larger franchises and brands to run brand-compliant ads at the local level, targeting by attributes like ZIP code, age, interests, and life events* (Source: Hearsay Social)

### Dos and Don'ts for Growing Your Network

DO

- Stay connected on social media before and after in-person meetings. Make it a habit to connect on social media with people you've met in person, such as at a tailgate party or Little League game.

- Provide links to your social accounts on your business card, email signature, website, event marketing, office signage, and more.

- Create an inviting profile and share great content so that people want to connect with you.

- Ask for testimonials, recommendations, and referrals. If there's someone specific you are trying to reach, look that person up and see if you have any mutual connections who could provide a warm introduction.

*continues…*

- Consider paying for social media targeted ads or for premium LinkedIn features such as InMail (which allows you to message prospects you aren't connected with and haven't met yet) and advanced search.

**DON'T**

- Don't invite people to connect on LinkedIn without customizing the default "I'd like to connect" message. Take some time to provide background on who you are and why you'd like to connect. Many people refuse to connect with a salesperson who can't be bothered to personalize the message. You'll want to use your desktop computer to do this; LinkedIn's mobile app/site only lets you use the default invitation text.

- Don't spam people. If you've reached out on Twitter and LinkedIn, left a voicemail, and followed up with two emails, chances are the person does not want to engage with you. Take a hint and move on. If you add too many contacts at once or anyone you add marks you as "suspicious," your account may be temporarily suspended.

## STEP #3. Research, Listen, and Act on Important Signals

No sales rep enjoys manually entering data into a CRM system. But if you think about it, LinkedIn and Facebook are like smart CRMs where all of the records you use to keep tabs on customers are consistently updated by the customers themselves.

Once you've established your "Rolodex" on social networking sites, it's time to put an ear to the ground and learn about your customers based on all the rich information they are sharing. Reps can scan their social feeds or search for news and commentary. People love to share on social media, and many of these posts contain buying signals or other good excuses to connect and establish a touchpoint. From mergers and acquisitions to home and auto purchases, a typical social media feed is a goldmine of data, waiting for you to discover the big nuggets and follow up.

Take the insurance sector, for example. Consultancy McKinsey and LIMRA found that rep knowledge of three or more life events in customers' lives on average resulted in a 10% lift in sales. Social media sites are among the first places consumers go these days to share life events, and so have become indispensable sources of information for insurance agents. Even if an immediate sale isn't at hand, acknowledging these major life moments is an opportunity for a relationship manager to reach out and build trust and rapport.

Reps, especially those with large networks, may find it daunting to manually scan through each of their social feeds and private messages on a consistent basis. But even without social media, many reps today fail to have *any* touchpoints with their clients between sales. There's a lot to be gained by adding a few warm touches a year, which are so easy to do around life events with a simple "Congrats!," "How are you?" or "Let's get coffee!" message.

Hearsay Social, as mentioned earlier, has built its business on developing automated algorithms that scan social network feeds for meaningful signals. Data analytics that combine social network activity with web traffic, click rates, and search engine optimization (SEO) can help reps understand customers' motivations and anticipate their future needs.

Of course, reps must take care not to be overly aggressive and introduce a "creepiness factor." When done right, customers appreciate reps who take the time to do their homework before reaching out. Today's buyers expect a highly tailored message and refuse to be bombarded by sales pitches until they are in a place to seriously consider them. Successful reps employ a strategy of staying at the top of the customer's mind and remaining low-touch until it's the right time to become high-touch.

### Dos and Don'ts for Listening for and Acting on Customer Buying Signals

**DO**

- Listen for "social signals" like birth announcements, job changes, office openings, and acquisitions; your connections are sharing valuable information on social media every day. Respond in the feed or take it offline and send flowers with a handwritten card.

- Always research contacts before a meeting, whether you are meeting them for the first time or they are long-time clients.

**DON'T**

- Don't launch into a sales pitch. Social media is about relationship building and the soft sell.

- Don't be creepy. The same social etiquette and courtesy that govern your offline interactions also apply online and on social media.

## STEP #4. Educate and Engage

The final step in mastering social sales is content marketing. Excellent content marketing allows reps to demonstrate expertise and add value, build trust and credibility, and stay "top of mind" without being annoying. The goal is to share relevant and useful content that educates, informs, and delights, rather than outright sells.

Like coaching a Little League team or running a financial wellness seminar, social media content marketing won't likely translate into sales right away. And it's true that many people who view your posts may never become paying customers. Even so, sharing targeted information proves that you are a trusted source for information about your products and meets people on social media where they begin their buyer's journey.

In today's jungle of over-information, reps who consistently post high-quality, high-value items hack a clear path that customers will follow. Think of each post as a deposit into the reservoir of trust with your customers. As their comfort and trust in your brand grow, so too will their willingness to buy from you and refer you to others.

If you are supported by a marketing organization, it's a good idea to take brand-level content and campaigns and make them your own. For example, through Hearsay, marketing teams populate a content library with suggested posts, tweets, and web and email copy for reps to customize and share. If you're on your own when it comes to content development, find people and companies whose opinions you respect and follow them on Twitter to get content ideas.

### Best Practices for Effective Content Marketing

**DO**

- Monitor media sources and influencers relevant to your customers, such as influential blogs and trade news publications, to identify and speak to the latest trends. Set Google News Alerts on important keywords so that you can be notified when developments occur in your areas of expertise. Sign up for Newsle (acquired by LinkedIn), a service that emails a daily digest of news about your LinkedIn connections.

- Post frequently (but don't spam) and consistently. As a rule, post three to five times per week on each social network. Post or schedule posts at times when your customers are likely to be active on social media—for example, share long-form articles during work hours and Facebook posts in the early morning or evenings.

- Mostly don't talk about yourself. Follow the 80/20 rule: 80% of your posts should be about other people and events, while no more than 20% of your posts should be about yourself, your company, or your products. Celebrate new hires, awards, and accolades. Share professional development content and promote local events and charities. Make it personal and authentic.

**DON'T**

- Don't go radio silent for months. Having an abandoned, neglected Facebook Page is worse than not having one in the first place.

- Don't spam (e.g., post 10 times a day or multiple times in a row). There's no quicker way to get a bunch of people to unfollow your page.

As with anything worthwhile, the transition to becoming a Social Sales Professional takes practice, hard work, repetition, and ideally support from your company and sales manager in the form of updated technology, training, and business processes. Tens of thousands of sales professionals have embraced this blueprint of the Hearsay Four Steps to establish richer client relationships, and their results are impressive. The Four Steps not only led to better sales and retention lift for reps, but clients surveyed about this process also said they felt their advisor knew them better, seemed to care more about their unique situation, and was able to offer more personalized and more valuable advice after being connected on social media.

## How Field Leaders Operationalize Social Selling

When I meet with heads of sales, the same question always comes up: "How do I nudge my mid- and late-career reps out of their comfort zone and into the dynamic, omnichannel reality of today's buyer's journey?"

If you are serious about modernizing, digitizing, and professionalizing your field organization into the kind of elite Social Sales Professionals who will thrive in the Facebook era, you must fully incorporate and ingrain the right mindset, technologies, and training. Your field social media program can't be treated as a mere side project with no dedicated resources. You must commit an adequate level of investment and hold your reps and sales managers accountable at every step along the way.

In my experience working with sales professionals at Google, Salesforce.com, and now Hearsay, I've come up with nine winning "plays" to operationalize social sales and field transformation:

- **Segment your field force.** Define and execute a differentiated approach for each group, starting with the early adopters:

  - *Early Adopters:* Start with the latent demand that already exists in your organization. Which of your reps have created social presences on their own? Partner with them to launch a pilot. Ask them for best practices and success stories, and encourage them to evangelize their success with their peers.

  - *Beginners:* They may understand social media and may be on social networks for personal use but do not fully grasp how to use it for business.

  - *The Uninitiated:* They may not be on social media at all and don't understand its value proposition. Some may be "technically challenged."

- **Drive zealous adoption through bottom-up evangelism.** Develop case studies and testimonials from successful early adopters and let them evangelize to their peers at national, regional, and local sales meetings. Celebrate early wins, such as sourcing a new client, and then convert the skeptics. It's always hard to teach an old dog new tricks, but the best teachers are often other "old dogs" who have actually mastered the new trick.

- **Provide an active role for top-down sales leadership.** The entire sales chain of command from the chief sales officer down must personally sign up for social media engagement to lead by example and support top-down transformation. They must stay closely involved, setting goals and monitoring and measuring progress. A key turning point for many Hearsay customers was getting front-line sales managers on board to help coach reps day in and day out on social best practices. An added benefit has been that socially savvy sales managers are now also utilizing social networking tactics for recruiting and ongoing rep engagement.

- **Ongoing training, rewards, and gamification.** Change management doesn't happen overnight. Create an ongoing program and system to ensure reps stay engaged and learn new skills as social network platforms evolve. Gamification and rewards, such as a social selling rep leaderboard, can be helpful to build habits early on and keep people motivated.

- **Focus on the "why."** Before you tell reps "how" to become a Social Sales Professional, you must first persuade them on "why." Your reps are smart. Show them the data. Draw parallels to how they've sold in the past and explain why social selling is better. Although social and predictive technologies are relatively new, the fundamental behaviors, activities, and relationship building underlying them are not. Conveying these linkages can make it seem less overwhelming for reps to make the leap.

- **Integrate social media into your selling process and sales methodology.** Social media selling can't be a program off to the side; it must become a core part of your sales methodology and standard operating procedure. Incorporate it into your new-hire training, sales conferences, and business KPIs. If you decide to commit to a social selling strategy, decide which existing program it will replace. You can't keep piling more onto your reps' plate indefinitely.

- **Set clear brand guidelines.** With or without an officially sanctioned program, reps are out on social media representing your brand. It's best to have an official program so you can set, communicate, and enforce brand rules and best practices. Especially in emerging markets, some companies have faced legal issues, negative public relations, or public backlash as a result of reps saying the wrong things on social media. A combination of training and software monitoring should mitigate any risks.

- **Commit the required resources.** Assign a dedicated point person with the time, social know-how, and respect of the field to drive the program. Ensure you have adequate resources when it comes to technical integration and a strong project manager to decide and configure business rules, schedule and run training workshops, analyze program effectiveness, and iterate and escalate to executive sponsors when the program gets stuck.

- **Partner closely with other functions.** Successful social selling programs are a team sport. Partner with marketing personnel on content strategy and development, integrating these efforts with brand-level campaigns, and analyzing how different types of content are received. Partner with legal and compliance to establish the right guidelines, policies, and procedures.

Even with the best of programs and the best of intentions, you may face resistance from some of your reps. Some sales organizations have moved to mandatory social selling programs, bringing social KPIs into the set of sales activities that are part of their compensation programs. Others are taking a slower approach. The following sidebar features one sales leader's experience in rolling out a social selling program in his organization.

## Perspective from a Field Leader

Marty Flewellen

Chief Distribution Officer, Transamerica Life & Protection

Some 30-plus years ago when I started my sales career, the mantra of the day was "10/3/1." You engaged with 10 suspects, which created 3 prospects, who turned into 1 sale. It didn't matter if you were a good sales rep; it only mattered if you followed the formula. We taught this approach because it was impossible to time your call with the consumer's interest level. Nine times out of ten, the product you were offering was not top of mind for them—or even on their radar.

Today, the odds are much more in sales reps'—and the customer's—favor. Using a robust social network and consumers' "digital exhaust," a Social Sales Professional can time engagement to coincide with the exact moment the customer is experiencing the need. This instantaneous relevance can change everything.

But reps have to do more than just reach out at the right time. We must offer credible, critical insights. Consumers crave clarity. In the past, people struggled to learn enough to make informed choices. Today they are inundated with data and pitches, so today's reps must help distinguish the facts that matter from the clutter. Even more importantly, sales professionals should be prepared to have potentially uncomfortable conversations that help customers challenge their preconceived notions—about their needs as well how to address them.

As the head of a sales organization with 100,000 reps, I see signs every day about how the sales dynamic is evolving. The world needs qualified sales professionals who not only relish the sale, but also take pride in providing a unique perspective. With the increasing commoditization of products, the value we deliver will be measured by our knowledge, insight, empathy, and clarity of message, and whether we can offer all of this right when the customer is ready.

Ultimately, you should set the right expectation with reps and field leaders: Social sales is a commitment, not a fad. It's not about optimizing for a transaction today, but rather about forging a lasting, high-value customer relationship over the long haul. There may be some early wins in social selling, but true success will come over time rather than overnight.

# Summary

Field transformation requires leadership, conviction, and decisiveness. Sales strategy and tactics have to change in the social, mobile, digital age. Sales professionals have an incredible opportunity to elevate themselves to a new class of elite professionals who are social in every sense of the word—omnichannel, collaborative, and trusted.

As always, the best reps listen first, taking advantage of the information and access now available to see what customers are posting about, and then connect with the right person at the right time with relevant content and useful recommendations. At Hearsay, we have been able to measure the impact that effective social sales can have on a company's bottom line—that is, upwards of 20% to 30% lift in sales between test and control groups.

Today's highest-performing sales organizations follow these four steps:

- Sales teams are encouraged to create an individual professional presence on social networks that is consistent with the brand, yet personal and authentic.

- Teams constantly increase their network connections and make a habit of social networking, including seeking out referrals and building relationships with customers and centers of influence.

- Reps establish methods for uncovering important events among their contacts so that they can quickly respond and turn prospects into leads.

- Every rep establishes a credible reputation by posting useful, relevant content and following contacts in a way that is friendly and demonstrates expertise.

Threatened by the rise of roboadvisors and automation, today's sales professionals occupy a unique place in the business ecosystem. These reps have been offered a unique and critical opportunity to upskill, prove their value, and double-down on the human element of customer interaction. With referrals and recommendations from social networks growing in influence, successful Social Sales Professionals must master the new rules for customer engagement—they must provide individualized service with a distinctly human touch, at scale. Doing this right will require time and commitment, but the ROI will more than compensate salespeople and sales organizations for their investment.

# 6

*"A brand is no longer what we tell the consumer it is—it is what consumers tell each other it is."*
—Scott Cook, Founder of Intuit

# Social Marketing: From Campaigns to Experiences

Just as sales organizations need to transform themselves, so too do today's marketing departments. The biggest change is that marketing is no longer solely the job of marketers. Today's brands are equally shaped by salespeople, customer service agents, and recruiters as well as customers, strangers, and influencers—often on social media. Marketers must consider and own the entire customer experience, even though much of it is beyond their direct control.

The other game-changer is the explosive growth in mobile capabilities and usage, particularly among millennials and Generation Z. The vast majority of these individuals say their smartphone never leaves their side, day or night. When they wake up, it is the first thing they reach for. In a survey conducted by Zogby Analytics, 60% of respondents believed that in the next five years, "everything will be done on mobile devices." In this chapter, we'll explore the different ways that marketers are going mobile; in the next chapter, we'll talk about how mobile messaging apps such as WeChat and Facebook Messenger are transforming payments and commerce.

We've already discussed at length how today's customers have sky-high expectations and incredible power—they can turn to social, mobile, and digital channels to research companies, read product reviews, seek friends' input, comparison-shop, and voice their opinions and complaints. For marketers, the key is shifting from a campaign mindset to an always-on, conversational experience mindset. Marketers must lead the way for Social Business and mobilize their entire organizations to continually engage the always-connected customer before, during, and after the sale in ever-more ways.

It wasn't always this way. For more than a hundred years, the purchase funnel, or AIDA (awareness, interest, desire, and action) model, has guided the marketing discipline.

Perhaps not surprisingly, this funnel no longer accurately describes today's nonlinear, multi-stakeholder world. A funnel implies that a purchase is the end of the buyer's journey, but we know in today's world of social media that it's only the beginning of a relationship.

In 2009, consulting firm McKinsey created an updated customer journey framework, dubbed "the loyalty loop," that added three post-sale stages to the traditional funnel—enjoy, advocate, and bond. In the loyalty loop, customers repeatedly reevaluate their decision to stick with a brand (Figure 6.1).

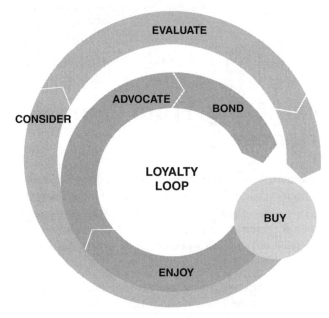

**Figure 6.1**
*The loyalty loop represents how modern customers evaluate, consider, and buy a product*
(Source: General Assembly)

When all goes well, brands entice customers to continually stay in the loop. When something goes amiss, however, customers leave the loop and have to start the consideration process all over. Marketers can target a customer at any stage in the loop through a content supply chain. The loyalty loop reminds marketers that the endgame isn't just acquiring customers, but keeping and delighting them at every turn.

But is the loop comprehensive enough? Interactions today between brands and customers are messy. Customers often find themselves in a tangle of conflicting messages and influences. We can no longer realistically target customers at any specific stage of a well-defined process. Instead, we need to plan for "meaningful coincidences." As shown in Figure 6.2, a spaghetti structure is perhaps a better depiction of this web of interactions.

Consider the task of marketing new shoes. A consumer might discover a brand on a fashion blog, visit the brand's website and social media accounts, read online reviews, go to a brick-and-mortar store to try on the shoes, and see that friends have 'liked' the shoe company on

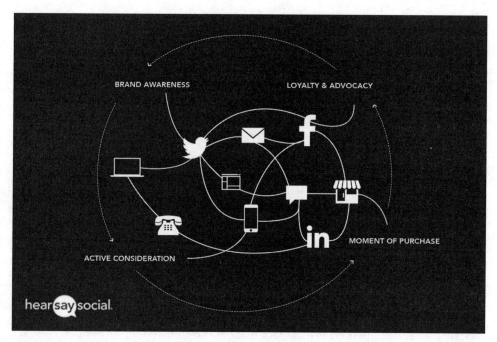

**Figure 6.2**
*The nonlinear stages of the modern omnichannel customer journey* (Source: Hearsay Social)

Facebook. This cumulative set of events works together to pull a customer toward the brand. Marketers can't control which events will take place, nor can they dictate the order in which they will take place, so it's important to have a strategy for each of the major channels, such as cultivating influential third-party bloggers, encouraging customers to review their purchases, and engaging regularly on social media platforms. Today's marketers must master the omnichannel spaghetti structure of multiple stakeholders and multiple rounds of evaluation and reevaluation across paid, owned, earned, online, and offline venues.

In the spaghetti structure model, there are still different buyer stages, but those stages are no longer neat and sequential. After a customer purchases, she may reconsider. One bad incident could change a loyal advocate into a brand detractor whom the company must once again win over. There are also many more opportunities to get it right and delight. And more than ever, every customer plays a role affecting the awareness, consideration, and customer experience of others.

## Five Marketing Pillars of Social Business

The new spaghetti-structure customer journey is rewriting the marketing playbook. There are five pillars in this structure that every organization needs to build and fortify: excellent content marketing, ambassadors and influencers, mobile-first mindset, data mastery, and seamlessly integrated campaigns.

# PILLAR #1. Excellent Content

In Chapter 1, we saw how the keepers of the digital last mile—Facebook, Google, Amazon, and their ilk—win the hearts, minds, and wallets of consumers because they have frequent digital touchpoints, and how they enjoy frequent digital touchpoints because they've won the hearts, minds, and wallets of consumers. Through excellent content marketing, every business, regardless of category and transaction frequency, can establish frequent digital engagement.

Customers are hungry for good content to consume during the increasing hours each day they spend scrolling through digital screens and social media feeds, but the bar for what constitutes good content has never been higher. The average consumer is bombarded with more than 3000 marketing messages *each day*. They have learned to tune out the vast majority. They can sniff out a sales pitch from a mile away and run the other direction. In fact, more than 200 million people around the world—twice as many as are on Pinterest—have installed ad blockers, up 48% in the United States and 82% in the United Kingdom, according to a study by Adobe and Pagefair. Ad blocking was estimated to cost publishers more than $20 billion in 2015.

Lengthy sales pitches, spam, and gimmicks are no longer tolerated by today's savvy customer. What customers crave is content that educates, entertains, delights, and delivers authentically on an organization's brand promise. Increasingly, an overly formal voice and corporate jargon, even in B2B situations, does not resonate with buyers. On social media in particular, there is an etiquette and expectation around being authentic (how you would talk to a friend or family member), approachable, and easily relatable. Successful social media marketers tend to use a more casual tone, shorter posts, photos and videos, and customer retweets. Social media is supposed to be a real-time stream and a place where people let their guard down, so anything that feels overproduced or salesy is not welcome. Moreover, in addition to authenticity and relatability, today's skeptical consumer demands transparency and expects companies to own up when they've made a mistake.

Beyond this, there are no hard and fast rules—in fact, the more creative, the better. Social media can consist of micro-content or long-form material; the content could be a photo, video, infographic, or comic strip. It just needs to tell a great story and offer something of value. That value could be as simple as offering a smile, a new perspective on an everyday occurrence, inspiration, educational knowledge, a tool, a comparison, or an apology. Value takes many different forms depending on the brand and product category. Taking risks and adding in whimsy and artistry are definitely advised, as they will help your content stand out and motivate shares and retweets. The Coca-Cola Company follows a strategy in which 70% of its content is tried and tested, so that the company knows that a certain audience percentage will respond to it. However, Coke aspires to have 20% of its content be something new and innovative and 10% "just plain risky"—in which case the company has no idea how people will respond. This kind of risk taking allows the organization's marketing team to experiment and grow.

My friend and *Socialnomics* author Erik Qualman often says, "Successful companies in social media function more like entertainment companies, publishers, or party planners than as traditional advertisers." I couldn't agree more.

### Red Bull: A Media Company That Happens to Sell Energy Drinks

Red Bull's content efforts have dominated the social media space, and sometimes space literally. A few years ago, the company sent Austrian skydiver and self-described daredevil Felix Baumgartner on a free fall from the edge of the stratosphere. Adding to the company's existing set of extreme sports events and videos, this world-record-breaking event won Red Bull nearly 1 million interactions on Facebook in a single day and boosted sales by 7%! Content marketing offered the company an incredible way to show—not just say—its motto, "Red Bull gives you wings!" The company's €5 billion in revenue in 2015 came solely from sales of its popular energy drink, yet Red Bull describes itself as a media company.

The most effective strategy for each company depends on its brand promise and the factors influencing its customers' purchase decision (Is it based on perceived quality, knowledge, or lifestyle?). Certain brands like RBC Wealth Management are more serious (most people want a financial advisor who takes managing their money seriously), while others like T-Mobile are more lighthearted and may make use of emojis, as shown in Figure 6.3. Companies with brand mascots, such as Allstate's Mayhem and Jack from Jack in the Box, find that social media can help the mascot come to life, injecting a sense of fun authenticity (which is ironic, given that the mascot is a made-up creature). As you develop your brand's social media voice, take into account your brand values and what your customers expect of your organization.

**Figure 6.3**
*A tweet from T-Mobile that fits its brand promise of being the "Un-carrier"—simple, fair, fun*
(Source: Twitter)

### Momentum Marketing as a Content Marketing Strategy

Retail brands in particular may consider momentum marketing (also called newsjacking) as a strategy for surprising and delighting customers around timely news. The idea is this: When a relevant news event occurs, you find a way to insert your brand into the conversation, generally by using the trending hashtag in your tweet.

*continues…*

Done well, this strategy is essentially a way to get your brand in front of thousands, if not millions, of people. But newsjack the wrong news or in the wrong way, and it can backfire in a big way.

Here are three examples of successful momentum marketing campaigns:

- During the Super Bowl power blackout in 2013, Oreo's marketing team quickly crafted this gem: "You can still dunk in the dark" (Figure 6.4).

**Figure 6.4**
*The clever photo Oreo tweeted during the Super Bowl blackout* (Source: Oreo)

- The company was able to inject some lighthearted humor in the midst of an unfortunate event, delighting customers and amassing nearly 16,000 retweets.

- Virgin Holidays took advantage of the newly passed same-sex marriage law in the United Kingdom to offer a timely message, which aligns with the company's progressive brand promise.

- Charmin used the Oscars to insert itself into a trending topic with humor and surprise, referencing a longstanding favorite joke of toilet paper being stuck to someone's shoe as they exit the bathroom (Figure 6.5).

Though there's no immediate connection between Oreo and the Super Bowl, Virgin and same-sex marriage laws, or Charmin and the Oscars, each company found clever ways to capitalize on the opportunity with some lighthearted humor. But newsjacking can also go terribly wrong, especially when companies try to distract people from hardship or suffering. Most consumers feel doing so is in poor taste and crosses a line that should not be crossed. If this unfortunate fate should befall you, take a deep breath and acknowledge, apologize, be transparent, and take steps to remedy the situation. You have to take risks to do anything great, and everyone makes mistakes sometimes.

**Figure 6.5**
*The clever momentum marketing tweet from Charmin during the Oscars* (Source: Twitter)

Generally, there are three good rules of thumb for newsjacking. First, you must do it early, just as the news is starting to break; otherwise, you won't reach the vast majority of people who will have already searched and tweeted about the news and moved on. Second, the tie-in to your brand must be made clear, because otherwise your message could be confusing and come off as trying too hard. Finally, be prepared for a negative reaction. After you newsjack, you should closely monitor the response and be prepared to @reply back. Keep in mind that momentum marketing is not a strategy for every day; you should employ it sparingly and opportunistically.

## Expert Knowledge and Thought Leadership

In the world of B2B and high-consideration B2C, marketers must cater to customers' desire to self-educate by building a repository of easily findable expert content. Customers in the consideration phase of their purchase journey will search on your company, product, category, key pain points, and competitors to learn best practices, understand the range of available options, and judge your solution. Your success will depend on the relevancy and findability of your company blog, website, social media pages, analyst reports, and press coverage. The higher the level of consideration applied to the purchase (think enterprise software, financial services, and real estate), the more research the customer will do and the more expert content your organization will need to have available across paid, owned, and earned channels to build credibility and demonstrate expertise.

You will need to provide the same content in multiple formats and at varying levels of depth and detail. Early on in the buyer's journey, the customer wants to quickly scan and narrow down her consideration set, so a lengthy whitepaper and two-hour webinar are overkill. More appropriate forms of content at this stage of the decision-making process would be a blog post or customer testimonial. The customer may also check out the social media accounts for your company and for the salesperson with whom she is working to see if they are keeping up with trends and are responsive to customers. All of these assets should be search-engine optimized and easily navigable from the company's website homepage.

I think of content marketing in terms of stock and flow. Having a rich "stock" repository is important because during the consideration phase, customers will do their own online research. Customers want to make an informed decision; to do so, they must seek out honest knowledge about the problem they are trying to solve. "Flow" is about getting your stock content into the attention stream of your customers and prospects, as we will turn to next.

## PILLAR #2. Content Distribution Through Employees, Customers, and Influencers

Equally important to developing excellent content is figuring out how and where to distribute it. The constant flow of content is also the lifeblood of social networking sites. Of course, you will tweet and post links to your stock content through your brand social accounts, but don't stop there. Here is where your employee brand ambassadors, customers, and influencers come in.

### Employee Brand Ambassadors

Marketing has been democratized—employees are on social media and whether you or they are aware of it, they are representing the brand and playing a role in shaping the customer experience. In parallel, customers are researching individual service professionals, from doctors and lawyers to realtors and financial advisors, before deciding to work with them and their company. It's no longer enough that so-and-so is affiliated with Mass General, Latham & Watkins, Coldwell Banker, or AXA, as respected as these brands may be. Customers want to get to know *the specific individual* with whom they will be working: Where did she go to school? Who might we know in common? Does she have expertise in the area where I need help? Will our personalities jive?

For marketers, no longer is communication tightly controlled—and that's a good thing. Your employees and in-house experts are your best and most authentic brand ambassadors. Most likely, they want and need your help, since they aren't marketers. Marketing teams must develop crisp brand guidelines and ideally provide or suggest content for the organization's externally facing sales and service professionals to share on social media.

Minneapolis-based wealth management firm Ameriprise Financial has done just this. As part of its award-winning GoSocial Program, the company has mobilized thousands of its financial advisors across the country to establish social media profiles and serve as brand ambassadors. Karen Goodwin, an Ameriprise wealth advisor based in Walnut Creek, California, has a vibrant and robust Facebook Page. As shown in Figure 6.6, Karen leverages a combination of Ameriprise-created content, such as her cover photo (featuring "Colleen Webb, Explorer"), and content she creates herself, such as her cookie bar recipe (see the lower-right image).

**Figure 6.6**
*Facebook Page for Karen Goodwin, an Ameriprise wealth manager based in Walnut Creek, California* (Source: Facebook)

The Ameriprise marketing team populates the advisors' Hearsay Social content library (shown in Figure 6.7) with suggested posts, linking both to third-party content and to Ameriprise's "stock" of website content. The content created for use by advisors might echo what the brand is posting, but needs to be created in a different voice that's authentic to an advisor.

Karen typically logs in a few times a week to select which items she will post immediately or schedule for posting later in the week. She injects her own unique personality into these posts, which resonates with her clients and community, and uses Hearsay's compliance features and approval workflow to stay within brand and securities regulations (see Chapter 11 for a deep-dive on social media legal and compliance considerations).

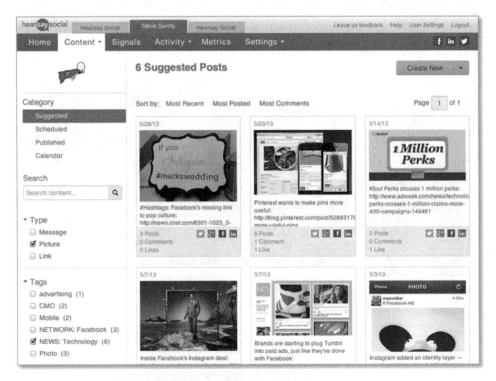

**Figure 6.7**

*The Hearsay Social content library for advisors (iPad version) filled with suggested posts developed by the marketing team and approved by the compliance team* (Source: Hearsay Social)

More broadly (and outside the securities industry), employee advocacy on social media is a hot and growing area. Several technology vendors, including Dynamic Signal, LinkedIn Elevate, SmarpShare, and PostBeyond, offer employee content-sharing solutions. Activate your employee brand ambassadors and you will unlock a passionate and authentic distribution channel for your content.

Marketing teams can benefit from granular and aggregate insights into which kinds of posts are resonating across which segments and geographies. Any brand campaign—be it a TV ad, sporting event sponsorship, or new product announcement—can be instantly amplified and pushed out through thousands of relationship managers' social profiles. For many organizations I've worked with, the engagement levels on individuals' pages often outperform those on the brand's homepage even when the message is identical— it's a testament to the immense power of one-to-one relationships and local networks and communities. Although it's important for marketing teams (along with their legal counterparts) to establish clear guidelines, companies should rely on letting their people represent them in creative ways that resonate locally and with their specific audiences, as the following sidebar about Farmers Insurance agent Joel McKinnon illustrates.

### "He's Just a Little Boy"

Joel McKinnon, a Farmers Insurance agent in New Philadelphia, Ohio, was incredibly moved when he stumbled upon a poem, "He's Just a Little Boy" (written in the 1920s by Chaplain Bob Fox) posted at a Little League field last year. He inadvertently ignited a national movement when he snapped a photo and posted it to his Facebook Business Page (see Figure 6.8).

**Figure 6.8**
*Farmers Insurance agent Joel McKinnon's Facebook Page containing the "He's Just a Little Boy" post, which went viral* (Source: Facebook)

*continues…*

His organic Facebook post instantly drew hundreds of 'likes,' comments, and shares in an age when parents sometimes get carried away and put too much pressure on their kids to excel in sports. The Farmers corporate marketing team, through their Hearsay dashboard, caught wind of the viral post. They shared the post on Farmers' corporate brand page on Facebook and added it to the agent content library on Hearsay, where hundreds of McKinnon's fellow agents across the country picked it up and shared the post on their respective Facebook Pages. The post continued to go viral.

In the post comments, a number of Farmers' customers from across the country asked how they could get the same sign for their local Little League field. The Farmers marketing team decided to have 1500 of these signs made and sent to various communities across America. To celebrate McKinnon's ingenuity, the company turned to his hometown print shop, Synergy Sign Company, in Strasburg, Ohio, to produce the signs.

Just when the company thought the campaign couldn't have turned out any better, Major League Baseball then picked up the story and posted about it on the MBL homepage (Figure 6.9). It took McKinnon less than five minutes to share the original post, and he spent zero advertising dollars. With some quick thinking and rapid execution, the Farmers home office marketing team transformed a local post into a wildly successful national campaign. The result was a level of authentic engagement that money can't buy.

**Figure 6.9**
*Joel McKinnon's viral post resulted in coverage on the Major League Baseball website*
(Source: MLB.com)

## Customers and Influencers

In addition to employee brand ambassadors, marketing teams need to cultivate relationships with customers and third-party influencers (such as bloggers, celebrities, research analysts, experts, and tastemakers), as they can be powerful contributors to both aspects of the "stock and flow" concept we introduced earlier. Examples of customer-created "stock" include online ratings and reviews, blog posts, and testimonials. Examples of their "flow" contributions include social media posts, shares, and retweets. McKinsey found that "marketing-induced consumer-to-consumer word of mouth generates more than twice the sales of paid advertising," with customers acquired via word-of-mouth having a 37% higher retention rate.

Successful customer relationships on social media first begin with successful customer relationships off social media. The following sidebar examines how retailer Warby Parker embraces social media to amplify its customer connection in stores and with online orders of its eyewear.

### How Warby Parker Has Mastered Customer Connection On and Off Social Media

New York–based eyewear company Warby Parker is one organization that has mastered customer connection, engagement, and delight both on and off of social media. First, the company has built immense customer trust by living its brand values of being environmentally friendly and giving back to the community. Efforts include Warby Parker's carbon-neutral pledge and "buy a pair, give a pair" program in which every pair of eyeglasses purchased causes the company to donate a pair to someone in need.

Second, the company has created truly spectacular experiences that customers love photographing and sharing on social media. Examples include its iconic brick-and-mortar stores as well as the Warby Parker Class Trip—an authentic yellow school bus reimagined as a mobile showroom and refurbished to look like a professor's study (it traveled to 16 cities nationwide!). Another example is the Home Try-On program, which has been a part of the company's business plan since its launch. The founders recognized that purchasing eyeglasses online can be somewhat of a non-intuitive process for most people, so they wanted to offer customers a risk-free introduction to the brand. With the Home Try-On Program, customers can order five pairs of glasses to try on, completely free of charge, which allows them to wear them around and get the opinions of friends and family for five days. Customers love the program, and many take to social media to share photos of themselves in the various pairs to solicit feedback from friends and from the Warby Parker team, using the hashtag #WarbyHomeTryOn.

*continues...*

Finally, the Warby Parker social media team takes time to engage with every mention on social media. Thousands of customers reach out every month soliciting styling advice, assistance with customer service inquiries, and someone with whom to share their excitement about the brand, so this is not easy to do.

All of this makes good business sense: Warby Parker has calculated that Home Try-On customers with whom the company engages on social media are converted into buyers at an up to 20% higher rate than the average customer. It has also found that customers consistently purchase the frame recommended to them by Warby's social media team, indicating that customers truly trust the social media team and brand.

Here are a few ideas on how to cultivate relationships with customers and influencers:

- **Follow them.** The first step is establishing a connection and starting a dialogue.
- **Shower them with love.** Retweet and always respond to customers and influencers, as Warby Parker does. Give them special discounts, perks, and access. Remember their birthdays. Find other ways to delight them and get them talking even more about how great you are.
- **Ask for their input.** Working on a new product or rebrand? Ask your best and most loyal customers for honest feedback. You could do so ad hoc on social media or create more formal customer and industry advisory boards. We've gotten great ideas and new directions from doing this at Hearsay Social. Marketers also play a key role in encouraging, measuring, and managing online reviews, such as getting a greater number of reviews and specifically encouraging your most delighted customers to create reviews.
- **Have your employee ambassadors connect.** One respected multinational organization coaches its advisors to tweet at local "celebrities" (like the high school football coach or mayor) to connect around local issues. Every so often, the celebrity will engage in conversation, and these tweets get retweeted significantly. It's an easy and often fun way for your people to connect to local issues in their community while influencing the influencers and getting their name and your brand out there in an authentic way.
- **Use a technology platform to manage these relationships.** Depending on how many customers and influencers you are trying to manage, it may make sense to use a software platform. Influitive, TapInfluence, and Traackr are great technologies that help with this effort.
- **Partner in a business capacity.** Often, enterprise customers will agree to do a joint press release or other testimonial in exchange for a discount. Some bloggers will agree to author and/or publish sponsored content in exchange for a fee or free services (just make sure this is clearly disclosed, per the FTC's Blogger Disclosure Regulations).

## Paid Content Marketing

As far as paid content distribution goes, many B2B and high-consideration B2C marketers as well as media companies are finding success utilizing paid "recommended related content widgets" that appear at the bottom of editorial articles in publications ranging from *Fortune* to *Wall Street Journal*. For example, an entrepreneur's Google search might result in her visiting Forbes.com to read an article about whether to incorporate as an LLC, C Corp, or S Corp. Beneath the article and comments section, a series of widgets offer additional paid links to related articles, videos, and slideshows, likely sponsored by a law firm or legal services marketplace like Priori.

Two New York startups, Taboola and Outbrain, dominate the buying and selling of this widget space. A big limitation of social network advertising today is the lack of purchase intent. Sponsored marketing based on related keywords (in the entrepreneur's case, the keywords might be "incorporation," "tax structure," "LLC," and "C Corp") can help marketers connect with intent. When it comes to long-form content, these sponsored widgets typically perform better than search marketing, because customers on editorial sites are already in content consumption mode.

Today's marketers must master the art and science of excellent content marketing. They have to generate both stock and flow, and customize content for multiple lengths and formats mapping to different customer need states and preferences. They also must create complementary but unique content for the corporate brand, employee ambassadors, customers, and influencers. At Hearsay, we call this approach #CODE—create once, distribute everywhere—and we apply it to every product launch, thought leadership piece, or other initiative we do. It's the only way to reach and connect with today's savvy customer while presenting a consistent omnichannel experience.

## PILLAR #3. Mobile-First Mindset

Any marketing discussion these days would not be complete without a focus on mobile apps. The world is not far from having 3 billion adults active on smartphones. Google recently reported that there are now more searches performed on mobile devices than on desktop computers. Many apps, such as Snapchat, WhatsApp, Vine, and Instagram, are not only mobile-first but mobile-only. Not surprisingly, mobile ad expenditures are growing faster than any other digital ad format in the United States and are expected to exceed $40 billion in the next few years, yet it isn't keeping up with the dramatic growth in the amount of time consumers spend glued to their smartphones. Internet analyst Mary Meeker found that print advertising remains "way over-indexed relative to time spent," whereas mobile advertising spend is proportionally far less than the amount that mobile media consumption might warrant.

For brands, this is a make-or-break moment—either master mobile or risk irrelevance. Five key mobile strategies can be deployed as part of the mastery pathway: mobile social media posts, responsive websites, mobile apps, text messaging, and mobile messaging apps. Across the board, marketers must adapt to smaller screens, shorter attention spans, and multi-device engagement.

To be fair, entire books have been written just on mobile marketing. I won't be able to do this topic full justice here, but instead will share some high-level thoughts:

- **Mobile social media posts.** More than 70% of social network users access social networks with their phones. Marketers need to optimize the content they post for the mobile screen (see the tips in the nearby sidebar). You should also consider mobile advertising on Facebook and LinkedIn, which is driving higher clickthrough and conversion rates than desktop social ads and is four times more effective in converting affluent customer segments.

- **Mobile apps.** Mobile apps are the ultimate direct channel to your customers. Most of the time, you can keep them logged in so that they are just a tap or push notification away. However, mobile apps are expensive to create and maintain, so this strategy typically makes sense only for big companies with a large installed base with a need to frequently transact with their customers. Alaska Airlines, Chase, Allstate, and Starbucks all have widely downloaded, top-rated apps that are worth checking out. Be wary of companies offering to white-label or otherwise build a low-cost mobile app for your business. It may sound tempting, but the vast majority of these are poorly done and will hurt your brand.

- **Text messaging (SMS).** Text messaging can be a very powerful channel for companies—more than 90% of people read text messages within three minutes of their receipt. However, the majority of customers don't want to receive marketing-related text messages from the majority of companies, so proceed with caution in this sphere. The most accepted use cases are for special offers and non-marketing-related updates, such as flight delays and order status. Vendors to look at for appropriate usage include Twilio, Waterfall, Tatango, and BrightTag. A word of caution, however: In my experience, text messaging is generally most welcome by consumers as a one-to-one communication channel rather than a mass-communication channel. A number of firms we work with at Hearsay have deployed our sales rep texting app but refrain from sending mass texts at the brand level. Whatever you do, make sure you adhere to the strict opt-in regulations when it comes to text messaging (such as TCPA in the United States and CASL in Canada), as the fines for noncompliance can add up quickly.

- **Mobile messaging apps.** Mobile messaging apps including SnapChat, WhatsApp, and Facebook Messenger are offering powerful ways for brands to reach customers in a more private setting (generally in the form of a paid campaign). Figure 6.10 shows an example—the World Wildlife Fund's recent Snapchat campaign, "Don't let this be my last selfie." But the potential for mobile messaging apps is far greater than messages, as WeChat has demonstrated and Facebook Messenger clearly aspires to become. In the next chapter, we will discuss how mobile messaging apps are becoming platforms for payments and transactions.

- **Responsive websites and email.** A responsive website or email automatically adjusts how it lays out content based on the device being used to access it (large versus small) and screen orientation (landscape versus portrait). Not only are responsive sites table stakes these days for your SEO ranking, but they also make for the best customer experience, allowing easy browsing and navigation. Note this is different than having a mobile site, which is a separate, usually stripped-down instance of your website. A mobile site is usually more work to maintain and will hurt your SEO. For email, shorter

**Figure 6.10**
*Example of the World Wildlife Fund's successful Snapchat campaign for endangered species: "Don't let this be my #LastSelfie"* (Source: World Wildlife Fund)

is better. Optimize it for shorter attention spans by summarizing your content and then including a link to a web page where users can access the full version.

## PILLAR #4. Data Mastery

Today's marketing teams must become experts at capturing, buying, accessing, and using data to become much more targeted and relevant to customers. The digitization of consumer

### Tips for Mobile-Optimized Social Media Posts

- Include a photo or video. Just as on desktop, posts that include a photo or video are the most eye-catching for consumers scrolling through their mobile feed. Opt for vertical (rather than wide) images and video to mirror the vertical orientation with which people typically interact with their phones. Users scrolling rapidly through content feeds will not typically stop to rotate their phones to view a wide-format photo or video.

- Keep it short. Twitter has always had a 140-character limit on posts, but it's tempting and easy to go over that for Facebook or LinkedIn posts. On a small mobile screen, you don't have the luxury of length.

- If your post includes a link, make sure the landing page is also mobile-friendly.

- For ads or high-stakes posts, test them first by publishing them to a dummy account; make sure it looks good on both the iOS and Android platforms before actually posting the message.

- If you are running a video ad on Facebook, consider hypertargeting users connected via WiFi to ensure the video loads and results in a smooth viewing experience. Many mobile networks are not yet predictably reliable when it comes to video streaming.

activity and interaction has created an enormous amount of data, which marketers can now use to learn about their customers, measure program effectiveness, and focus and refine their efforts over time. These days, there's no excuse for "spray and pray" marketing. The rapid proliferation of data has put the Holy Grail of marketing—the "segment of one"—within reach.

On social networking sites, the ability to target ads to very specific audience profiles based on characteristics such as interests, gender, hashtags, and friend activity is known as hypertargeting. Essentially all social profile data, posts, and hashtags are all now targetable by advertisers. If your company produces golf clubs, for example, you might wish to run a Facebook campaign targeting people who list golf as an interest and live in areas where your company's products are sold. You might also wish to run a LinkedIn campaign targeting the owners, managers, and buyers at golf shops to encourage them to stock your products and give them favorable in-store placement.

As shown in Figure 6.11, marketers can hypertarget customers based on demographic information such as location, language, income level, and age, as well as across a variety of preferences such as favorite films, TV shows, websites, and restaurants. Table 6.1 summarizes the different kinds of social media ad targeting. Hypertargeting narrows the playing field, allowing companies to reach only the most relevant potential customers or tailor specific messages to different audience segments.

**Figure 6.11**
*Facebook's self-service advertising tool allows hypertargeting based on age, gender, language, interests, behaviors, page connections, and more* (Source: Facebook)

**Table 6.1    Summary of Social Network Ad Targeting Types**

| Targeting Dimension | Description and Examples | Social Networks Supported |
| --- | --- | --- |
| Demographic targeting | Target self-reported demographic information on social profiles such as age, race, gender, religion, education, career, or memberships. | Facebook (richest data set), LinkedIn (primarily job, education, and association data) |
| Interest (psychographic) targeting | Target what people report as their interests, activities, skills, and pages they have 'liked.' | Facebook, Twitter, LinkedIn, Pinterest, Instagram |
| Behavioral and connection targeting | Reach users based on prior purchase behaviors or the use of a particular device. Connection targeting finds people who are linked somehow to your app, page, group, or event. | Facebook, Twitter, LinkedIn |
| Look-alike targeting | Reach people who have profile and post attributes similar to those of your existing followers. | Facebook, LinkedIn |
| Targeting on existing customer database | Upload a list of email addresses, phone numbers, or usernames, and their profiles will be found and targeted. Also works on visitors to your website (by including a pixel from Facebook on your website). | Facebook (known as custom audiences), Twitter (known as tailored audiences) |

## Programmatic Advertising and Retargeting

With so much data available about consumers, such as which sites they are visiting, which mobile apps they've installed, and what they're sharing on social media, many advertisers are turning to programmatic, or automated, methods of buying, placing, and optimizing direct online advertising campaigns. According to eMarketer, programmatic expenditures recently eclipsed $10 billion, about half of the total US digital display ad market.

Programmatic advertising automates the ad placement process by deciding, usually in real time, which consumers to serve an ad impression to based on data the advertiser believes is pertinent. For example, Tesla might run a programmatic campaign targeting consumers in a certain age range who have visited a different luxury car manufacturer's website in the last 60 days. Tesla would decide ahead of time the ad bid price range, daily budget, and desired reach, and the algorithms would then do the rest.

The consumers being targeted by this hypothetical Tesla campaign might see the ad on Facebook, LinkedIn, other websites, or during a mobile app's installation—on any publisher site that is part of the ad network running the campaign. A different customer visiting an identical social or web page will likely be shown a completely

*continues…*

different ad. Programmatic campaigns hypertarget consumers based on third-party behavioral data (such as "people who visited a certain website or downloaded a certain mobile game") or audience data (such as demographic information from a Facebook profile) to automatically cherry-pick the best impressions for the campaign.

One particularly fast-growing area of programmatic advertising is retargeting, a form of behavioral targeting on people who have visited a particular site but didn't complete a purchase transaction. The retargeted ad is delivered to those users on a different site (usually in a completely different context) to try to lure them back. If you've ever viewed an e-commerce item, say a pair of shoes, and then kept seeing an ad for those shoes on Facebook and other places you visited on the web, this was retargeting at work. It's effective but some consumers find it creepy.

There is a nice measurable aspect to programmatic media, but a few challenges remain beyond the creepiness factor. The first challenge is fraud—specifically, whether ad views and clicks are from the real human beings the brand is paying to reach or from "bots" (you may have heard of the term "click fraud"). The fraud issue is not limited to programmatic advertising, but it's more rampant in this realm because advertisers no longer have a direct relationship with publishers. The second challenge is viewability—that is, whether a viewer scrolls to the part of a web page where an ad loads. Finally, family- and children-oriented brands in particular worry about brand safety and relevance. Programmatic ads can appear anywhere in an ad network. Certain companies may not want their logo and ads to appear next to an article about their competitor or on a site that contains graphic images, violence, or other media that do not fit with their brand promise and values.

Generally, marketers have much more data to work with these days. With new data comes new metrics, such as viewability. For instance, if an ad loads at the bottom of a web page and the consumer visits the page but doesn't scroll down to where the ad is, the ad is not considered viewable. If you've ever wondered why you could click "skip this ad" on a YouTube video or click the "X" on a pop-up ad, it's because the website publisher is verifying viewability by making sure you are a human being.

In the past, it wasn't possible to verify viewability of web pages, much less viewability of television, radio, print, or billboard ads. Some make the mistake of trying to compare social media viewability, such as in the Facebook News Feed or the Twitter stream, with these traditional channels, but it's comparing apples to oranges.

With increasing pressure on marketers to deliver results, lots of people are jumping into the fray to help measure and verify media effectiveness. For example, Facebook shifted to only charging for ads that are viewable. The company also works with advertising clients to conduct "conversion lift" studies to see whether and to what extent campaigns led to improved online and offline sales, as well as other calls to action. To do this, Facebook compares the data between a control group (not shown the campaign) and a test group (shown an ad campaign), and then compares these outcomes with the advertiser's data (generally from pixel tracking or an in-store point-of-sale system). Third-party data companies such as Datalogix, comScore, and Nielsen Catalina Solutions also partner with brand advertisers to measure ROI across various campaigns and channels. So far, the metrics look pretty darn good. In the United States, social network–driven e-commerce is projected to top $14 billion in sales this year, representing approximately 5% of all online retail revenues.[1] According to a recent Business Insider Intelligence report, social media is the fastest-growing referral source of any online channel for retail e-commerce traffic.

## PILLAR #5. Integrated Multichannel Campaigns

The final pillar of social marketing excellence is integration across channels and stakeholders to create a situation where the whole is greater than the sum of its parts. Integrated campaigns provide clarity, consistency, and greater return on investment, as customers are more likely to notice, remember, and then act if they see something repeated in complementary ways across different channels and mediums.

Not every campaign needs to incorporate every channel every time. Sometimes an integrated campaign involving just two channels can be very effective, such as a hashtag printed on a storefront display.

Integrated campaigns can also be more resource efficient, because you can reuse creative assets developed for one channel on others. For example, you might embed a YouTube video on your website or post it to your social channels.

Often the greatest challenge in multichannel campaigns is organizational in nature. Your sponsorships team might not be in regular communication with your web team, which is not talking every day to your social media marketing manager or to the in-store promotions team. Not surprisingly, successful integrated efforts tend to be driven by the chief marketing officer. Otherwise, the lack of consistency from message to message leads to loss of credibility and the brand being perceived as insincere. To quote Jim Collins, "The hallmark of mediocrity is chronic inconsistency." With multiple marketing channels, employee brand ambassadors, customers, influencers, and members of the public talking about your brand at all times, these integrated efforts have never been harder to execute and yet more important.

With this exact goal in mind, Penn Mutual Chairman and CEO Eileen McDonnell decided to combine the roles of chief marketing officer and chief digital officer to closely align the brand's growing set of digital activities with its offline initiatives. She brought Jeff Fleischman into this combined role. Soon after joining the company, Jeff helped to spearhead an ambitious national rugby campaign that included a sponsorship of the Collegiate Rugby Championship and Varsity Cup Championship, TV partnership with NBC Sports, radio partnership with CBS Radio, outdoor and on-site events (Figure 6.12), web, and brand social media efforts; he even mobilized Penn Mutual's financial advisors to post about the partnership on social media (Figure 6.13).

---

1. http://think.withgoogle.com/customer-journey-to-purchase/

**Figure 6.12**
*A team competing in the Penn Mutual Collegiate Rugby Championship*
(Source: Penn Mutual Collegiate Rugby Championship)

**Figure 6.13**
*A Penn Mutual financial advisor, Sheldon Sweeney, posting about the company's rugby sponsorship on his Facebook Business Page* (Source: Facebook)

The result has been measurable increased brand awareness, recruitment, and lead generation for Penn Mutal. Nearly 7 million impressions were driven on Twitter alone, with such hashtags as #TeammatesForLife, #Rugby, and #CRCFan. Approximately 22% of the company's newly appointed advisors, especially millennials, cited rugby as having "some or strong impact" on their decision to join the company.

Brands maximize ROI and the relationship with their customers when every offline and digital touchpoint reinforces and builds on the other channels, across stakeholders, offering a deeply powerful and cohesive experience despite the journey being nonlinear.

# Four Steps to Successful Social Marketing

With the foundation now established for content, content distribution, mobile, data, and integrated campaigns, we can focus on the tactics of setting up and growing an effective social marketing presence.

## STEP #1. Establish a Brand Presence

Just as individual social profiles help sales reps be findable, so too are social brand presences an important "home base" that make companies and brands easily findable by their customers. Websites are still important, but having only a website these days is not enough. Today's customers expect to find brands and companies on social networking sites, which they view as a more authentic and conversational complement to websites.

For large organizations and brands, Facebook Pages, Twitter brand accounts, and LinkedIn Company Pages have become important extensions to existing web strategies to engage existing audiences as well as reach new audiences. For small business proprietors, brand presences provide a clean separation between their personal and professional identities.

### Which Social Network?

The most popular social networks worldwide are Facebook, Twitter, LinkedIn, Pinterest, and Instagram. Approximately 71% of Internet users engage with Facebook, making it arguably the most important outlet for most marketers. Twitter is the ideal tool for marketers to participate in real-time, fast-moving conversations and tap into sharing and virality. As the world's largest database of professionals, LinkedIn is the key platform for B2B and high-consideration B2C sectors such as luxury goods and real estate. LinkedIn Company Pages are also often used by prospective job candidates to gain an understanding of a company's culture, mission, and existing employee base. Pinterest, now the third-most popular social platform in the United States, and Instagram are ideal venues for highly visual marketing, such as that dealing with restaurants and food, lifestyle brands, home improvement, fashion, salons, travel, and the like.

Depending on whether your business is B2B or B2C, or in retail, consumer packaged goods (CPG), professional services, or another sector, and depending on the geography and demographics of your current and ideal customer, being on one particular social networking site may make more sense than participating in others. The new 'buy' button and payment capabilities within Facebook, Twitter, and Pinterest (covered in Chapter 7) should also drive your decision of where to set up shop, virtually speaking. Each presence you choose to support will require ongoing investment and resources, so think hard and test your options before committing to a social network.

In other cases, the expanded audience engagement opportunity may justify investment in maintaining multiple presences. This strategy works well for Starbucks, which is active on numerous social platforms including Facebook, Twitter, LinkedIn, Pinterest, Instagram, and WeChat (Figure 6.14).

**Figure 6.14**
*Starbucks does a great job in spreading its presence across multiple social media platforms*
(Source: Facebook, Twitter, LinkedIn, Pinterest, Instagram, and WeChat)

## Corporate Versus Line of Business or Local Pages

Many companies have multiple lines of business and products. In this case, it generally makes the most sense to create separate presences for each major brand. For instance, the majority of consumers are not familiar with Mondelēz International, whose corporate Facebook Page has slightly more than 115,000 'likes,' whereas Oreo, Toblerone, and Trident Gum—brands within the company's portfolio—each have millions. Another example is Chase Bank, which has its own branded Facebook Page in addition to separate pages for its products, such as the Chase Sapphire and Chase Freedom credit cards (Figure 6.15).

**Figure 6.15**
*Chase Bank has done a good job creating different Facebook Pages and experiences across multiple lines of business* (Source: Facebook)

Similarly, on LinkedIn, you can create Showcase Pages to highlight specific brands relating to a LinkedIn Company Page. For example, Adobe's Company Page links to several of its Showcase Pages (Figure 6.16).

**Figure 6.16**
*The LinkedIn Page for Adobe has links to its showcase pages* (Source: LinkedIn)

Local place pages can also be very powerful. Facebook, Google Places, Yahoo! Local, and Yelp (Foursquare pioneered much of this space, but has since declined in popularity) all automatically create a page for every local business based on publicly available directory data. Customers can also create local pages by "checking in" on Facebook or Yelp. It's best to periodically check and claim these local pages so you can begin managing them as part of your content "stock."

Maintaining local pages takes a lot of work, but the SEO benefits can be enormous. Local pages rank high in Google searches, Google Maps, and social media results. Local store or franchisee websites often show up higher in search results than corporate websites. A local agent's Facebook post will probably reach about five times as many people and spur eight times as much engagement as a corporate headquarters Facebook post.[2] The reason is that customers are drawn to and click on local results.

## STEP #2. Build Your Follower Base (Grow Your Network)

Now that you have your social brand presences, you need to build your follower base. A great place to start is with employees, friends, and trusted customers. Seeding your presence (inviting friends, family, and loyal customers) with some initial level of followers and activity makes it more attractive to strangers. From there, start spreading the word about your social presences by including links, Twitter handles, and hashtags on your website, employee email signatures, print campaigns, billboards, and product packaging.

Aspirational, lifestyle, and beloved local brands have it the easiest when it comes to attracting 'likes' and followers, as they come to the proverbial social media table with an existing following. For example, Maserati, Nike, and Chicago hometown favorite Lou Malnati's Pizzeria don't have to do much to amass very large followings, because people naturally wish to publicly identify with these brands.

The rest of us have to work harder to provide clear and compelling reasons for people to visit and connect with our brand pages. Depending on your industry sector and brand promise, different strategies, such as being funny, helpful, or inspirational, can work to attract followers. Whichever strategy you choose, make it readily apparent to customers when they visit your page (more on this in Step 4).

It probably goes without saying, but one of the best ways to build a follower base is to regularly engage, care, and provide interesting/funny/useful posts. In other words, be worth following.

## STEP #3. Listen ("Hear")

Although a social media presence can offer great opportunities for getting your brand and message out there, it is an equally crucial—if not even more valuable—source of audience insights. Every day, hundreds of millions of people turn to social media to express their delight or disappointment with a brand in real time. Sentiment analysis

---

2. http://www.adweek.com/socialtimes/local-facebook-pages-outperform-corporate-pages-in-terms-of-reach-engagement-percentage-study-finds/277160

tools such as Viralheat, Sysomos, and Radian6 (part of Salesforce Marketing Cloud) are helpful for taking the pulse of the social buzz, scrutinizing social share of voice, and staying ahead of social media crises and on top of suddenly viral tweets, across owned social media accounts as well as public social posts.

But don't be surprised if not all of the comments are positive. Especially on Twitter, complaints are commonplace. If you see multiple complaints about the same issue, your customers are likely onto something that legitimately needs fixing. We'll cover Social Customer Service in detail in Chapter 7, but for now recognize that complaints on social media can have a big impact on your brand—a sometimes hard lesson for marketers.

Depending on the volume of customer interactions relative to the size of your social media team, you may wish to set a service level agreement (SLA) for responding to tweets, posts, and comments. For some organizations, it may simply not be realistic to try to respond to everyone.

If you read between the tweets, so to speak, social media can be full of rich, interesting, and real-time insights into how customers and noncustomers perceive your brand, products, and recent company announcements. Listen, but be careful not to overreact to a vocal minority. Also watch out for sarcasm.

## STEP #4. Educate and Engage ("Say")

With your brand presence, followers, and basic level of insights in place, the golden moment arrives to engage through permission marketing. Brand presences on social media are the ultimate opt-in marketing channel. Anyone who 'likes' or follows your brand has actively elected not only to receive your brand updates (as they would by joining your email list), but also to publicly identify with your brand: By default, Facebook, LinkedIn, and Twitter display brand 'likes' on member profiles. Therefore, your social media followers are likely some of your hottest leads and most loyal customers with whom you should invest in cultivating relationships and community, which is primarily done through excellent content posts.

### What to Share

What should brands post about? Well, let's first consider what brands should *not* post about. With a few exceptions (i.e., offer-driven businesses with low customer loyalty), posts should not be solely about brands, products, and transactions. Whether on or off social media, nobody likes companies or people who talk only about themselves.

Brands should seek to provide audiences with something valuable in every post. Value can come in many different flavors, and the right strategy for each brand depends on its brand promise and the objectives for its social media presence. Here are some typical content strategies, one or a combination of which may be best for you:

- **Educational and informative.** The lowest-risk strategy is to provide helpful information and educational content to build credibility and a trusted authority. For example, an insurance company might provide earthquake readiness tips or a reminder to file your taxes on time. A home improvement company might share a how-to video on DIY wallpaper application. A fitness club might share a recipe for a healthy meal using seasonal local ingredients.

- **Funny and lighthearted.** On social media, a little personality goes a long way. Funny jokes, stories, and puns can work for certain brands. @Charmin and @OldSpice are great examples of brand accounts that inject humor into their social posts in ways that tie back to their brand and products.

- **Community-oriented.** For some brands, what works best is to make their social media presence all about their customers and community. This strategy spans everything from featuring customer videos and stories to contests and polls to wishing people a Happy New Year or Happy Thanksgiving.

- **Inspirational.** Brands that challenge the human spirit often amass quite a following on social media. Take lululemon athletica, for example. A recent post quoted Kate, the company's global editorial manager: "Standing at the top, I wept with pride and sheer exhilaration in spite of myself. Even though I'm tethered to a safety system, make no mistake: walking across a 60-metre long suspension bridge between that mountain's two spires and then standing 600 dizzying metres above the valley floor with sheer drop-offs in every direction is completely humbling. Once the tears stopped, though, elation set in, which I think is fairly accurately captured in this image. I'd do it again tomorrow." This strategy works especially well for athletic and fitness brands, military/police/firefighter recruiting, and volunteerism.

- **Company and product announcements.** Although it's not good practice to talk only about your company and products, doing just that every so often is generally welcome and expected. Previews of new product launches in particular do well on social media, as does giving fans early or exclusive access to special deals or events. A good rule of thumb is to talk about your company or product no more than once every four to five posts. The exception is if you manage a beloved aspirational, lifestyle, or local brand where your product speaks for itself and already has a large offline following; in that case, you can get away with posting about your product much more often.

Include photos and videos when possible to capture people's attention and boost engagement. Whether you should include links in your posts depends on which strategy you choose. Lighthearted posts, quick news, and photos or videos typically stand on their own. Educational posts and meaningful announcements may require more explanation than fits in 140 characters and therefore more often link to long-form content. Longer-form content can be from the company blog or from third-party sites (in this case, the brand is acting as curator and commentator). The paid strategies we discussed earlier can help drive further reach and engagement.

## When and How Often to Share

In an ideal world, brands should post at least once a day, but not so often that followers are inundated with their messages. As in any relationship, you are setting expectations with your customers and followers, so consistency is important, too. It's better to consistently post once every other week than to post daily for a month and then go radio silent for the next month.

Responding in real time to audience posts, comments, and trending topics is an important aspect of social marketing, but many brands complement this with longer-term campaign calendars. Often, social posts can be prescheduled and coordinated with off-social-media campaigns such as TV ads, athletic or charitable sponsorships, and certain times of year (such as graduation time, holidays, or National Retirement Planning Month). Popular tools such as Tweetdeck, Spredfast, Sprinklr, Hootsuite, and Salesforce Social Suite allow posts to be scheduled ahead of time.

Finally, brand marketers should think about the best time of day and days of the week to maximize impressions and engagement. Technologies like Hearsay Social (Figure 6.17), SproutSocial, and Oracle Marketing Cloud can analyze historical audience behavior to suggest when to schedule posts to coincide with your particular audience's tendency to check and engage with their social media feeds. An earlier sidebar discussed momentum marketing (also called newsjacking) as a one-off strategy, but timely content is also generally valuable. A motivational quote about sisters might do OK any day, but on National Sisters' Day it would probably be particularly meaningful.

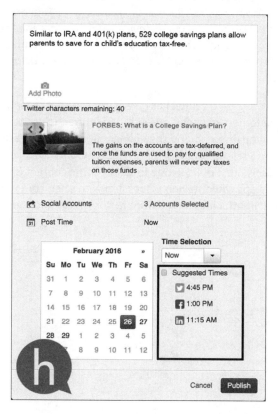

**Figure 6.17**
*Hearsay Social's predictive analytics suggests and schedules social media posts for the time of day and day of week each user's connections are most likely to be active and engage* (Source: Hearsay Social)

## Summary

It's an exciting time to be a marketer. Increasingly, marketing teams need to reach across and outside their organizations to influence the influencers, be they employee ambassadors, customers, bloggers, or members of the public at large. Social marketing has moved far beyond simple banner ads and one-size-fits-all campaigns to sophisticated conversations that hypertarget segments of one and are integrated with multichannel initiatives.

From an organizational perspective, social marketing must move from a practice to an operating model. Esther Lee, who is global chief marketing officer of MetLife and has also run marketing organizations in the telecommunications and consumer packaged goods sectors, says:

> Though social media practices are difficult in and of themselves, we can hire headcount, agencies, and consultants to help with the practices. What we can't outsource is reorganizing our companies to create a social media engine across marketing, technology, legal, customer service, and sales to provide a truly integrated presence, engagement, and relationship. In order to drive the right content, marketing needs to engage everyone from PR and HR to product development and compliance, and the organization needs to be agile enough to execute on something before it's no longer timely and relevant.

The traditional linear marketing funnel has given way to a messy spaghetti-structure customer journey. Customers' expectations of brand authenticity, their willingness to conduct their own online research, and their connections via mobile devices have all transformed the art and science of marketing. To survive and thrive in this new era, marketing organizations must build a mobile, data-centric content foundation and execute the four key steps while staying in lockstep with sales, commerce, and customer service to present a delightful and united front to customers and the world.

# 7

*"If I had to guess, social commerce is next to blow up."*
—Mark Zuckerberg in 2010

# Mobile Messaging and Social Commerce: Going from 'Likes' to 'Buys'

In the first decade of the Facebook era, social media permeated the entire buyer's journey, becoming an integral part of marketing, selling, customer service, product development, and more. Social networks became the place where people go to discover, research, and validate purchase decisions, and then to talk about their purchases after the fact. But until recently, social networks did not directly facilitate actual commerce in any meaningful way.

All of this is changing right now, thanks to the explosive growth of mobile messaging apps, many of which have incorporated payment capabilities. Six of the top 10 most used mobile apps today are messaging apps. WhatsApp, Facebook Messenger, WeChat, and Line each has hundreds of millions of monthly active users (WhatsApp has more than 800 million!). Especially in Asia, many of these apps are already being used for far more than messaging—for example, for gaming, virtual goods, media, payments, commerce, and summoning real-world services such as food delivery, hailing a cab, or checking in to a flight.

In parallel, many of the major consumer-oriented social network companies, including Facebook, Pinterest, and Twitter, have introduced 'buy' button and virtual shop capabilities in their feeds and pages. These companies have high hopes and aspirations that consumers will soon go from merely browsing, 'liking,' and talking about products on their platforms to actually paying and transacting.

A 2014 analysis of channel attribution for e-commerce conducted by the Google Analytics team had found that two-thirds of the time, social media plays an "assist" role leading to a transaction; only one-third of the time does social media play a role in the "last interaction" (Figure 7.1). Social media has always seemed to suffer from attribution issues, but this will soon change in a big way. Social commerce—for both online (products) and offline (services) interactions—is about to get real. In fact, in China, it already has.

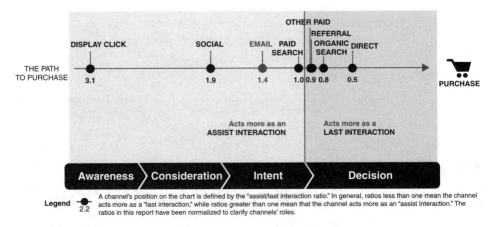

**Figure 7.1**
*Google's attribution analysis of e-commerce in 2014 found social media played a limited role in driving transactions, but that's about to change* (Source: Google Analytics.[1] Google and the Google logo are registered trademarks of Google Inc., used with permission.)

Facebook, in particular, is well positioned to play an important role in commerce. First, the company has not one but *both of the top two* mobile messaging apps—Facebook Messenger, which it carved out of the Facebook mobile app in 2015 to create a stand-alone messaging app, and WhatsApp, which it acquired in 2014 for $19 billion. As WeChat has demonstrated in China, mobile messaging can be a powerful platform for transacting between buyers and sellers. Facebook Messenger, run by the former head of PayPal, David Marcus, is building robust payment services. Facebook also brings to the mix more than 2 billion existing users (if you include Instagram and WhatsApp), their friend connections, and their brand preferences.

Consumers spend more time on social media than any other digital activity, and while they're on those social networks, they're often talking to or about brands. With every 'like,' click, and post, Facebook learns more about every consumer and becomes better able to match her with products and services likely to be of interest and relevance. Just as WeChat has done in China, Facebook will likely become an even more important channel

---

1. Google Analytics, Q4 2012. $N$ = US: 130M conversions (12K profiles); UK: 78M (8.3K); DE: 52M (4.4K); FR: 36M (5.2K); BR: 35M (2.6K); JP 20.5M (2.0K); CA: 7.4M (1.4K). Note that the purchase paths in this report are based on interactions with a single e-commerce advertiser. http://think.withgoogle.com/customer-journey-to-purchase

for businesses around the world, no longer reserved just for marketing, customer service, and employee brand ambassadorship, but actually facilitating transactions for both products and services, online and offline.

## A History of Fits and Starts

The road to social network commerce has been long and bumpy. There have been more than a few failed experiments and plenty of learning along the way. Here are some of the past attempts and lessons learned:

- **Transaction sharing.** Facebook Beacon, launched in 2007, broadcast a user's activity while on third-party partner sites (such as purchasing movie tickets on Fandango or a coffee table on Overstock) to that user's profile. This happened without the user's permission and resulted in a huge privacy uproar. Facebook quickly dismantled the program. In 2009, a startup called Blippy raised $13 million to create a platform allowing consumers to share their real-time credit card purchases with friends. That didn't last long, either.

- **F-commerce.** In 2010, Facebook launched the ability for retailers to create e-commerce experiences on Facebook. Major retailers including 1-800-FLOWERS, Gap, J.C. Penney, and Nordstrom participated in the test, creating virtual stores on their Facebook Business Pages. However, F-commerce was shut down after just two years, as consumers seemed to prefer to directly transact on each retailer's existing e-commerce website.

- **Social gifting.** Several attempts at social gifting have failed to strike a chord with consumers. The initial version of Facebook Gifts, which was launched in 2007, allowed users to buy virtual stickers (for $1.00 each) to share on friends' walls. The idea didn't take off, and Facebook Gifts was shut down in 2010. Two years later, Facebook Gifts relaunched as an online shop to send digital gift cards as well as physical gifts to friends (based on Facebook's acquisition of a social gifting startup, Karma). But it, too, was shut down in 2014 due to warehousing challenges and low consumer uptake. Besides Facebook, a number of social gifting startups, including SendSocial, Wrapp, and Treater, have all shut down or pivoted to new concepts.

- **Facebook Card.** In 2013, Facebook experimented with a universal stored-value gift card called Facebook Card that consumers could use to make purchases in brick-and-mortar retail stores such as Sephora, Target, and Olive Garden. The plastic, reusable card could hold value from multiple different retailers; for example, a friend could gift you with $10 at Sephora, a different friend might give you $25 at Target, and yet a third friend could load $20 for Olive Garden on your card. Alas, this was not a huge hit and the program was wound down in 2014.

Facebook's journey toward unlocking commerce is full of important lessons for traditional businesses. First is the Facebook team's persistence, which epitomizes the Silicon Valley mantra of fail early, fail fast, learn, and try again. Second is their laser focus and refusal to settle for anything less than a home run—the Facebook team has repeatedly shut down programs such as Facebook Gifts that may have been profitable but not "big enough." This has freed their attention and resources to focus their efforts on scoring a home run. Finally, I admire the company's ability to adapt and learn not only from its own failures but also by studying the success of others. As we'll see later in this chapter, a big source of inspiration for Facebook has clearly been the Asian mobile messaging companies.

## Mobile Messaging Apps as Payment and Transaction Platforms

In Asia, three mobile messaging apps have been on a tear since 2010. WeChat (created by Chinese Internet giant Tencent), Line (developed by the Japanese subsidiary of Korean Internet giant Naver), and KakaoTalk (founded in 2010) dominate the Chinese, Japanese, and Korean markets, respectively, and are quickly expanding across Asia as well as the rest of the world.

There are some interesting qualities worth noting about the Asian messaging apps. First is how Asia leapfrogged the West in embracing mobile devices, apps, and commerce. In North America and Europe, high PC Internet penetration and the wealth of robust PC-first websites delayed smartphone adoption and app development. The nascency (or, in many cases, nonexistence) of e-commerce in Asia paved the way for the earlier and faster rise of smartphone penetration, apps, and commerce.

Second, the Asian mobile messaging companies have all been successful in getting their users to pay for their services. Most of their revenue comes from in-app purchases of virtual goods (for use in their highly addictive, free-to-play mobile games). They also make money off of virtual stickers featuring cartoon characters. Users buy and send these as messages (think of it as taking emojis to the next level). The smallest category of revenue comes from official accounts for businesses and celebrities who pay to send promotional messages to consumers who opt-in to their messages. This is in stark contrast to the patterns seen in America and Europe, where for decades the conventional wisdom has touted ad-driven business models that totally subsidize consumer apps and services. This pattern has now started to change—WhatsApp charges users $0.99 per year and Snapchat charges users $0.99 for three Snap replays (in the past, Snaps would disappear after viewing them one or two times; Snapchat also experimented with paid image filters in 2015 but rolled them back).

But perhaps the biggest difference is that these Asian messaging apps are not just messaging apps, but robust platforms for managing much more, including transacting commerce. Take WeChat, for example: It offers the most far-reaching set of applications through a robust third-party ecosystem of partners.

### WeChat: The Everything Platform

The bulk of WeChat's revenue originally came from virtual goods purchases for use in the company's free mobile games, but the true genius behind the sale of these virtual goods was that they provided a mechanism for WeChat to capture and store user payment credentials. Today, one in five users has linked a bank account or credit card to the user's WeChat account (WeChat is on track to exceed 1 billion users by 2018). These same WeChat payment credentials can be used to book flights, buy movie tickets, hail a taxi, post product reviews, top-up their mobile phones, and buy financial products from ecosystem partners. In select cities across China, WeChat even has a City Services section that allows consumers to book doctor's appointments, pay home utility bills, pay traffic fines, report incidents to police, and monitor real-time traffic camera feeds and air quality (sadly, a huge problem in China).

But that's not all. As venture partner Connie Chan describes on the Andreessen Horowitz blog, WeChat harnesses the full power of the sensors on our smartphones and connects users to both on-demand collaborative economy services and the Internet of Things:

> Where most US apps confine the smartphone camera to just taking photos of people and places, WeChat engages the camera to scan English text and translate it into Chinese, or to pay directly for a transaction [to scan a QR code]. WeChat also better utilizes all the other smartphone sensors as sources of data input: It uses GPS when users search for businesses nearby. It calls upon the microphone to identify a TV show or a song on the radio. It uses the accelerometer when a user shakes a device to find strangers nearby to chat with. And it uses Bluetooth [to enable users to] add friends in their vicinity.

> Put it all together, and you can get some pretty creative results. Take Chinese toy company Dan Dan Man, which created Mon-Mon, a Bluetooth-enabled stuffed animal that integrates WeChat with the offline world [shown in Figure 7.2]. Parents can use the Mon-Mon official account in WeChat to send personal voice messages and pre-recorded … bedtime stories to the toy while they are at work or traveling. Kids immediately get those stories or messages, and can even press Mon-Mon's belly to reply to their parents' WeChat account in a message delivered back as a voicemail.

**Figure 7.2**
*Mon-Mon, an Internet of Things stuffed animal that can send and receive voice messages recorded for kids from their parents' WeChat app* (Source: YouKu)

Businesses, municipalities, celebrities, and other entities can become part of the WeChat ecosystem by creating an official account. This allows them to access APIs to build apps within WeChat, utilize WeChat Payments, send up to four broadcast messages per month, show up in their subscribers' accounts in-line with personal contacts, reply to any user message (must be within 48 hours), and access analytics. Users can add (i.e., subscribe to) any official account just as they would add a friend and immediately begin engaging with that account. There are millions of ecosystem apps in WeChat today, ranging from local restaurant delivery services and municipalities to Didi Kuaidi (the "Uber" of China), Burberry, and Starbucks.

WeChat now has the leading platform for *service transactions* (also known as online-to-offline transactions) in China. It is eyeing the $1 trillion prize for *e-commerce product transactions* as well. Merchants with official accounts linked up to WeChat payments can now set up virtual stores, enabling consumers to transact with them without leaving WeChat. Whether WeChat will be successful in gaining meaningful share against the 800-pound gorilla of Chinese e-commerce, Alibaba (whose Alipay payment service competes with WeChat Wallet), or will go more the way of F-commerce remains to be seen. In any case, the dominance of WeChat as a payment and transaction platform is both indisputable and amazing.

## Here Comes Facebook Messenger

WeChat's expansion into all of these myriad areas was possible because of China's low PC penetration and shortage of digital-last-mile players for many of the services that had already become popular for the PC web in the West. In the early 2010s, there was no Chinese equivalent of PayPal, OpenTable, YouTube, Amazon, Google Maps, or websites for booking hotels, paying traffic fines, and checking in to flights—at least none that was widely used—and many of the Western PC-first websites either did not do business in China or were blocked by government censors. Tencent created WeChat and, in some cases, helped seed ecosystem partners (with funding and go-to-market support) to fill the void. It was a wide-open land grab, and WeChat executed its strategy beautifully.

In the West, there's far more entrenched competition. The PC-first Internet giants have all reinvented themselves in the mobile market, so there is no single dominant platform. As a result, running the WeChat China playbook is not how the West will be won. The F-commerce lesson suggests that businesses and consumers don't merely wish to recreate the same shopping experience inside of Facebook that they already have today directly on the retailer's website. For Facebook-driven commerce to truly take off, it must offer something valuable and new. My guess would be that the Messenger team will pursue many different strategies when it comes to commerce. They have already launched two types of integrations, focused on on-demand services and product concierge services, which we explore next.

### On-Demand Service Transactions

In Chapter 3, we talked about how Facebook Messenger has begun integrating with the large and burgeoning collaborative service economy, starting with ride-sharing service Uber. Users can now hail an Uber ride from within the Facebook Messenger thread in which they are making plans with friends. Those friends can then see estimated waiting and arrival times, as well as order their own Uber rides from within the thread. I would expect other service integrations to come soon, similar to WeChat's many service provider integrations in China.

For now, Facebook Messenger integration makes the most sense for services between or involving friends, such as ride sharing, vacation rentals, food delivery, and groceries (e.g., allowing you to collaborate with your spouse or housemates on a shopping list). Facebook Messenger would make less immediate sense as a means to transact for individually consumed or private services, such as booking a medical consultation, until and unless those types of services providers come onto Facebook Messenger in a big way (which could totally happen at some point).

## Product Concierge Services

Facebook Messenger has also partnered with select product retailers, including Everlane and Zulily, to accept orders, send confirmations, confirm delivery, and generally provide personalized customer service within Messenger. Everlane, for example, has introduced a personal shopper-like concierge service (Figure 7.3), although the actual transaction still occurs via the retailer's existing commerce site. Consumers can message the retailer with questions, such as "Could you help me find some new tops?" and "Which navy blue silk tops do you have in size small?" and a live human will respond back, generally a few minutes later.

**Figure 7.3**
*Retailers including Everlane (featured in the interaction shown here) now offer a customer service and shopping concierge through Facebook Messenger* (Source: Facebook)

Click-to-chat functionality isn't new but comes to life in a whole new way when combined with Facebook. For one thing, many users are continuously logged in. Persistent Messenger conversations including order history and past customer service issues are viewable at a glance to both customers and retail service staff. Facebook knows who your friends are, so it's easy to imagine a scenario where friends might weigh in on certain purchases or collaborate on buying something together. Facebook also offers trusted identity, stored payment credentials, and knowledge of which brands consumers like and have talked about in the past.

In 2015, the Facebook Messenger team also launched M, a personal digital assistant (think Apple's Siri or Microsoft's Cortana) that finds information and completes tasks on users' behalf, powered by a combination of artificial intelligence software and humans who supervise and continually "train" the software. Tasks include purchasing items, having flowers or other gifts delivered to loved ones, booking restaurant reservations and travel, and more.

If M takes off, the implications for merchants will be profound. Just as Google search came to dominate the PC web as the most powerful tool for capturing purchase intent (e.g., most people searching for "Alaskan cruise" are likely in the market to book just such a trip soon), M could come to dominate both purchase intent *and* transactions in the mobile era, thanks to recent advancements in machine learning and stored login and payment information on mobile devices.

Of course, Facebook isn't the only player attracted by this enormous opportunity. Several startup companies—most notably Operator (described in the sidebar), Magic, and Mave—are also building personalized concierge offerings.

### Operator: Routing Layer for Retail Services

Created in 2014 by Robin Chan, Phil Fung, and Uber co-founder Garrett Camp, Silicon Valley startup company Operator seeks to reimagine the commerce experience, using the messaging paradigm. No more lengthy web searches or long lines at the mall—users simply message the Operator app about what they'd like to buy, such as dress shoes or a new dining table. Users can get as specific as they want, such as "Find me a decently priced live-edge dining table that can be delivered by March 1."

Behind the scenes, the company employs a combination of artificial intelligence and a network of product specialists—human operators, if you will—who will research and send you the best available options online and offline. Then, after you confirm your choice, that same combination will help you place your order.

Operator is betting that today's impatient consumers would rather send a simple text request than spend time trying to search, compare, and decide on purchases, especially while they're using a mobile device. Operator is a future expression of how search capabilities might look as the world moves toward mobile messaging.

Over time, Operator should get better at knowing what each individual customer wants and likes. Eventually it could become a starting point for all kinds of goods and services purchases, similar to how Uber and Postmates are a logistics layer for transportation. Operator has even partnered with UberRUSH to compete against Amazon by aggregating and delivering inventory from local stores for instant delivery. As of this book's writing, Operator is not integrated into Facebook Messenger, but that could be an interesting next step.

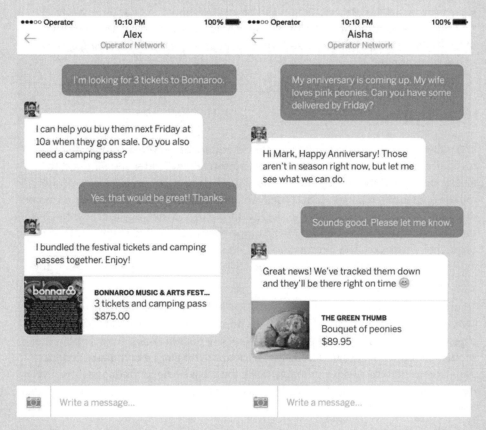

**Figure 7.4**
*Two examples of on-demand commerce requests sent to Operator via mobile message*
(Source: Google)

Magic, another Silicon Valley startup, provides a high-end concierge service for "anything"—its website promises to fulfill any request that's not illegal, supposedly including everything from meeting your favorite celebrity to setting up a private concert in your home (currently available only in the United States). All you have to do is send your request via text message to "MAGIC" (83489). Similar to Facebook Messenger and Operator, Magic is also powered behind the scenes by a combination of artificial intelligence and humans.

Mave, the personal assistant service founded in 2015 by former Snapchat COO Emily White, takes concierge services to an even higher level. Mave can actually decide which services you may need—from buying gifts for friends and delivering them on time, to planning birthday parties, to finding great schools and child care, to maintaining your home and paying the bills. When possible and where it makes sense, Mave selects, orders, and stitches together services from existing on-demand marketplaces, such as Instacart, TaskRabbit, Kitchit, and others presented in Chapter 3. White's bet is that busy dual-income households will be willing to pay to relieve the cognitive load of having to decide what they need while saving time and actually doing a better job at the tasks at hand.

## 'Buy' Buttons

In parallel with mobile messaging and concierge services, another commerce-focused revolution is brewing on social media: 'buy' buttons. From Twitter and Pinterest to Instagram and Facebook, 'buy' buttons have been showing up across their websites and mobile apps, both in pages ("stock") and stream ("flow"). The idea is simple: Consumers discover a product on social media, 'like'/tweet/pin it, and then buy it, all without leaving the site. When users click 'buy' for the first time, they're prompted to enter shipping and payment information. This information is saved so that subsequent transactions are a one-click (or one-tap) experience. Figure 7.5 illustrates an example of Twitter's 'buy' button for a Nest thermostat.

To provide consumers with context for its 'buy' buttons, Twitter has launched Twitter Product Pages (Figure 7.6). Retailers populate the page with images, videos, a description, and price. Twitter then automatically pulls in recent tweets about the product along with an option to buy (or click to the retailer's e-commerce product page). Twitter Product Pages probably make the most sense for frequently, positively tweeted-about products (a Product Page with no tweets, few tweets, or only negative tweets is not very enticing).

**Figure 7.5**
*'Buy now' button on Twitter* (Source: Twitter)

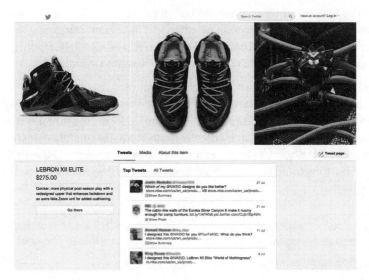

**Figure 7.6**
*Twitter Product Page for the Lebron XII Elite basketball shoe by Nike* (Source: Twitter)

As a social network that is essentially all about products, Pinterest is well positioned to capitalize on its 'Buy it' button (Figure 7.7). 'Pinning' demonstrates strong purchase intent: Nearly 90% of Pinterest users have bought something as a result of browsing on the site, even before the 'Buy it' button was available, and nearly half have bought five or more items they have pinned.[2]

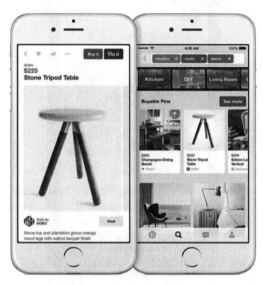

**Figure 7.7**
*The Pinterest 'Buy it' button appears next to the 'Pin it' button* (Source: Pinterest)

On Facebook, which currently accounts for half of total social referrals and more social commerce revenue than Pinterest, Twitter, and Instagram combined,[3] brands can incorporate 'buy' buttons in both paid and organic posts, and allow consumers to complete a transaction without leaving Facebook (illustrated in Figure 7.8).

It's still early days for social network 'buy' buttons, but they could eventually become a powerful way for product manufacturers to reach consumers directly. They might also help with the cart abandonment problem. The Baymard Institute estimates that 68% of interested buyers drop out of an e-commerce purchase flow before completing the transaction, most often because they get distracted on another site.[4] Potentially, social network 'buy' buttons could reduce friction because users are already logged in, have

2. According to a study conducted by branding and media agency Millward Brown: http://www .forbes.com/sites/kathleenchaykowski/2015/06/30/buyable-pins-go-live-on-pinterest/

3. According to a BI Intelligence Report: http://www.businessinsider.com/social-commerce-2015- report-2015-6

4. http://baymard.com/lists/cart-abandonment-rate

**Figure 7.8**
*Merchants can add a 'Buy' button to paid and organic news feed posts as well as brand pages*
(Source: Facebook)

stored their payment credentials, and can complete the transaction without leaving the social network app. Reducing clicks and steps is especially important on mobile devices, as it's clunky and slow to load a new browser window and have to type in all of your credit card and shipping information on a small screen.

The challenge will be not to make the same mistake as F-commerce and merely replicate e-commerce sites within social media sites. Some merchants and consumers have, for example, complained that WeChat's virtual shops lack the robust ratings and reviews, advanced search and filters, and other shopping features that more mature commerce sites have trained customers to expect.

## Summary

Both the social networking companies and mobile messaging companies are racing to stake their claim in commerce territory. They all aspire to be clearinghouses for much more than 'likes' and messages. As the behemoth that has both the largest social network *and* the two most-used mobile messaging apps, Facebook is in a strong position to win big in commerce, in terms of both product e-commerce, as exemplified by the company's partnership with Everlane, and on-demand services, as evidenced by its partnership with Uber. Over time, the immense data that Facebook amasses could enable ever-more powerful customer experiences—such as personally tailored 'buy' buttons inside of Messenger based on segment-of-one targeting.

To succeed in this quest, Facebook will need a "killer recurring payments use case" to compel consumers to store their payment credentials—similar to what in-app virtual items did for WeChat. Facebook will also need to onboard the right merchant and service provider partners and convincingly navigate user privacy, data, security, and trust issues.

Should companies integrate with commerce capabilities on mobile messaging apps and via social media 'buy' buttons? On the one hand, companies like Facebook and WeChat very clearly own the digital and mobile last mile and could be very powerful partners. On the other hand, they are so powerful that they could someday intermediate (with a service layer that commoditizes) your much smaller company, much like how some businesses now feel pushed into a corner by Google. One-tap buying without having to leave Facebook could mean your brand potentially loses control of merchandising, cross-sell, and upsell opportunities, and data, and no longer directly owns the customer relationship. But that might happen anyway—and it's obviously better to be there and stay relevant than to be totally cut off from today's always-connected, social customer. Brands will need to weigh the benefits of reaching new audiences, achieving potentially higher conversions, and managing the customer experience against these threats. One thing's for sure: The proliferation of mobile messaging apps as our stored identity and payment wallet will dramatically change the future of transactions and commerce.

## 8

*"Cheers to a new year and another chance*
*for us to get it right."*
—Oprah

# Social Customer Service

From the Arab Spring and Ice Bucket Challenge to the FedEx deliveryman "monitor toss" and hit-YouTube music video "United Breaks Guitars," consumers today are very much aware of the power they wield on social media. When there's an issue, they no longer email or write letters or wait on hold for "the next available customer representative." Those days are over: Today's customers take to social media to sing your praises—or voice their displeasure.

A survey by Twitter found that 80% of its users have mentioned a brand either positively or negatively in their tweets.[1] Unfortunately for businesses, more consumers (53%) tend to tweet about a bad experience than a good one (only 42%). McKinsey estimates the volume of tweets specifically targeted at brands and their Twitter customer service accounts has grown 2.5 times in the last 24 months. According to call center company LiveOps, 65% of customers prefer to interact with customer service agents via social media (Figure 8.1), and 83% have walked away from an intended purchase or canceled a subscription due to poor customer service on social media.[2]

---

1. https://blog.twitter.com/2014/study-exposure-to-brand-tweets-drives-consumers-to-take-action-both-on-and-off-twitter

2. http://www.liveops.com/social-customer-service

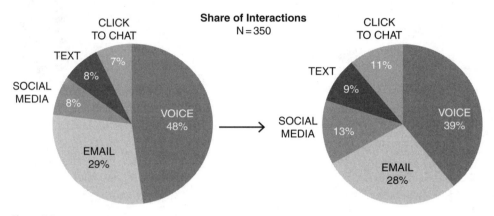

**Figure 8.1**
*Social media represents the fastest-growing channel for delivering customer service, as*
*shown by the change in share of interactions taking place on social networks from 2010 to 2015*
(Source: LiveOps)

# A Big Opportunity

For many organizations, customer service is the initial foray into social business. Often, before the marketing team has put up an official brand presence, someone in the company discovers customers are already complaining on Twitter. The company is "pulled" into social media sometimes before it is ready. Consumer demand becomes a powerful forcing function to mobilize a social presence.

While there is valid concern that social media outlets have become a cesspool of customer complaints, a growing number of companies are realizing they have little choice but to engage with customers in these forums due to the spaghetti-structure journey introduced in Chapter 6. Today's reality is that one happy customer can drive incredible word of mouth and goodwill, and one angry customer can do a lot of damage. Happy customers, angry customers, and indifferent customers all play a role in influencing prospective customers. The good news is that beyond mitigating the downside, there's also a huge potential upside: Social media provides ample opportunities to delight customers and convert them into loyal fans.

Finally, social customer service can be faster and more effective than traditional methods of customer service. For example, customers can perform self-help by reusing solutions provided to others who faced similar problems. In addition, Gartner found that customer service agents could handle four to eight times as many issues per hour on social media compared to call center interactions. This is not terribly surprising; both Twitter and Facebook Messenger, for example, are designed for short, speedy interactions. Nielsen calculates that social customer care on average costs less than $1 per interaction, compared with $2.50 to $5 per email (the actual amount for each organization obviously depends on the industry and customer profile). Most importantly, the metrics show customer satisfaction seems to dramatically increase when they interact with companies' customer service via social media, perhaps due to the faster resolution time or the good feeling that comes from venting one's frustration.

Social networks are no longer just a place for brands to market and sell—they are a place for companies to really listen to and engage with their customers, and ultimately provide excellent customer care efficiently and expediently. When done well, managing customer service over social media can both reduce costs and help build brand equity. McKinsey found that the best organizations harnessed social customer care efforts to unlock value through cross-selling, upselling, and reducing churn, improving year-over-year revenue per contact by nearly 7%, compared to the 12% decline experienced by "socially inept" customer service organizations.[3] But the benefits don't stop there: Consumers who experience positive social customer care interactions are also nearly three times more likely to recommend the brand to friends and followers.[4]

# How Customer Service Has Changed

Before social media emerged, customers had few channels to contact a brand if they had a question or problem. They could write a letter. They could call. More recently, they could send an email, fill out a web form, or click to chat. In each of these cases, the communication is private, one-to-one, and transient. Social media, however, completely changes the rules of customer service. In the era of Facebook and Twitter, customer complaints are persistent and often public. They can be broadcast to customers' friends and followers, and amplified through retweets and sharing.

Here are a few key ways that customer service rules have been rewritten.

## RULE #1. Customers Want an Immediate Response

In Chapter 3, we talked about how today's customer has come to demand instant gratification. This principle applies to customer service just as it does to ordering an Uber ride. When customers have an issue, they want it resolved as soon as possible. No one likes being put on hold or waiting for days or even weeks and months to hear back from a company. Social media interactions have the benefit of being both real-time and asynchronous, making them an ideal customer service channel. Phone calls are real-time but not asynchronous—you have to stand by until a customer service rep is available. Letters, email, and online forms are asynchronous but not real-time, so while you typically

---

3. *Harvard Business Review* article: https://hbr.org/2015/07/your-company-should-be-helping-customers-on-social

4. NM Incite Report: https://drive.google.com/file/d/0BwJJf0P4IF0oc0h0M1kxb3d6S0k/view?usp=sharing

aren't held up waiting for someone to get back to you before going on with the rest of your day, you often do have to wait a long time before your issue is resolved.

Social media and mobile messages are short, sweet, and to the point. Tweets are limited to 140 characters, so customers and companies alike tend to cut to the chase, resulting in a speedier resolution that is good for everyone. A handful of companies have the means and business justification to staff their social customer service channel on a 24/7 basis. Dutch airline KLM is a good example: No matter what the time of day or day of week, there is likely a KLM flight somewhere en route. For most companies, it is not feasible to be "always on," so it's important to clearly set expectations. Verizon Wireless manages to do this by listing hours of operation on its @VZWSupport Twitter profile and by signing on and off each morning and evening, respectively.

## RULE #2. Transparency and Accountability

As consumers, we are sometimes told that "this call will be recorded for training purposes" but for all intents and purposes, we know the call is a one-to-one conversation. Customer support emails and online form submissions are similarly not usually made public. On social media, it's different. Customer service interactions are always recorded and often transparent for all to see—tweets are public, Facebook posts are semi-public, and Twitter Direct Messages and Facebook Messages are private but persistent. Negative feedback must be handled diplomatically. If the company is at fault, it needs to own up to it. If not, it needs to be gracious in sharing the facts.

Easy sharing on social media has also meant that customer service interactions (both good and bad) tend to get amplified. Happy and angry customers alike want to tell their friends and the world about their experiences and opinions. On average, consumers who experience a positive social customer service interaction tell 42 people about it, versus 15 people for non-social service channels.[5] The net effect is that companies are being held more accountable (fortunately, unreasonable customers are also held more accountable) and the stakes are higher for having excellent customer service.

All of this means that today's customer service agent requires a different set of skills from the traditional service agent. As someone who may potentially interact with the public, that person needs to be hired and trained as a brand ambassador. The agent adopts the brand's voice and must be personable, articulate, and empathetic. She also needs to be resilient and confident, relying on her instincts to respond to customers quickly and appropriately.

## RULE #3. Authentic Human Interaction

In Chapter 6, we saw how today's consumers crave authentic brand voices that they can relate to. Being authentic and approachable is even more important when it comes to customer service and support. Most customers going into an interaction already feel

---

5. LiveOps study.

frustrated, so the more the brand can humanize and empathize, the better. It's easy to hate a faceless corporation; it's much harder to hate a friendly human being who is trying his or her best to help you resolve an issue.

As Figure 8.2 illustrates, Verizon Wireless humanizes its customer service efforts on Twitter in two ways. First, its cover photo features the customer service team members. Second, these agents use a friendly and authentic voice in their tweets. As mentioned under Rule #1, Verizon also properly sets expectations with customers regarding response times by clearly signing off and on each day (see the top tweet) and specifying customer support hours of operation in the account description.

**Figure 8.2**
*@VZWSupport humanizes the brand and builds a more meaningful connection with customers*
(Source: Twitter)

Another way to build customer trust and connection is to share the name or initials of the customer service agent currently tweeting. For example, @KLM reps sign tweets with their initials (e.g., ^CS) and @Zappos_Service reps sign on with a simple "Hey Twitter, Nicole here for a couple hours" so that customers know who is behind the tweets.

## RULE #4. No More Departmental Boundaries

Today's best customer service organizations are not just getting on social media, but are actively integrating social media conversations into the traditional phone, portal, and email channels and workflows, and across the entire company, as the sidebar on Wells Fargo illustrates.

# Case Study: Wells Fargo's Social Media Command Center

Renee Brown, Head of Social Media, Wells Fargo

Two years ago, Wells Fargo launched a social media command center to improve our ability to listen and respond to customer feedback. Situated in a dedicated physical space at our headquarters in San Francisco, the command center is staffed by customer service and marketing personnel who monitor trends via a dashboard and respond in real time to incoming tweets. It has become an invaluable way for us to gauge customer sentiment, collect feedback, and to respond and engage on the social and digital channels increasingly preferred by our customers.

Here are five lessons we've learned thus far:

- **Speak in the language of the customer.** One of our best lessons learned—and this is an ongoing lesson—is that the way corporations (especially in financial services) communicate oftentimes confuses consumers. The ability for us to continue to use plain language and be crisper in what we are saying is one of the things we see as an opportunity through social listening.

- **Social media is often the first responder and can reduce time to resolution.** Given the real-time nature of social media, our team is often the first to identify and respond to issues impacting our customers. For example, we have become the leading indicator of any potential issues with our ATM network. If we pick up more than a couple mentions of an ATM not functioning, we route that information to the right team so they can investigate and resolve the issue.

- **Social media can't sit in a silo.** We now have more than 200 critical business processes connected to our social technology. Just as in the ATM example, our social media insights must expand beyond the command center itself and be fully integrated into each specific area of business. An important step to securing buy-in across an organization is to involve business leaders early and agree upfront on goals, metrics, and process, such as an escalation path and formula for calculating metrics such as customer engagement, reach, and sentiment.

- **HR is a critical partner.** There are more than 265,000 team members. Although we've invested in clear guidelines and training to help our team members understand what they can do on social media, any command center listening on the public web will invariably intercept employee conversations, activities, and posts that need to be addressed separately from customers. Integration with the human resources department early and often is essential—it will be a key constituent in your listening and response efforts.

- **Crisis situations can happen at the worst times.** Sometimes it feels that the most critical social media issues happen late on a Friday night or over long weekends. Your team must be 24/7 and ready to react on a moment's notice. While our main location is in San Francisco, we have a backup location in Charlotte and also have after-hours support from a location in the Philippines. Be ready for salty and strong content. Social listening is not for the faint of heart. Prepare your teams and leadership to read words they are not accustomed to seeing in typical work settings—it is part of the social media environment and our customers' everyday reality.

Wells Fargo has always prided itself on being a leader in the social space. We are leading not only because of the technologies we've implemented, but also because of how we've integrated these tools, processes, and metrics across the company to keep the customer at the center of our focus. The command center has allowed us to do less talking and more listening. Our belief is that the more you listen, the more you can improve your customer experience and meet your customer needs.

Customers expect a consistent experience from companies, whether they are visiting a brick-and-mortar location, chatting with a customer service rep on Facebook Messenger, or scrolling through a marketing email. Because of this, the role of customer service is no longer confined to the customer service department; constant collaboration and handoffs must occur across sales, marketing, public relations, investor relations, and R&D. We live in a customer-centric, customer-driven world, and customers don't care about departmental boundaries and politics. They expect seamless and cohesive interactions with your organization every time. Sales and marketing teams must think about how to serve and delight the customer after the sale is made. In the same vein, customer service teams must think about upselling, cross-selling, and referrals.

## RULE #5. Social Return on Delight

In today's spaghetti-structure buyer's journey, customer delight translates into influential earned media,[6] brand lift, and referral sales. For companies that deliver delight, the prize is not only customer loyalty, but also a positive ripple effect across that customer's friends, followers, and acquaintances.

Certain brands, such as Nordstrom, Ritz-Carton, and Zappos, have always prided themselves in exceptional customer service online and offline. Social sharing amplifies the ROI of creating these moments of delight, turning previously one-on-one interactions between a brand and a single customer into powerful brand storytelling campaigns that get shared again and again.

Take the story of Joshie, a stuffed animal that was left behind at the Ritz-Carlton hotel in Amelia Island, Florida. Riley, the young boy who was Joshie's owner, was devastated over

---

6. Earned media, also known as free media, refers to publicity via third parties gained through unpaid promotional efforts other than advertising. Examples of earned media include unsponsored mentions in a newspaper article, on a television program, or on social media.

the loss. To console Riley, his father said Joshie was just taking a few extra days of vacation and then asked hotel staff to help corroborate the story. Days later, Joshie came home with a binder detailing his trip, complete with photos of him at the Ritz-Carlton spa (Figure 8.3), pool, golf course, and even the loss prevention office, where he got an honorary security clearance badge. Riley and his family were so delighted that they shared their experience with friends and family, and before long, the story of Joshie the stuffed giraffe had spread to the local television news as well as across social media. This is yet another example of how social business blurs the lines between marketing and customer service and how investing in customer delight can pay dividends in the form of customer loyalty and earned media.

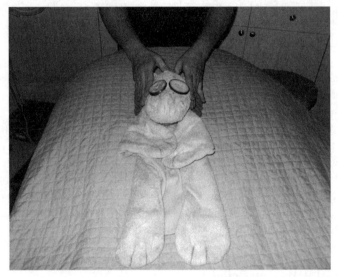

**Figure 8.3**
*Ritz-Carlton's treatment of a young guest's beloved stuffed animal morphed into a successful media campaign, initially on social media but later making its way to TV and print news*
(Source: Facebook)

## Four Steps to Effective Social Customer Care

Now, we are ready to talk about tactics. In the preceding chapters, we introduced the key steps to social selling and social marketing, respectively. There are similarly four steps to social customer service: (1) establish a social care presence, (2) listen for feedback, (3) respond and resolve, and (4) track trends and metrics. We'll discuss each one in turn.

### STEP #1. Establish a Social Care Presence

Many brands already have customer support forums and communities as part of their websites, but these days, when customers run into a problem, they increasingly gripe on

Twitter or Facebook. Forrester Research shows that in the United States, company website FAQs, call centers, and online forums remain the dominant customer service channels for now, but Twitter has been the fastest-growing channel (Figure 8.4). In the coming years, Facebook Messenger will also become a big player in customer service, based on the success of its recent integrations with select retailers, including Zulily.

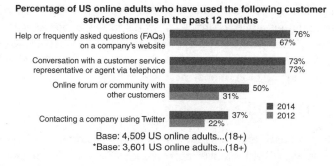

**Percentage of US online adults who have used the following customer service channels in the past 12 months**

Help or frequently asked questions (FAQs) on a company's website — 76% / 67%

Conversation with a customer service representative or agent via telephone — 73% / 73%

Online forum or community with other customers — 50% / 31%

Contacting a company using Twitter — 37% / 22%

■ 2014
■ 2012

Base: 4,509 US online adults...(18+)
*Base: 3,601 US online adults...(18+)

Source: Forrester's North American Consumer Technographics® Customer Life Cycle Survey 2, 2014

119674          Source: Forrester Research, Inc. Unauthorized reproduction or distribution prohibited.

**Figure 8.4**
*Website FAQs and call centers are still the primary channels used for customer service, but online forums and Twitter are catching up* (Source: Forrester Research, Inc. report, Brief: Take Social Customer Service Beyond Your Own Walled Garden, February 19, 2015)

Depending on the volume and nature of customer care tweets that your brand receives, it may be a good idea to create a separate social profile specifically for customer service so that support issues and angry complaints don't get comingled with content marketing and offers. This is what Netflix has done, as shown in Figure 8.5. The main @netflix handle is used to promote new releases, trailers, and memorable quotes, while @netflixhelps is specifically designated for customer support, such as streaming issues, technical difficulty, account lock-out, and so on.

**Figure 8.5**
*Netflix maintains separate Twitter handles for its marketing (left) and customer service (right) efforts* (Source: Twitter)

Other businesses, such as Southwest Airlines, opt to respond to customers through their standard brand Twitter handle. On the one hand, a dedicated customer service channel allows a brand's customer service department to own the channel, create a distinct tone, and manage, track, and analyze customer service metrics (as opposed to public relations and marketing metrics). It also allows the brand to provide dedicated customer service updates, especially for those customers who don't want to be inundated with marketing and promotional updates. On the other hand, customers may not find and access the brand's dedicated customer service channel—or won't bother to look for it. Having a single social media account means that the brand can have a consistent voice, no matter the message, and the brand will have the opportunity to add more followers who can receive future marketing and promotional messages.

## STEP #2. Listen for Feedback

There are several ways social care teams should "listen" for customer feedback on Twitter, including direct messages (DMs), @replies, and mentions. DMs and Facebook Messages are one-to-one (or group) private messages. One advantage to using them is the ability to take potentially embarrassing or mundane back-and-forth conversations into a private forum. Another advantage is the persistent nature of the messages—a service rep responding to a customer can easily see the historical context of interactions between the company and customer (the customer can see it, too).

@replies are tweets that begin with @username (in this case, your social care team's Twitter handle) and show up in Twitter's Notifications tab. These messages are directed at your social care team and, just as with DMs, customers generally expect a response. But your team shouldn't stop there. Likely, there are other people on Twitter who are venting about a service issue—a New York University study found that 37% of all tweets are related to customer service but less than 3% use the @ sign. Your team should be able to easily locate these other tweets through a saved search on your company and product names and related keywords.

Prior to the advent of social media, brands weren't privy to customer conversations about their products and services unless the customer reached out first—therefore customer service was always reactive. That's all changed now. Brands that search and listen not only to tweets specifically directed at them but also all potential brand and related keyword mentions have an opportunity to get proactive, such as for crisis management as discussed in the nearby sidebar.

### Crisis Management Using Social Media

If a crisis hits, social media accounts will most likely be the first to "hear" about it; these messages can be an early warning system for brands. But no matter how a brand discovers it may be entering crisis mode, it must think about the role of social media in the response and have a mitigation plan in place that addresses social media.

Ideally, brands should prepare a version of their "emergency response" or template holding statement for social media. Social care agents should have a clear escalation path for sounding the alarm—for example, if they come across a product safety issue that may warrant review for a potential recall. Especially on viral media like Twitter, early response is key to containing the damage and minimizing rumors, false information, and panic.

## STEP #3. Respond and Resolve

Auto-responders or canned template replies are not a good idea; customers are savvy and can tell immediately if they're receiving a canned message. Sometimes I see customer care teams use the same phrasing over and over (clearly copy-and-paste)— even though they are staffed by live humans, they come across as mechanical. Make sure your reps mix it up to keep their responses fresh.

While brands don't want to resort to templates and automated responses to customers, they do need to adopt a playbook for managing customer service on social media networks. Agents need to prioritize which customer and message they respond to first. If the customer is asking a direct question on social media, for instance, an answer should be provided quickly. Indirect references to the company, in contrast, can be bumped lower in the priority list. Drawing an escalation map also helps agents gauge which messages they can respond to, and which need to be passed on to a supervisor.

Social care reps need to be judicious in deciding whether to take a social customer service conversation to a different channel, such as DM, email, or phone. In some instances, a customer's question can be resolved quickly while remaining on a public forum. At other times, when a complaint involves personal information such as an address or order number, it will be necessary to move the conversation to a private channel. But once the issue is resolved, a best practice is that the conversation must move back to the public sphere to "close the loop" and let the customer as well as others know it's been taken care of. British online retailer ASOS does this, as shown in Figure 8.6.

**ASOS Here to Help** @ASOS_HeretoHelp · Jul 27
Hey ▒▒▒▒▒▒▒▒▒ sorry to hear about this, we've replied to your DM.

3:52 PM - 27 Jul 2015 · Details

Hide conversation

**Figure 8.6**
*The ASOS customer support team follows tweets and lets customers and others know when they move a discussion into a private forum* (Source: Twitter)

What's the best way to manage all of this? At low volumes, it's easy to use a free tool such as TweetDeck or even plain old Twitter search to find and respond to mentions.

At high volumes, consider using a paid social media tool like Spredfast or Sprinklr to create different queues, assignment workflows, and analytics. As with other customer service channels, speed matters.

On social media, the expectations for response and resolution are even higher. When customers reach out to a brand over social media with a customer service issue, they expect a rapid response—32% expect a response in 30 minutes and 42% expect one in an hour. It also doesn't matter if it's the weekend or after normal business hours: 57% of customers expect a response on any given day, at any given hour.[7]

## STEP #4. Track Trends and Metrics

It may not be realistic or remotely possible to respond to everyone, but it's worth aspiring to that goal and measuring the actual performance. Tracking key metrics helps managers staff their customer service channels appropriately, improve over time, and evaluate social care channels relative to traditional channels like phone or email.

The most basic metric is volume, which offers a baseline to understand changes and make comparisons. How many incoming messages does your social care team receive on social channels? What percentage is responded to? Which types of messages do they receive—are they marketing messages, public relations messages, or customer service messages? Are they related to deliveries, a product, the website, or an in-store experience? Categorizing messages by major customer issues provides a much more meaningful analysis than just how many absolute tweets are coming in.

Brands should also track average initial response time as well as average resolution time. Especially on a public forum like Twitter, the former is important for letting customers know that the brand has received the message and is working hard to find a solution, even if it may take a while. The goal, as customer care teams track these metrics, is to ensure that the team is providing consistent service across all channels. Also, if volume suddenly spikes in one channel, the company needs to be ready to bring in additional agents as needed. The best customer service organizations are now training all or a subset of reps to respond on multiple different channels so they can flexibly be assigned back and forth between Twitter, phone, email, or web as demand on one or the other channel waxes and wanes.

Because of the asynchronous nature of social media communication, it can be tricky to measure time-to-resolution, as it cannot be compared "apples to apples" with other customer service response times. With social media, an agent may respond to a tweet, but not hear back from the customer for several hours. At the same time, handling time can be a helpful metric to compare how quickly it takes for an agent to resolve an issue. An issue, for instance, could overall take 10 minutes to resolve over email, but only 5 minutes to resolve over social media—a clear demonstration of the ROI for social customer service.

---

7. http://www.convinceandconvert.com/social-media-research/42-percent-of-consumers-complaining-in-social-media-expect-60-minute-response-time/

## *Identifying Trends*

Sometimes, social media feedback causes companies to change a product or aspect of their business operations. That's what happened to discount retailer Target in 2015, when an Ohio mom named Abi Bechtel (@abianne) posted a tweet complaining about a sign in a Target store referencing "building sets" and "girls' building sets," and the tweet went viral. To its credit, the company reviewed its merchandise labeling product and decided to switch to gender-neutral signage for kids' toys, bedding, and books. As we mentioned earlier, social media can be the first to "hear" about issues and can help companies spot changing consumer preferences.

Aggregate customer sentiment can be measured to gauge overall customer satisfaction and brand health. Brands can track change in sentiment over time, during different seasons, and when there are known issues such as a drop in product quality, new product launches, discontinuation of products, and product recalls. Some of the major technology providers for tracking sentiment include Viralheat (Figure 8.7), Sysomos, and Radian6 (part of Salesforce Marketing Cloud).

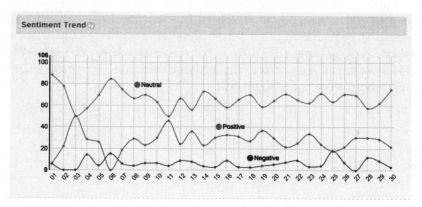

**Figure 8.7**
*Tools such as Viralheat enable brands to analyze the social voice of the customer by sentiment, trending over time* (Source: Cision blog [www.cision.com/us/blog]. ViralHeat is a Cision Company.)

# Summary

In the Social Business era, customer service teams face a daunting new set of challenges. They must respond quickly and succinctly in the voice of the brand. They must sift through the noise, bots, and trolls to identify customers who need assistance, and to prioritize the ones who need a response right away. Customer service teams must know how to filter the constant stream of social media conversations to identify and direct a customer to the appropriate agent. Service agents must also navigate multiple social media channels, along with both public and private messages, which can be confusing and difficult to keep track of. And the entire process comes with high stakes. A single tweet could misfire and go viral—and not in a positive way. American Airlines learned this a few years ago, when it responded to all tweets, even negative ones, with an automated "Thanks for your support!" Its tone-deafness was subsequently mocked by the Twitterverse and splashed over the Internet.

Brands have no choice except to invest in excellent social customer care. It is the new SEO in the continuing struggle to stand out. Excellent customer service leads to glowing customer reviews. Glowing reviews, in turn, lead to higher search engine rankings— Google's search algorithm, for example, now includes customer reviews as a key factor, and even weights reviews differently based on the person leaving it. Simply put, great customer service begets more online marketing power and a greater online presence.

A bad review isn't the end, either. If a customer is upset—and says so on social media—it gives the company a second chance to get it right. Ignore the complaint, and lose the customer. But reach out to the customer with an apology and a heartfelt attempt to find a solution, and the company could turn a bad relationship into a good one.

Social customer care requires brands to establish a totally new process for handling customer queries. It requires new tools to listen, filter, and measure social media chatter. It requires training agents with a fresh set of skills. But the payoff is worth it: Not only can excellent social customer care cut down on costs, but it can also bolster the brand's image and mobilize a new legion of evangelists who contribute to the buyer's decision journey of friends, followers, and strangers.

# 9

# Social Recruiting: How Recruiting Is Becoming Like Marketing

Just as all customer-facing aspects of business have been totally transformed by Social Business, so too have recruiting, retention, and engagement of an organization's employees undergone a sea-change as a result of the social media explosion. Today's social, always-connected consumer is also your employee. The ubiquity of consumer social media profiles on LinkedIn, Twitter, and Facebook has made it possible for the first time to reach and connect at scale with passive candidates—that is, those not actively looking for a job but open to exploring new opportunities—which vastly increases the addressable candidate pool for any organization. As a result, the recruiting discipline is starting to resemble a marketing function, from talent brand-building and demand generation to lead qualification, nurturing, and analytics.

Social media can be a fantastic recruiting tool that allows hiring managers and recruiters to find and vet people, keep in touch with a pool of top candidates, and continually stay top of mind and engage with potential employees. Social networks are where hundreds of millions of the world's most qualified job candidates can now be easily found and reached. Among the candidates for the most in-demand job positions—engineering, IT, sales, marketing, and operations—social network usage is especially high. Many candidates actually *expect* to find their next career opportunity via social media..Social networking sites have rapidly overtaken company career websites, employee referral programs, and internal transfers as one of the top sources of job candidates (Figure 9.1). Similar to the buyer's journey, the candidate decision journey today resembles a spaghetti structure in which social, mobile, and digital sources of information and influence play a greater role than ever before.

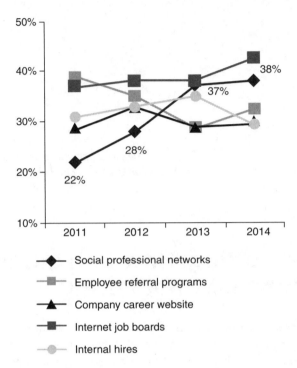

**Figure 9.1**
*Social networking sites are a fast-growing source of recruiting leads* (Source: LinkedIn Global
Recruiting Trends Annual Report[1])

Social media does not just represent a new channel to reach candidates—it offers a
totally new way to recruit. Just as in sales and marketing, the network effects and data
targeting aspects of social media are game-changers. At the end of the day, recruiters
and hiring managers can send out only so many messages one at a time. If this is your
strategy, all you are doing is changing the medium from email to social networking
sites. Savvy companies are going further by using technology to automatically search
and promote relevant jobs to the right candidates—technology that can help them
reach into second- and third-degree connections. This is what creates the network effect
needed to fill the top of the funnel and start to treat recruiting like a sophisticated sales
and marketing operation.

The good news is the majority of companies are already on board with social recruiting.
According to career advice blog The Muse, more than 90% of companies today use or
plan to use social media in some capacity for hiring, and these figures continue to climb

---

1. https://business.linkedin.com/content/dam/business/talent-solutions/global/en_US/c/pdfs/
recruiting-trends-global-linkedin-2015.pdf

each year. Nearly half of *Fortune* 500 firms include links to social media on the careers section of their websites.[2] Yet despite acknowledging that social recruiting helps with successful placements, higher candidate quality, less time to hire, and an increase in employee referrals, 82% of recruiting professionals today describe their social recruiting skills as "barely proficient or less."[3] So they will need your help, especially when it comes to training and tools.

## The New Rules of Recruiting

In the olden days of yore, recruiters would post job openings in newspaper classified ads and on generic job boards. Then they would sit back and wait for reams of résumés to pour in, at which point they would use impersonal tracking systems to weed out the vast majority of applicants based solely on their résumé and cover letter. The Internet unleashed greater reach and efficiency, allowing job applications to move online and recruiting teams to search for specific keywords among candidate applications. Online job board Monster ruled the day, and 'Apply Now' buttons beckoned from dozens of other online résumé aggregation sites.

But social recruiting is an even greater step-change than recruiting via the Internet was. As the world's largest professional social network, LinkedIn is the social network par excellence for job searching (35% of job seekers use the site[4]) and, therefore, recruiting, especially in business roles. At the time of this book's writing, LinkedIn was 50 times more valuable than Monster in terms of market capitalization. Although less often associated with recruiting, Facebook and Twitter also have become powerful tools for recruiting (Figures 9.2 and 9.3). On the technical recruiting side, online communities such as Quora, GitHub, and Stack Overflow are useful places for discovering great software engineers, though they can be harder to navigate if you don't have a technical background.

The shift to social recruiting is deeper than one company (LinkedIn) replacing the other (Monster) in a competitive landscape. Social networks actually offer a whole new paradigm for hiring that solves many of the problems of the old system, dramatically expanding the addressable market. The following sections outline the new rules.

---

2. https://www.themuse.com/advice/job-seekers-social-media-is-even-more-important-than-you-thought

3. Jobvite Recruiting Survey: https://www.jobvite.com/wp-content/uploads/2014/10/Jobvite_SocialRecruiting_Survey2014.pdf

4. Adecco Global Social Recruiting Survey: http://www.adecco.com/en-US/Industry-Insights/Documents/social-recruiting/adecco-global-social-recruiting-survey-global-report.pdf

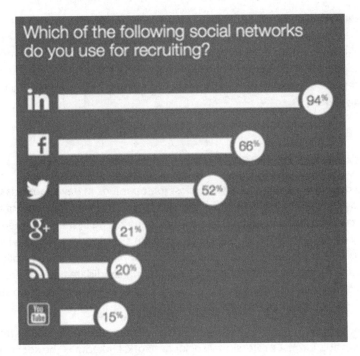

**Figure 9.2**
*Among companies that use social media for recruiting, 94% are using LinkedIn, 66% are using Facebook, and 52% are using Twitter* (Source: Jobvite)

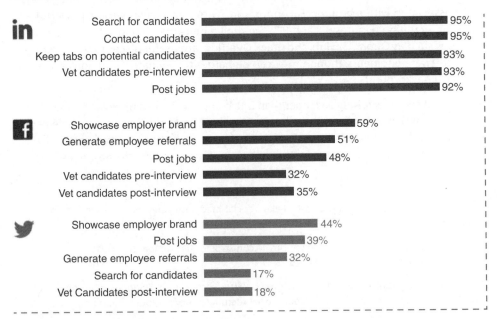

**Figure 9.3**
*Top social recruiting use cases for LinkedIn, Facebook, and Twitter, respectively* (Source: Jobvite)

# RULE #1. Prospective Candidates Are Researching Your Company

Amidst the war for talent, especially for highly skilled professionals, it has never been more important for companies to invest in their talent brand—in other words, how companies are perceived by current, past, and prospective employees. In a survey of millennials by student guidance platform ConnectEDU, nearly 58% reported that they would take a 15% cut in pay to work for a company with a great culture, values, and leadership.[5] And it's not just millennials who want "something more" from an employer. Talent branding—which spans everything from the careers section on your company's website and social media profiles to a candidate's interview experience and what employees say about the company to friends—has become table stakes for recruiting the best people across the board. Just as today's customer likes to drive the buying process and do her own research online before engaging your company, so too does today's recruit.

In particular, an organization's LinkedIn Company Page and (premium) Career Pages, job posts on Twitter, internship page on Facebook, and LinkedIn profiles and Twitter handles of recruiters, hiring managers, and key executives have all become essential components of talent brand-building. Those are some of the first places job candidates go to learn more and make up their minds about a prospective employer.

A company's talent brand is generally correlated with, but sometimes distinct from, its marketing brand. Amazon and the former Lehman Brothers are examples where the talent brand and consumer brand were perhaps more divergent—Amazon is beloved by consumers but has received media coverage for allegedly being a tough place to work, whereas Lehman Brothers had a strong talent brand but a negative public brand, especially after the mortgage crisis. One way to get a pulse on your talent brand is to visit Glassdoor, where current and former employees as well as job candidates write anonymous reviews regarding their experience interviewing with or working at specific companies.

## Appealing to Millennials

Millennials are already the largest segment of the US workforce and will make up more than 50% of the total workforce by 2018, according to the US Bureau of Labor Statistics. Employers must put strategies in place to appeal to this important group of current and future workers. As noted in earlier chapters, millennials are always-connected and incredibly social, and they expect employers to be, too. Young people are more likely to use social networks to search for jobs, research companies, and connect with employees in companies of interest. An Aberdeen Group study showed that 73% of 18- to 34-year-olds found their last job through a social networking site.

Millennial candidates expect to be able to find key information online about what it's like to work for a company. Moreover, when they apply for a job, they expect the process to be seamless and completely online. Even before they begin a job search, they are using the "Students and Alumni" feature on their university's LinkedIn Page to explore the careers of

---

5. http://www.fastcompany.com/3031513/the-future-of-work/where-the-class-of-2014-is-turning-for-jobs

alumni and to network, joining industry-related groups on Facebook, and searching Quora and Glassdoor for honest answers on your corporate culture and working conditions.

But social recruiting is important not just for millennials. Conveying a strong talent brand on social media is important for persuading the vast majority of passive candidates who are happily employed elsewhere to take your call, attracting the kinds of people you want, building greater awareness of your company and your recruiting efforts, and differentiating your organization against competing offers. The same social marketing best practices discussed in Chapter 6 similarly apply here: Use an authentic and relatable (versus stiff corporate) voice, invest in content marketing (about your organization as an employer), and integrate your social efforts with other digital and offline recruiting efforts to provide a seamless candidate experience. You need to help prospective employees picture what life would be like working at your company, much the same way that marketers help customers imagine how life will be improved by their product or service.

## RULE #2. Passive Candidates May Be Your Best Next Hires

It has always been the case that many of the best potential recruits are already gainfully employed elsewhere, which means they are generally not posting their résumés on job boards. In the past, it was difficult to identify these passive candidates. Recruiters relied on one-off referrals and even cold-calling the desk phones of their competitors' employees. Yet despite these tactics, most recruiters were not able to get meaningfully beyond the roughly 25% of potential recruits who are actively looking at any given time. They were, in essence, leaving behind an additional 60% of potential recruits who were not actively looking but were open to talking to a recruiter (Figure 9.4). In other words, these passive candidates were not findable.

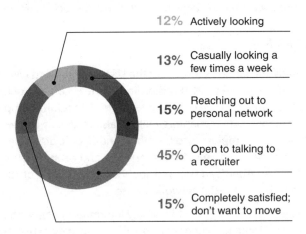

12%  Actively looking

13%  Casually looking a few times a week

15%  Reaching out to personal network

45%  Open to talking to a recruiter

15%  Completely satisfied; don't want to move

**Figure 9.4**
*Prior to social networking, recruiters were generally able to reach only the roughly 12% of active job seekers, but consumer social networking has unlocked the other 73% of passive job seekers*
(Source: LinkedIn Talent Solutions)

The proliferation of individual social network profiles has made it possible for the first time to systematically recruit passive candidates, unlocking a candidate pool that is three times larger and generally higher quality. Yet nearly 40% of global companies today have no strategy for recruiting passive candidates,[6] so there is tremendous opportunity waiting to be exploited by more social-savvy organizations.

## RULE #3. Candidates Expect Hiring Managers to Play a Bigger Role in Recruiting

Candidates want and expect to be able to check out their prospective manager via social media and get to know him or her before agreeing to a phone screen or even replying to a recruiter's initial message. Accordingly, today's hiring managers must also play a bigger and more active role throughout the recruiting cycle, using social networking sites to source new talent, keep tabs on and tap into their own networks, periodically touch base with key talent, and brand themselves and their organizations in the right ways.

Doing this right requires a commitment from each hiring manager and a new level of partnership between hiring managers and recruiters. At Hearsay Social, we add recruiting goals to each hiring manager's annual review and include recruiting as a top agenda item alongside sales pipeline in our weekly executive team meetings. We have the recruiters for each department sit with that department; attend the department's meetings, offsite events, and social gatherings; and have weekly one-on-one meetings with each hiring manager to sync on candidates in the pipeline.

Excellent recruiting has always been about building relationships with the people you hope will eventually work with you. Staying in touch is even more important when dealing with passive candidates, since by definition they are less likely to be open to switching jobs at the moment you happen to reach out. In the past, this was difficult and time-consuming, but social networking sites have changed the math on staying in touch. By listening to, commenting, and 'liking' social feeds and posting relevant content, today's hiring managers can remain top of mind and keep tabs on when a candidate is ready to consider his or her next role.

## RULE #4. Digital Marketing and Data Tactics Are Changing the Game

The confluence of the first three rules is causing recruiters to aggressively adopt marketing tactics, from generating brand awareness to consideration, evaluation, and closing the deal (i.e., a successful hire). Social recruiting resembles a sales funnel. In fact, many of the terrific new digital marketing capabilities discussed in Chapter 6 are being successfully utilized to segment and target prospective employees with the most relevant messages and jobs, and then to nurture these candidates until they are ready to "convert."

---

6. LinkedIn Talent Solutions Blog: http://talent.linkedin.com/blog/index.php/2014/11/the-global-trends-that-will-shape-recruiting-in-2015

For example, recruiters now are paying attention to tried-and-true marketing tactics such as measuring message open rates, tracking optimal time of day and day of week to send messages, and A/B testing subject lines and body text. They are rewriting job descriptions to have a more authentic and approachable tone and to reflect the organization's culture and values.

Targeted demand generation—social campaigns, email campaigns, landing pages, and advertising—applied to recruiting can also lead to a bigger pipeline, higher offer acceptance rates, and more condensed recruiting cycles. Today, companies are launching their own direct marketing campaigns to drive everything from diversity hiring and campus recruiting to building relationships with the most skilled talent. Jobvite, Greenhouse, and Lever are the leaders in the applicant tracking system (ATS) space. A number of large companies, including Schneider Electric and PG&E, use Jobvite Engage to build online campaigns and grow their database of passive prospects who are not yet candidates, similar to how marketing automation software works.

Predictive analytics born out of e-commerce and marketing, such as Amazon's "Frequently Bought Together" and "Customers Who Bought This Item Also Bought X" features, have now been applied to social recruiting. Such algorithmically suggested connections include LinkedIn's "People Similar to X" and "People Also Viewed Y" sections.

Referral marketing has also been made easier by the fact that recruiters and hiring managers can now see if an existing employee or other common connection might be able to provide a warm introduction, so that they can avoid reaching out cold to the candidate. A study by recruiting technology provider 1-Page found that 93% of prospects will read a job-related message from a friend, whereas 20% will immediately click the 'delete' button when the same message is sent by a recruiter they do not know.

### L'Oréal's Digital Marketing Playbook for Recruitment

Based in Paris, L'Oréal Group is the world's largest cosmetics and beauty company. Despite global brand recognition, L'Oréal's recruiting team struggled with finding high-quality candidates for prestigious internships. Job boards yielded a high volume of applicants, but few were qualified.

To improve their success rate, the L'Oréal recruiters turned to digital marketing on Facebook. First, they established a dedicated L'Oréal Careers Page (Figure 9.5). They installed an app from third-party vendor Work4 (disclosure: I'm an investor) that allowed them to post internship openings as well as allow fans and employees to then share these jobs with their respective networks.

Also using Work4's platform, the recruiters ran paid advertising campaigns on Facebook for these internship openings, hypertargeting specific schools and majors, work history, and location. As a result, L'Oréal was able to reach and attract higher-quality candidates and fill its internship positions much more quickly.

**Figure 9.5**

*The L'Oréal Careers Page on Facebook* (Source: Facebook)

As Figure 9.6 shows, L'Oréal's job ads on Facebook followed a typical digital advertising conversion funnel: The ads generated 5.88 million impressions, which led to 4,167 clicks and ultimately 153 applicants, almost all of whom were prequalified for the internships based on the education and work experience ad targeting criteria.

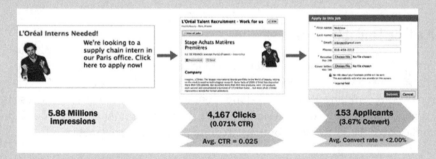

**Figure 9.6**

*Conversion of L'Oréal's Facebook ads to internship applicants* (Source: Work4, Inc.)

Instead of relying on traditional job boards, which its ideal internship candidates typically do not visit, L'Oréal has adapted its recruitment strategy to go to Facebook, where these candidates are already active, and then appeal to them through highly targeted advertising.

*(Source: Work4 Website: https://www.work4labs.com/loreal)*

Work4 and Jobvite both offer applicant-tracking solutions for driving referral hires through social networking sites. Data on Jobvite's platform show that referrals are the fastest and largest source of hires, outpacing all other sources, including career websites, job boards, advertising, and agencies. Also, employee-referral sourced hires last longer than employees found through any other source of hire.

## Four Steps to Social Recruiting

When an organization has a robust, engaged presence on social networks, that activity provides a huge boost to recruiting, just as it is does to sales, marketing, service, and commerce. When job seekers see and experience a company's committed social presences, the overarching message they receive is that the company understands how to connect with and demonstrate it cares about customers, employees, and potential recruits. The company burnishes its reputation as a contemporary, socially savvy, flexible, and adaptable organization, appealing particularly to younger applicants. Just as customer testimonials help with sales, so there is nothing more compelling than employees authentically advocating for an organization.

In the social era, those companies that can lead with purpose and show that they genuinely care about their people will be the most attractive to top talent. The following sections present steps organizations can take to build their social recruiting prowess.

### STEP #1. Be Findable

The first step is for companies, recruiters, and hiring managers to be findable on the channels where candidates expect to be able to find and research them. The careers section of your company website is no longer enough. The best candidates will research your organization, interviewers, hiring managers, peers, and former employees, and the most efficient and effective way for them to do so is through social media.

#### Six Faces of Social Recruiting

There are six kinds of social media presences that candidates examine when evaluating prospective job opportunities. Recruiting teams should be thinking about each one:

- **Recruiting-specific company pages.** Establish a "home base" for your talent brand with a LinkedIn Company Page, LinkedIn Careers Page, Twitter account (such as @StarbucksJobs and @BofACampus_Jobs), or Facebook Page dedicated specifically to recruiting (such as facebook.com/KPMGrecrute). Which social networks the company should invest in to build its presence depend on the industry.

- **General company pages.** Keep in mind that candidates will likely visit your customer-facing presences as part of their research on your organization. Although these presences are optimized for customers and prospects, if recruiting is a top priority for the company, it's not a bad idea to periodically share a "we're hiring" or employee spotlight message through these channels: Loyal customers sometimes make terrific, highly motivated, and knowledge-able employees.

- **Recruiter profiles.** Individual recruiters should build up their own personal social media profiles and personal brand to help them stand out from the crowd. Instead of blasting out job descriptions, the best social recruiters share interesting and helpful content, such as exciting company announcements, interview tips, and advice on how to grow one's career, and they interact with contacts about these issues. Over time, recruiters demonstrate they are cred-ible and helpful, building trust with prospective candidates.

- **Hiring manager profiles.** The best employees tend to be focused on career development. They know the importance of working for the right person and will spend extra time researching their prospective manager. Hiring manag-ers need to invest in building their brand, generally on LinkedIn and Twitter, and post regularly. They can tweet team photos to provide a glimpse into the work culture, share thoughts regarding their management philosophy, and curate or ideally blog original content about subject-matter expertise to garner the attention and respect of prospective candidates. Hiring managers can ask current and former direct reports to write LinkedIn recommenda-tions describing their management style. Managers should be prepared to engage with their followers—one of them could be the next top recruit in waiting. Finally, it's always a nice touch to share something personal, such as an interest, hobby, or community involvement.

- **Executive profiles.** In addition to becoming familiar with their direct manager, today's prospective employees want to understand the vision, direction, mission, culture, and values of an organization. These insights can be hard to glean from explicit corporate communication channels such as press releases and annual reports. Instead, job seekers are increasingly looking up key executives on social media to understand them as people and decide whether they are "my kind of leader." As we explored in the "Social CEOs Lead by Example" section in Chapter 4, millennials in particular have a favorable view of executives who actively share on Twitter and author long-form posts on LinkedIn. Some organizations have also enjoyed success, particularly among millennial candidates, by creating and sharing short videos of leaders discussing their vision and values, and why they care about creating a great workplace.

*continues…*

- **Employee voice.** As part of their online research on a prospective employer, candidates research their would-be coworkers to evaluate passion for the company, competence, and social fit. Employees with thoughtful profiles evangelizing the organization contribute positively to the talent brand and have an ideal foundation from which to share job opportunities and generate referrals (see the "Unilever's Presence on LinkedIn" case study later in this chapter). Employees whose profiles are full of grammar/spelling errors and gripes have the opposite effect—Jobvite's Recruiter Nation survey found that 72% of recruiters respond negatively to spelling and grammar mistakes on résumés and social posts. Finally, creating a dedicated recruitment blog linked to and from your careers website also creates great opportunities to showcase different employees or hear from them directly in the form of guest posts.

Just as for salespeople, social recruiting presences needs to be branded and consistent, yet personal and authentic (Figure 9.7 is a good example). LinkedIn profiles in particular have become the place for professional branding; they are how potential candidates are evaluating whether you're someone they would like to work with, just as you are evaluating them as a potential hire.

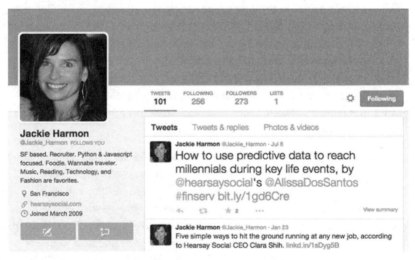

**Figure 9.7**
*Jackie Harmon, a recruiter at Hearsay Social, conveys the company culture as well as her personality through her Twitter profile description and tweets* (Source: Twitter)

With so many windows for prospective job seekers to peek into your organization, it's paramount to educate managers and recruiters on how they should be communicating authentically but within company guidelines. Every recruiter, hiring manager, department head, and C-level executive should have a freshly tuned profile that includes target key words for job searchers. It can be very powerful when everyone in the company is sharing updates to their networks about open job opportunities and general news about the organization.

Apart from these general principles, which are applicable across all social networks, there are also specific tactics to increase your chances of being found and building a good reputation on the big three social sites, as described in Table 9.1.

Table 9.1   Best Practices for Establishing a Social Recruiting Presence

| Network | Best Practices |
|---|---|
| LinkedIn | • Add recruiting and employment information to your organization's LinkedIn Company Page. |
| | • Encourage hiring managers, recruiters, and other employees to have a high-resolution head shot on their profiles, update their headline and summary, regularly share updates, and publish long-form posts that showcase their expertise on specific industry topics and trends to build the talent brand. Candidates want to work with smart, passionate people. |
| Facebook | • Establish a Careers Page separate from the brand page and use it to aggregate employee testimonials. |
| | • Offer apps from within your Careers Page that recommend positions for applicants, show calendars of recruitment events, or drive traffic toward webinars and recruiting-specific content. |
| | • Have real employees post to the page (versus the page admin posting) to humanize the company and be authentic. |
| Twitter | • Create a recruitment-specific handle (e.g., @googlejobs, @UPSjobs) and monitor it during regular hours, just as you would a customer service channel. |
| | • In the bio section, encourage candidates to ask questions and interact with you as a recruiter. If the bio is for an individual recruiter, make it specific so that you stand out. |
| | • Build up your list of followers by strategically following top talent candidates and occasionally retweeting them. |
| | • Share content about skill building and career opportunities. |
| | • Retweet content from other company handles. Share videos, pictures, and information about new products and job openings. |
| | • Promptly respond to candidate queries. |

Prospective customers don't respond to companies that blast out sales pitches, and prospective candidates are no different. Social recruiting isn't about loading up the company Twitter feed and Facebook posts with open job positions. Instead, it's about telling a compelling brand story about why your company is the best place to work and grow one's career (Figure 9.8 illustrates an example from Hearsay Social). Enable each of your employees to easily share job opportunities with their networks when they believe it is relevant—and take advantage of the power of social targeting and vetting.

**Figure 9.8**
*Many executives and employees at Hearsay Social have shared the company's YouTube video on Facebook, LinkedIn, and Twitter with their networks* (Link: hearsaysocial.com/careers)

## Going Mobile

An important aspect of being findable is having a great mobile presence. According to Glassdoor, three in five job seekers used their mobile device to look for a job in the past 12 months, while one in four job seekers say they would not apply to a job if a company's career site was not mobile optimized.[7]

There are four major bases to cover when it comes to mobile channels: social network presences, a mobile-optimized career site, mobile job application, and staying in touch during the interview cycle. The good news with social network presences is that Facebook, LinkedIn, and Twitter are already fully mobile optimized. When it comes to your mobile career site and application process, make sure the number of clicks and amount of scrolling candidates must go through stay at a minimum. Scroll filtering, selectors, and drop-down menus all help streamline the process. The application should ideally take no more

---

7. http://www.glassdoor.com/blog/infographic-rise-mobile-job-search

than a minute or two, as people's attention spans and patience tend to be minimal when on a mobile device. As Figure 9.9 shows, Starbucks, Prudential, and Abbott Laboratories all have best-in-class career sites that are optimized for mobile platforms.

**Figure 9.9**
*Starbucks, Prudential, and Abbott Laboratories are members of very different industries, but they all boast excellent mobile-optimized careers sites that appeal to today's job candidates* (Source: Company websites)

Finally, today's savvy recruiters are staying in touch in real time and keeping candidates warm with frequent updates and check-ins, often sent via text message, Twitter DMs, or Facebook Messenger.

### Unilever's Presence on LinkedIn

Unilever is a British–Dutch multinational consumer goods company with more than 400 brands, including Dove, Ben & Jerry's, and TRESemmé, and distribution in 190 countries. It is also one of the highest-followed companies on LinkedIn, with nearly 1.7 million global followers. As follower count has increased over the years, so too has traffic to the company's Careers tab, job applications, and successful hires from LinkedIn.

The Unilever team attributes its social recruiting success to three factors. First, the company sets and follows a content calendar to ensure the LinkedIn Company Page is regularly updated with interesting posts showcasing company culture, community involvement, and consumer impact (Figure 9.10). The Careers tab is similarly full of rich content appealing to the types of candidates the company hopes to attract. Second, the company has added a LinkedIn 'Follow' button in employee

*continues…*

email signatures so that there is a clear and easy call to action in every message sent. Finally and perhaps most powerfully, Unilever has mobilized 45,000 of its employees on LinkedIn to act as brand ambassadors promoting the Unilever talent brand, company updates, and job posts by sharing brand updates in their personal status updates. Unilever's efforts are a wonderful example of an organization's recruiters, marketing team, and employees coming together to create a virtuous circle of enthusiasm and engagement on social media.

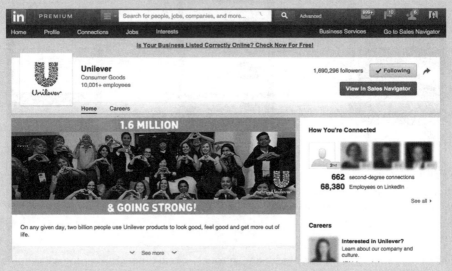

**Figure 9.10**
*Unilever's LinkedIn Company Page* (Source: Link Humans: http://linkhumans.com/case-study/unilever)

## STEP #2. Target, Identify, and Reach Out

Just as your marketing personnel should create profiles of your ideal customers, so too your recruiting teams and hiring managers should work together to develop ideal candidate profiles. One easy way to do so is to review the backgrounds and experiences of your current top performers and look for trends, such as previous employers, schools and degrees, and keywords. Assembling this data can help you craft a strategy for pinpointing your ideal candidates and pursuing them in a highly focused and targeted way. The new version of LinkedIn Recruiter helps to automate this process. Hiring managers can choose the profiles of "rock star" employees, and then LinkedIn Recruiter will automatically find and suggest people who are professionally similar as well as indicate mutual connections through which recruiters could obtain a warm introduction.

As always, referrals are the easiest and best way to identify and connect with candidates. LinkedIn Referrals is a tool that can be given to employees to help them source potential hires from their personal networks on behalf of the company. Software company 1-Page's Source.hr tool similarly allows recruiters to search pools of passive candidates and indicates which of the recruiter's company connections might be best suited to provide the referral. These can be incredibly high-yielding investments, especially when used in concert with an employee referral bonus.

Facebook, Twitter, private groups on LinkedIn and Facebook, Quora, GitHub, Stack Overflow, and Reddit are also good places to meet and build relationships with candidates over specific subject matter, such as big data analytics or direct marketing. Talent search engines such as TalentBin (acquired by Monster) let recruiters search across all of these sites at once.

Often, group moderators won't allow in recruiters or others who are not subject-matter experts themselves, so hiring managers have to be the ones to engage directly. Although this type of engagement can be much more time-consuming, joining and participating in these groups can lead to authentic connections with great potential candidates (Table 9.2).

**Table 9.2    Best Practices for Finding and Engaging Candidates**

| Network | Best Practices |
| --- | --- |
| LinkedIn | • Join LinkedIn groups relevant to your company. |
| | • Use the Advanced Search function to hone in on your ideal recruits. |
| | • Look at the automatically generated suggestions from LinkedIn showing other candidates with a similar profile to the one you are viewing. |
| | • View candidate recommendations and validate candidate claims through their profile and common connections. |
| | • Use Referrals to refer connections that are good fits for open job opportunities and share job opportunities to their individual LinkedIn status updates. |
| Facebook | • Facebook's built-in search functionality is not optimized for recruiters. Utilize third-party applications such as Work4, Jobvite, and 1-Page Source. |
| | • Use hypertargeted advertising (as described in Chapter 6) to drive traffic to the Careers Page. |
| | • Encourage existing employees to 'like' and follow other Facebook users to help with earned performance. |
| Twitter | • Create private lists of top performers to watch and strategically interact with. |
| | • Utilize hashtags to get in front of ideal candidates. |
| | • Use Tweetdeck to stay up-to-date on mentions of people you're following and to collect ideas about who and what to retweet, engage, or reply to. |
| | • Be responsive to candidate DMs. |

When you use social networks to reach out to appropriate job candidates whom you have identified and/or connected with, it's important to remember these guiding principles of effective interaction: Be authentic, highly targeted, helpful, and responsive. Getting aggressive or seeming insincere with a generic message does not work on any medium.

The best outreach starts with a short, creative subject line, which is then followed by a highly personal and personalized message. Instead of talking only about the organization and job, the best recruiters talk about how the candidate's specific experience at XYZ company caught their eye and would be a good fit for the specific job.

If your recruiting team is new to social media, it's a good idea to have social media–savvy colleagues (perhaps from the marketing team) provide a coaching session and ongoing feedback, as companies like Intuit have done (see the "Social Recruiting at Intuit" sidebar later in this chapter).

### Targeted Job Ads

LinkedIn's "Work With Us" ads as well as the Facebook advertising tools for recruiters from companies such as Work4 and LinkUp can be another powerful way to source candidates and improve close rates. For each role, determine the social network on which your ideal candidates are likely to be most active, and then create an ad for each open position on the appropriate network. As explained in Chapter 6, the hypertargeting capabilities of the social network platforms are quite powerful—you can target and tailor ads to candidates based on location, current/previous employer, education, languages, and interests.

On Facebook, you can even target friends-of-connections only to tap into first-degree referral networks. You can also use the Custom Audiences tool to target and tailor ads to certain email addresses or visitors to your website.

Once candidates click on your job ads, you need to send them to a landing page to learn more or begin the application process. This landing page could be on your careers website (most common) or Facebook Page, where potential employees can learn more about your company and even apply directly on Facebook if you have added this functionality with apps such as Sprout Social Job Board, Jobvite Work With Us, or Work4 Facebook Career Page.

### Reference Checks and Verification

Profiles on social media are far richer than a résumé for truly understanding who someone is. You can view photos, posts, and connections of a contact going back years and years. The cumulative social data paint a vivid picture of the individual's habits, preferences, decorum, professional interests, and hobbies. It is possible to make a character assessment and assess the maturity and honesty of someone through a quick skim of his or her social profile. Nowadays, recruiters see social media as a way of prequalifying candidates, while phone interviews and in-person meetings are seen as the candidate's opportunity to verify the first impressions provided by social media.

In the social era, formal recommendation letters are disappearing because better tools are available. Hiring managers, in particular, can not only view recommendations, but also check up on the recommender herself to evaluate whether she is credible and trustworthy. Hiring managers can also easily reach out to common connections to conduct more reliable and impartial "backdoor" references.

In certain industries, such as entertainment, sales, and even recruiting, where success can be largely determined by the size of your network or following, social media provides much greater visibility into the suitability and likely success of potential candidates. In the fashion world, for instance, some modeling agencies and fashion labels will now only sign models who have a certain number of Instagram followers, putting social media likeability on par with traditional measures of beauty or skill.[8] The chief sales officer at a *Fortune* 500 organization with which I work has similarly adapted his candidate vetting process. Any sales rep candidate is now also evaluated on how many relevant LinkedIn connections and Twitter followers she or he has, in addition to the usual interview feedback, reference checks, and track record of quota achievement. Sales manager candidates are evaluated on how many reps they are connected to. This chief sales officer told me, "In our business, success is a function of how large your network is. Social media provides perfect transparency and has markedly improved our ability to hire the right people who can actually succeed here."

Finally, a growing number of recruiters and hiring managers are also reviewing candidate profiles and posts for red flags, such as profanity; spelling and grammar errors; references to illegal drugs, guns, or alcohol; and sharing too much about politics or religion.

## STEP #3. Stay in Touch

Often when you come across and engage an excellent candidate, for a variety of reasons, the timing doesn't work. That individual may be in the middle of an important project, or may be new on the job, or you may not have the exact right role for the person. Instead of letting the outreach and interaction go to waste, it's a good idea to stay in touch. Follow him or her on Twitter and connect on LinkedIn.

Just as marketing and sales teams must invest in high-quality, relevant content to engage prospects throughout the buyer's journey, so today's recruiting teams need to share honest, authentic insights about their organization throughout the candidate's journey. Beyond that, there's no set formula for social content marketing, although LinkedIn's Talent Solutions team suggests a mix of thought leadership/industry news, talent brand posts, company news, event promotion, and fun content (Figure 9.11). Social media updates can be 140 characters or link to a long-form blog post. The content could be a team photo, animated video, product launch blog post, or emoji; it could be curated from a third party or original content. It just needs to tell a great story, offer new information, or add something else of value to help the recruiter stay top of mind and build the talent brand. Then, in the near or distant future when your ideal candidate has a bad day or decides she's finally open to moving on, you will most likely be one of the first people she contacts.

---

8. http://www.complex.com/style/2015/04/models-better-have-at-least-10000-followers-on-instagram-to-book-their-next-gig

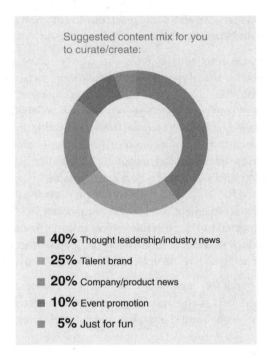

Suggested content mix for you to curate/create:

- **40%** Thought leadership/industry news
- **25%** Talent brand
- **20%** Company/product news
- **10%** Event promotion
- **5%** Just for fun

**Figure 9.11**
*Suggested content mix from the LinkedIn Talent Solutions team* (Source: "5 Steps to Boosting Your Talent Brand Through Content," LinkedIn Talent Solutions, July 23, 2015)

## STEP #4. Listen and Act on Job Change Signals

Social media venues today are not only where hundreds of millions of prospective candidates can be found; they're also full of insights about these candidates and what they are thinking at any given time. People tend to update their LinkedIn profiles soon after they've been promoted or changed jobs. Many people will proactively update their profiles to be more complete when they are still employed but looking.

Recruiters should regularly scan through their news feeds to uncover these clues and reach out to catch up and be helpful.

### Social Recruiting at Intuit

Intuit—a company that offers services and resources to help people and small businesses with their finances—has been a trailblazer in social recruiting over the past few years. Once it realized that traditional recruiting methods like print ads were becoming obsolete, the company overhauled its hiring methods by taking to social networking sites, live chats, and blogging. Intuit's aggressive social networking strategy has been so successful that it was placed number two on *Fortune*'s list of "Top 100 Companies to Work For"; *Huffington Post* also ranked Intuit as the second most social company, behind *The New York Times*. So what makes the company's new social media presence so wildly popular?

To remain on the cutting edge of social recruiting, the Intuit Global Recruiting Team partakes in a six-week boot camp to learn how to use sites not only for posting job advertisements, but also for enhancing company branding.

Intuit began its social network strategy by constantly generating pertinent content and information for prospective employees on its LinkedIn Company Page. Intuit also curated its Facebook Page by sharing job openings, useful apps, and financial tips. Recruiters similarly use their Twitter Page to post job advertisements and respond to potential candidates' questions faster than would be possible through email. The company also has dozens of boards on Pinterest, which it uses to promote its brand. Intuit Careers channels on YouTube feature dozens of videos about various careers, which link to job postings and are used to pump up prospective employees before or after an interview.

How does Intuit know that its social media strategy is working? The company measures the efficacy of its recruiting techniques through Google Analytics and analyzes tweets and comments on Facebook. Finally, it continually requests feedback from applicants—both those who accepted the offer and those who didn't—on how to improve the candidate experience, including social media presence and engagement.

## Once You've Hired Them . . .

An in-depth discussion of employee engagement is beyond the scope of this chapter and book, but I would be remiss if I didn't at least mention the importance of focusing on what happens after candidates have accepted your offer. First, it is essential for hiring managers to keep in close touch with new hires from the point that offers are made and accepted up until they show up for the first day on the job. After all you've invested in recruiting these newbies, you'll want to ensure that they stay motivated and hit the ground running (and that there is no chance someone else might poach them or persuade them to stay at their current job).

New hires are the most enthusiastic referrers to recruiting, so make sure to engage them early in identifying candidates for other roles at the company. One way to do this is by asking new hires to update their social network profiles with suggested marketing copy about the company and to share links to company job postings via their social network accounts.

Hiring managers must also equip new hires with social, mobile, and digital technologies to do their jobs. More than 40% of millennials, for example, say they're likely to download and pay out of pocket for apps they use for work purposes over the next 12 months, and nearly half use their personal smartphones for work. More than one-third of millennial workers prefer to collaborate online at work as opposed to via phone or in person.[9] Organizations that invest wisely in technologies for their employees will not only drive profits and productivity, but are also more likely to retain and motivate the people they've spent so much time, money, and resources to bring in the door.

Of course, your company isn't the only one prowling the social media recruiting jungle. What should you do about other companies poaching your employees who are on social media? The truth is that no company can fully insulate itself from restless employees and aggressive recruiters, especially in a strong economy. A recent Jobvite report showed that 45% of job seekers are satisfied in their current job but open to a new one. Millennials are twice as likely to job-hop as are members of older generations. But companies can't prevent their employees from signing up for social media and certainly can't prevent competitive recruiters from reaching out to them (they already are).

So what can companies do? Company leaders and hiring managers must continually re-recruit the people they already have. Social media can be a great place to do this—for example, celebrating team wins, calling out star employees, and sharing management philosophy. But the effort can't stop there. More than ever, today's managers need to periodically sit down with their people, really listen to what matters, and help them continually grow to cement their loyalty and recommitment. At Hearsay Social, we run an employee survey each fall, and every year for the last three years we've been conducting the survey, the top employee request has been more professional development and career planning. We've tried a number of different strategies and tactics, and so far the best received has been our managers' pledge to schedule a one-on-one meeting with every employee every six months to talk about career goals, progress, and next steps.

## Summary

Conveniently, the same social rules that apply to sales, marketing, and customer service also apply to recruiting. Social network interaction is totally changing the hiring game, prompting companies to engage authentically and responsively with job candidates on LinkedIn, Facebook, and Twitter and to adapt their own actions to the spaghetti-structure decision journey today's candidates go through. No more soliciting unqualified résumés on job sites with bulleted, boilerplate job ads, and getting overwhelmed by the unfiltered responses (thankfully!).

---

9. "Generation Y: Understanding the Work Habits of Millennials," Halogen Software Blog, 9/14; "The State of Workplace Productivity Report," Cornerstone OnDemand, 8/13; "Millennials at Work: Reshaping the Workplace," PWC, 2011.

Not only recruiters but also hiring managers and company leaders—in fact, all employees—need to set up smart, authentic social media profiles that position them as experts in their field. Maintaining these profiles, continually offering up useful content, engaging contacts with helpful advice, and targeting job information to the right candidates at the right time have become table stakes.

From there, today's social recruiters are analyzing their organization's top performers to identify the experience, skills, and qualifications the company needs for current open positions, and creating an intelligent search strategy to find them. They can then connect, interact, build relationships, and guide these prospects toward considering the employer and job when the time is right.

As with any aspect of Social Business, it may take a while to achieve success. Social recruiters and hiring managers are not just looking to fill positions for today. They want to build lasting relationships that will benefit their companies for years to come, through means ranging from enhancing the talent brand and reaching a greater pool of prospects to nurturing contacts and collecting referrals. Social networking has allowed passive candidates to become findable and reachable by recruiters, and as a result, recruiting looks more and more each day like a sophisticated marketing and sales funnel.

# PART III

# ENTERPRISE EXECUTION PLAYBOOK

## How to Make Social Business Change Happen

# 10

*"Plans are only good intentions unless they immediately
degenerate into hard work."*
—Peter Drucker, Management Guru (1909-2005)

# How to Operationalize Social Business

What do the most successful Social Business organizations have in common? That's
the question *Harvard Business Review* sought to answer in a recent survey of more
than 2000 companies.[1] It found the companies with the greatest Social Business ROI
typically have a dedicated team and a budget line item expressly for social media.
These companies are omnichannel (four or more channels), share rich multimedia content
(such as mobile-friendly videos), and participate in review sites, forums, and blogs. They
integrate their social media marketing with existing campaigns and email marketing.
The best Social Businesses use social media not only to monitor trends relevant to their
businesses, but also to research new product ideas, solicit online user feedback, and
aggregate customer reviews. They are great listeners—tracking and understanding where
their customers are likely to mention them, and making those mentions actionable, as
ideas for improving products or services. Finally, exemplary social brands distinguish
themselves by using metrics and analytics on a wide range of factors—from quantifying
consumer sentiment to using social media channels as focus groups, they appreciate and
tap into the social media data to unlock better customer engagement and relationships.

In the preceding chapters, we examined how each externally facing function can adapt to
today's social and always-connected customer. Now, we turn our discussion to how best
to operationalize Social Business across an organization—that is, how to weave together
these various social marketing, sales, commerce, customer service, recruiting, and employee
engagement initiatives across multiple lines of business and geographical regions.

---

1. *The New Conversation: Taking Social Media from Talk to Action,* report by Harvard Business Review
Analytic Services: https://hbr.org/resources/pdfs/tools/16203_HBR_SAS%20Report_webview.pdf

Social Business starts with a strong vision, but it can't end there. Conquering the digital last mile requires commitment, execution, iteration, communication, and coordination. The key is to do so without slowing things down with undue bureaucracy and never-ending committee meetings! As we discussed in Chapter 4, the Social Business Imperative starts with the CEO and management team making a commitment to incorporate social, mobile, and digital innovation into the organization's standard operating procedures. As in any change management situation, more than just executive sponsorship is needed: Executive *championship* is required, along with clear program owners, objectives, metrics, and the flexibility and expectation that the organization will learn as you go.

This chapter is divided in three sections: (1) common pitfalls and solutions; (2) tips on how to coordinate social media efforts across a large enterprise; and (3) ways to think about measurement, including calculating return on investment when the time is right.

## Common Pitfalls and Solutions

There are a variety of reasons why Social Business efforts might not achieve their full potential or fail entirely. Table 10.1 highlights some of the most common pitfalls, along with suggested solutions or mitigation strategies.

**Table 10.1    Social Business Pitfalls and Solutions**

| Social Business Pitfall | Downside | Solution or Mitigation Strategy |
| --- | --- | --- |
| Managers and leaders don't model the behavior and importance of Social Business. | This sends mixed messages to people when you ask them to adopt technology and strategies that their managers and organizational leaders don't fully understand and aren't using themselves. People begin to question whether Social Business is truly strategic. | Before rolling out a program, first brief and onboard key executives and managers. |
| The company jumps in with no clear goals or strategy. | It's easy to spend a lot of time and money with no results to show for the investment. | For each Social Business initiative, a clear owner should be named who is responsible for defining clear metrics and held accountable to those metrics. |
| Social Business efforts are disconnected from core initiatives. | There is lost opportunity to have a strategic Social Business program. It could also be confusing for customers if the Social Business elements aren't consistent with the company's other touchpoints. | Establish executive sponsorship and championship from the get-go to ensure Social Business is fully integrated with core priorities as well as with offline, web, and mobile initiatives. Do not just delegate social media to a summer intern. In large corporations, there is a big divide between executives and summer interns. There needs to be a focus on empowering the doers in the middle who truly operationalize Social Business. |

| Social Business Pitfall | Downside | Solution or Mitigation Strategy |
|---|---|---|
| The company gets stretched too thin, leading to an inability to sustain a consistent social media presence. | Impact and ability to execute are limited. | Be honest about how many resources you can devote to Social Business and don't try to do too much (e.g., don't launch on every social media channel on day 1). If company leaders want to do more, they must commit to investing more. |
| The company applies a one-size-fits-all shared services model. | Especially in larger organizations, a centralized social media team may find it difficult to understand each line of business and functional department whose Social Business efforts they are trying to support. Typically what happens is that those brand efforts followed by social customer service receive the most attention at the expense of social selling and social recruiting, which are typically less understood by centralized teams. | Most organizations shift ownership to each business unit and geography to truly interweave Social Business into their standard operating procedures. However, it's important to maintain links between these units so that efforts are coordinated. One French multinational company does this with quarterly check-in calls. Each time, every entity presents for 8 minutes on best practices and lessons learned from the previous quarter, and one entity (which rotates each time) presents a more in-depth set of insights for 30 minutes. |
| Each department or region reinvents the wheel when it comes to social media. | While a shared services model tends not to work across the disparate use cases for Social Business, failure to share best practices is a costly missed opportunity for many large organizations. | Consider setting up a cross-functional social media council, task force, or center of excellence to share best practices. Just make sure it doesn't become overly bureaucratic. Rather than impose a one-size-fits-all strategy, treat this center more as an open sharing and learning forum. |
| After initial excitement, end users feel discouraged that their hours spent on Social Business efforts aren't yielding immediate ROI. | They may quit the program before reaping the benefits. | Continue to lead and motivate participation by talking about clear business benefits, but set expectations that Social Business is a long game. |
| The social media team runs out of fresh content. | Social presence becomes less engaging over time, either as content gets recycled too often or post frequency diminishes. | Don't feel you have to create all original content. It's actually better to include a mix of curated content from other sources, including your customers and employees. If possible, invest in a dedicated social media content person or outside agency. |
| The social media team hits a wall or loses momentum when going through sign-off by IT, legal, compliance, and/or procurement processes. | Especially in large and heavily regulated companies, business enthusiasm for a program tends to wane during the lengthy approval process, IT integration, contract negotiation, and other prerequisites. | Establish executive sponsorship and engage cross-functional stakeholders early (see Chapters 11 and 12 on the roles played by legal/compliance and IT, respectively). A dedicated program owner should be tasked with quarterbacking the initiative through all the necessary checks and hurdles. |
| The company has no time for Social Business. | Either the project never gets off the ground or, once it does, efforts taper off. | Social Business programs must be fully integrated into the daily and weekly routines of end users, from salespeople and recruiters to customer support agents and marketers. Hold these individuals and their managers accountable for Social Business activities and metrics, as what gets measured tends to be what gets done. |

Ultimately, successful Social Business requires mobilizing the entire company around an innovation mindset. It can be a tricky balance, however. On the one hand, everyone needs to feel a sense of ownership for Social Business. On the other hand, you really do need specific people driving this effort, from the executive level down to program owners and end users.

### Maintaining Brand Assets Across The Digital Ecosystem

From Yelp pages with old store hours and orphaned landing pages that no one knows how to get rid of, to former employees' LinkedIn profiles that still show them as working at your company, the web can sometimes seem like a graveyard for forgotten and unused accounts. It's a good idea for organizations to experiment with new platforms and then have the discipline to wind down these experiments when they don't meet the bar, but often this happens without deleting the profiles that were created during this phase, especially when the employees who started the project move on.

Remember Second Life? Circa 2007, it was de rigeur for every company and institution to set up its own virtual site on this platform. But surfing around Second Life today is like riding through a ghost town, which reflects poorly on the many organizations that set up shop and then abandoned those efforts when the winds changed. The same thing is beginning to happen on social networks.

Enterprises should be careful to track every brand profile created to minimize the risk that abandoned accounts could linger and confuse or alienate customers who may stumble upon them. This is a special hazard that arises when you're integrating social media across multiple departments and initiatives, so it's important to have a protocol in place to track all of the identities established that may be out there representing the brand. There should similarly be a protocol for handling individual employee profiles when people move on from the organization.

## Social Business Initiatives

In the beginning, companies tend to have few major social campaigns, a scattering of minor initiatives, and a lot of informal and decentralized social media activities going on. Many organizations find themselves dipping their proverbial toe into the social media pool almost by accident, and usually without a well-constructed context or guiding strategy. Perhaps a firm picks out a Twitter handle and haphazardly launches a social marketing campaign without figuring out its long-term trajectory. Such campaigns can be momentarily successful, for a time driving significant traffic to the company's site. However, ultimately, many issues will be overlooked and won't be integrated into the core business, making the social strategy unsustainable.

From producing greater work efficiency and driving brand awareness to sourcing ideas and feedback for R&D, nurturing leads, engaging influencers, building community, and gathering competitive intelligence, the possible use cases for Social Business are many and diverse. How should organizations coordinate these disparate activities and programs across business units, departments, and regions?

## Transformation Starts at the Top *and* Bottom

For most companies, the initial foray into social media is led by a grassroots effort on the part of customers and employees. For Social Business to continue to be effective, however, it cannot lose this grassroots element, which lends employee passion, authenticity, and a human voice to company–customer interactions.

But Social Business also requires organizational transformation, a shift in mindset and action from defense to offense, cost center to revenue center, competing channel to complementary channel, and intern project to standard business practice embraced by C-level executives, beginning with the CEO.

A new generation of C-Suite leaders now author their own blog posts and oversee the presentation of their image and content on numerous social networks. Today, Social Business has become part of the expected skill set of a business leader, both for guiding business strategy and because today's customers and employees demand authentic leadership. The head of a prominent executive search firm revealed that more than half of her CEO and board placements and more than 90% of her chief marketing officer placements in 2015 had established social, mobile, and digital fluency as a mandatory or "strongly preferred" criterion in the executive search.

As we've noted multiple times, the absolute first step for operationalizing Social Business is to get buy-in from the C-Suite. This involves a general education process on the various forms of Social Business, including both opportunities and risks, as well as specific education for each executive tailored to her or his business unit, function, and geography. The leaders who are most effective at navigating their organizations through seas of change are those who have embraced the change personally and can deeply relate to their socially savvy customers and employees.

At some point, when enough disparate groups have developed their own business cases, ideas, and goals, it makes sense to bring together representatives from each unit to share best practices. Many large organizations end up creating an ad hoc social media council that cuts across different business units and departments, and that meets on at least a quarterly basis to share ideas.

## Social Centers of Excellence

Some organizations wish to go beyond sharing ideas to develop shared principles and even basic guidelines or standards. They may create a more formal version of a council that is more like a steering committee, often referred to as a center of excellence (COE). A social COE is responsible for setting the company's social media policy, making sure legal and compliance concerns are appropriately addressed (see Chapter 11 for discussion of common issues), and training everyone involved in these shared best practices. This cross-functional team generally includes stakeholders from the company's marketing, business development, sales, training, communications, compliance, supervision, IT, and human resources organizations.

Done well, social media centers of excellence can facilitate continual cross-functional alignment, learning, and sharing of best practices up, down, and across an organization. Overdone or done poorly, they can become bureaucratic, political quagmires that stand in the way of innovation.

Generally, the first task of a social COE will be to fill in the gaps in the social media ecosystem and construct a meaningful long-term strategy for the company. Every need must to be identified so that the COE can provide support and guidance according to strategic business priorities. Gradually the COE will introduce consistency throughout the organization in terms of policies, workflows, and processes for social media.

The COE formulates an enterprise-wide strategy for social media, making what was previously fragmented and scattershot a unified, proactive, and on-message network throughout the company. As the COE assists all of the different departments, it rolls out standardized reporting, measurements of ROI, and company-wide educational programs. In organizations that have a robust social media strategy and framework, the COE is often made up of 5 to 10 full-time employees under the direction of at least one manager. Over time, these employees generally move back into their respective business units or regions so that Social Business can become truly part of the organization's standard operating procedures.

As COEs work to streamline social media interactions at the company, they frequently amass portfolios of tools and technologies that can grow unwieldy over time. It is their job to carefully consider each new social management system so as to avoid redundancy while not imposing a one-size-fits-all mandate on truly disparate use cases. For this reason, it is very helpful to have an IT representative contribute to the work of the COE, as described in Chapter 12.

The COE should continually reevaluate the company's social media efforts and make sure that existing goals are being met or new ones are being formulated. Its most important contribution, however, is team members' growing expertise in what works best for the company. Organizing this knowledge into a usable format allows both scale and sustainability. Here are some typical deliverables:

- Playbooks and best practices for typical social media interactions for each type of user at the company
- Lessons learned, or what *not* to do
- Directory of all social media assets of the company

- Flowcharts for typical crisis scenarios and facilitation of actual simulations

- FAQ or wiki of company policies that is available for instant querying

Centers of excellence are not a certain recipe for success and do not work for many companies. Sometimes they end up duplicating work, introducing a stifling bureaucracy, and creating hurdles for innovation and progress. COE efforts can also be wasted if there isn't a clear path to implementation and regular check-ins with every department. Success requires every business to feel total ownership and accountability for Social Business—the danger with COEs is that they may become too far removed from the everyday operation of the organization.

The following sidebar examines how one multinational, multi-business-unit organization, Raymond James, has struck the right balance between coordination and autonomy across businesses and regions.

### How Raymond James Operationalizes Social Business

Raymond James, a St. Petersburg, Florida, *Fortune* 500 financial services company, has struck the perfect balance between the tricky area of compliance and a robust social media presence. In many cases, the two agendas are working against each other, but Raymond James, under the direction of CMO Mike White (@MikeWhiteRJ), has found a way to operationalize social media from vision to practice.

For one thing, all three company presidents at Raymond James are active on Twitter (@BillVanLawRJ, @TashElwynRJ, @ScottCurtisRJ, respectively), and two-thirds of the sales reps are active on Facebook, LinkedIn, and Twitter.

White says that the effort is centralized around a content blog that puts out the Raymond James point of view. It has themed sections that address all of the major areas of concern to the company's clients. For example, one recent content collaboration was with the MIT AgeLab, focused on longevity planning and implications for retirement, intergenerational wealth transfer, and beyond.

Memorable, useful content like this is disseminated on all of the company's social network channels following a well-thought-out editorial calendar. Each network is used for different purposes. The company's sales, marketing, and customer service operations have coordinated activities on the major three social networks. Public relations content goes out on Twitter, the government component and social responsibility content is posted to Facebook, and HR and recruiting posts are oriented to LinkedIn. The content hub for prospective advisors is well trafficked on LinkedIn and has led to many new hires; it is complemented by the Twitter handle devoted to Raymond James careers. As shown in Figure 10.1, establishing different handles for different parts of the business has allowed the organization to diversify its audience while amplifying each tailored message.

*continues…*

https://twitter.com/raymondjames

https://twitter.com/RJadvisorchoice

https://twitter.com/RJIS4wealthmgrs

https://twitter.com/RJCfoundtaion

https://twitter.com/raymondjamesCDN

https://twitter.com/rjcareers

**Figure 10.1**

*Six of Raymond James Financial's Twitter presences, each tailored to a unique audience (clockwise from top left: global brand, U.S. advisors, U.K. advisors, Raymond James Canada Foundation, Canadian brand, and global recruiting)* (Source: Twitter)

To coordinate across geographical regions, the Raymond James team conducts regular phone calls and meetings among representatives from each office; these get-togethers draw from a central editorial calendar and use a similar, agreed-upon tone and style, but each is targeted to a different region and clientele. On an ad hoc basis, regional managers look to one another for ideas, inspiration, connections, and synergies such as retweets.

For instance, if they post something for the capital markets business on solar energy, the PR team can also pitch that content to an editor on social media. There is no single social guru who brings it all together, but the process of communication ensures that no department steps on another's toes. Instead of individuals whose job it is to handle all social media efforts, everyone has social media engagement as a part of their job (much like most people use the Internet as part of their job).

Having the three company presidents and other executive leadership active on social media has brought benefits, both in recruiting financial advisors and prospective clients and in engaging with the company's existing advisors, employees, and clients. When potential recruits and clients can witness first-hand how effectively senior management and regional management are using social media, it sends a powerful message that the company is forward-looking and cares about connecting with its people.

## Social Business Measurement

Ultimately, Social Business programs, like any corporate initiative, need to drive ROI. Some use cases are easier to measure, such as tracking a social ad campaign from click to e-commerce conversion. Some are of medium difficulty to measure, such as tracking social customer service. It's possible to quantify this sort of interaction but requires some integration work to figure out customer satisfaction scores and resolution time—when a particular Twitter exchange ends, has the issue been resolved or merely taken offline to another channel? In my own experience, measuring social media return for salespeople has been the most difficult of all given the multichannel, multitouch attribution problem.

One common danger for transformational initiatives is holding fledgling programs accountable to hard metrics too soon and failing to build in time for organizational acceptance, change management, and process integration. Harvard Business School professor Clayton Christensen, who coined the term "disruption," has researched and written extensively about this problem.

Christensen defines three types of innovation: empowering innovations, which democratize expensive products into affordable ones; sustaining innovations, which replace older models with new ones; and efficiency innovations, which reduce costs. The first two types of innovation drive growth, whereas the third drives the bottom line, sometimes at the expense of growth. Christensen believes many businesses today have been held back in large part because they are focused almost entirely on efficiency—"streamlining and wringing bottom line savings and additional profits out of existing organizations [and practices]." He believes universities and business schools are training business leaders and investors to focus on fast and efficient return on capital investment; efficiency innovations provide ROI in 12 to 18 months, he says, but empowering innovations take 5 to 10 years to yield a result.

Sometimes it's the executive sponsor who demands this quick result, but often the culprit is the well-intentioned staff under the executive who want to do a good job.

These personnel may mistakenly put the same metrics in place for Social Business (or other innovation initiatives) that they do for efficiency innovations.

Last year, the CEO of a large Canada-based multinational company (and a friend of mine) realized this was happening in his organization—an unintended consequence of perfectly rational cost-cutting measures that needed to be put in place. Wanting to be good corporate citizens, his business leaders invested less and more slowly in empowering innovations, and his procurement team approached disruptive vendors with the same singular focus on cost as they did efficiency vendors. The CEO quickly stepped in. He said, "What if 30 years ago we had decided to not invest in putting phones on every desk, or only piloted with a few phones for a few people, because we couldn't measure the ROI of being able to make and receive calls? We wouldn't be in business today."

Social Business has elements of both empowering innovations and sustaining innovations. It is a long-term, transformational bet. But that doesn't mean there aren't metrics. At the outset, every program should begin with defining success, even if the early objective is just learning and observation. These objectives should be periodically reviewed (quarterly at first, then annually) to provide a focal point around which the organization can hold stakeholders accountable, prioritize competing objectives, and focus resources.

Although I agree with Christensen's 5- to 10-year time horizon (it's hard to argue with the great data he has collected suggesting this), I have also seen Social Business deliver results in a shorter period of time. Many leaders I work with have been pleasantly surprised by how soon they were able to achieve hard results, after just two to four years.

Let me share one concrete example in detail. My colleagues Weifang Zhu, Karin Zabel, Sarah Pedersen, and Abhay Rajaram collaborated with a number of *Fortune* 500 firms to develop an ROI evaluation and analysis framework in the Social Sales realm. Key inputs are the organization's internal rate of return (IRR) sensitivity, free cash flow (FCF) model, new deal uplift data, and value of brand reach. Next, they run a regression analysis to correlate sales lift and other KPIs with social activity data (e.g., posts, comments, 'likes,' retweets). They adjust for other variables, such as representative tenure and experience level, geography, support staff size, and baseline sales achievement, by comparing the Social Sales personnel to a control group of similar personnel who are not placed in the social selling program.

Each participating organization had been running a program for at least 24 to 36 months and ran its own analysis, but generally followed this framework. In each case, organizations have calculated a double-digit percentage lift in each of four key dimensions measured: customer acquisition, high-value customer acquisition (defined differently by each company), upsell and cross-sell, and net promoter score ("On a scale of 1 to 10, how likely is it that you would recommend this sales professional to a friend or colleague?").

In conjunction to these hard metrics, Hearsay Social's customer success services team has pioneered a Social Business Scorecard to help organizations benchmark themselves against their peers and identify key opportunity areas for improvement and focus as they work toward the long-term empowering innovation and organizational transformation. The next sidebar explains how this scorecard works.

### Social Business Scorecard to Guide Program Execution

In 2015, Hearsay Social introduced its Social Business Maturity Model and Scorecard to enable firms to objectively evaluate their enterprise Social Business programs and compare how they rank relative to their peers and industry benchmarks.

The first step in developing the maturity model was to identify all of the attributes of each enterprise's social media program ($n = 100$) and then run a regression to determine which attributes were ultimately most predictive of success, as measured by average sales uplift per sales representative.

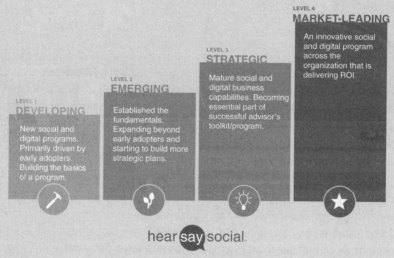

**Figure 10.2**

*The four levels of social media maturity and ROI actualization from the Hearsay Social Business Maturity Model and Scorecard* (Source: Hearsay Social, Inc.)

The data suggest there are seven critical practice areas:

- Dedicated project team assigned to the program

- Active championship and sponsorship from the C-Suite

- Robust content marketing strategy and development resources (could be in-house or agency)

- Adoption across the entire field organization or, better yet, the entire firm

- Ongoing engagement, education, and incentives at the individual user level

*continues…*

- Integration with overall sales methodology and practice management
- Ongoing value measurement and communication to end users to provide the "why" of what they are being asked to do

The Social Business Scorecard has been one way for organizations to operationalize their social media efforts with an actionable benchmark and roadmap. The feedback indicates that companies are now better able to keep learning and prioritize which steps they need to take to accelerate their programs as well as track their progress in delivering higher sales and value across the business.

## Summary

Here is how a well-oiled Social Business works: Specific initiatives are driven by each respective department, business unit, or region, with a light layer of best practices sharing and oversight across the entire organization. Everyone shares information across departments and has regular check-ins about content and strategy. Content is published independently, but is guided by organizational goals. As the next chapters will explore, legal and compliance teams as well as IT organizations should be engaged early in the process to ensure buy-in and alignment.

When all of these pieces are in place, organizations will be set up to deliver a cohesive omnichannel customer experience, and true business transformation and ROI can be achieved. Over time, a company will be able to leverage the outcomes of engagement and harness the power of social data to make more strategic decisions.

But don't be too quick or aggressive with the timeline for social success, or your innovation may stall out before it has a chance to take hold. State your goals realistically. It takes years to reach a point where social media becomes integral to every role and department and is coordinated across the enterprise. What's more, organizations must continually evolve as the technology rapidly evolves. It's a long road to travel, but with Social Business lighting up the future, it promises to be a fun, exciting, and profitable journey. Today's social, always-connected customer is counting on it.

# 11

*"The man who achieves makes many mistakes, but he never makes the biggest mistake of all—doing nothing."*
—Benjamin Franklin (Author's Note: I'm sure he meant women, too!)

# Legal, Governance, and Compliance Frameworks

Every organization today faces a Social Business Imperative to adapt to the always-connected, social customer. Among *Fortune* 500 firms, more than three-quarters now have an official presence (often multiple initiatives) on Twitter, Facebook, LinkedIn, or YouTube. But along with the unprecedented opportunities for marketing, sales, customer service, human resources, and nearly every departmental function or business unit, Social Business—like any disruptive technology—also introduces new risks. From PR fires and fines for regulatory noncompliance to the fraudulent tweet that caused the Dow to fall 150 points,[1] the risks are real and important to address.

Yet, given the seismic changes in customer and employee behavior, the greatest risk of all is doing nothing. For smaller, privately held businesses, the legal and compliance risks are generally minimal, and common sense is usually sufficient. Larger, publicly traded, and highly regulated businesses have a longer list of to-dos when it comes to risk mitigation. One challenge is that many regulations as well as internal corporate risk management policies and procedures were created for a slower-moving, offline world and do not easily translate to the real-time, constantly evolving reality of Twitter or Facebook.

Another challenge is company culture. If your legal organization, for example, is far removed from the business and unaccustomed to change, it may cite legal and compliance risk as an excuse to do nothing. Yet doing nothing on social media today would be akin to firms

---

1. "Syrian Hackers Claim AP Hack That Tipped Stock Market by $136 Billion. Is It Terrorism?" *Washington Post,* April 23, 2013. https://www.washingtonpost.com/news/worldviews/wp/2013/04/23/syrian-hackers-claim-ap-hack-that-tipped-stock-market-by-136-billion-is-it-terrorism

15 or 20 years ago refusing to set up a website due to fear of legal and compliance risk. In addition, if you don't offer an officially sanctioned program, your employees and associates will likely "go rogue" and proceed anyway, without guardrails or oversight of any kind.

Fortunately, things are changing for the better in this area. Regulators and corporate legal and risk leaders increasingly understand the huge importance and opportunity presented by Social Business. More and more, legal and risk teams realize that no matter what a company's official policy or presence may be, there are inevitably customers, prospects, employees, and members of the public talking about the company all the time on social media and that it's best to listen and mitigate any risk rather than to turn a blind eye.

The best legal, risk, and compliance officers recognize the critical role they must play in leading their organizations to embrace Social Business. Even regulators have acknowledged the critical importance of social media as a channel for providing fair and equitable access to information and have updated their rules accordingly. As described in Chapter 4, Netflix initially got in trouble for violating Regulation FD when its CEO Reed Hastings posted what was a potential material disclosure on Facebook. However, after investigating the matter, the SEC decided social media is an appropriate channel through which companies can disseminate material, nonpublic information, so long as the company informs investors ahead of time that it will be doing so and provides accessibility to all investors.

Across the board, business leaders should consider six primary areas of risk:

- **Strategic.** Sensitive information leaked on social media channels could dramatically affect the company's ability to achieve strategic objectives, such as the secret development and impending launch of a new offering that competes with a current partner.

- **Legal.** Companies need to consider all the legal risks involved with the use of social media, from hiring practices (decisions made from pre-employment social media screening) and employee monitoring to social media in litigation and e-discovery, social advertising laws, and intellectual property (IP) protection and misuse. Traditional legal risks can become magnified on social media due to the large number of employees actively sharing and participating and the public nature of many posts.

- **Market.** Employees on social media could inadvertently share insider information or purposely release false information that affects the company's stock price.

- **Reputation.** Whether intentional or malicious, truth or rumor, companies today are exposed to the possibility of a significant amount of brand damage being done in a short amount of time, starting with a disgruntled current or former employee or upset customer tweet gone viral.

- **Regulatory.** Businesses that are highly regulated, such as those in the financial services, pharmaceutical, and healthcare industries, have many enforceable obligations to consumers, investors, and the public.

- **Network and cybersecurity.** Malware and social engineering are increasing threats on social media. Employees using the same passwords for corporate and personal accounts also create vulnerabilities to identity theft, hacking into the corporate network, and theft of corporate digital assets and IP.

The Social Business era is here, and there is no turning back now. Mastery of and willingness to embrace technological change have become critical skill sets for today's board directors, CEOs, CMOs, CIOs, heads of sales, and heads of recruiting. The same is now true for general counsels, chief compliance officers, and governance and risk teams. As the pace of innovation continues accelerating, successful leaders will be defined by their ability to evolve and adapt their organizations to capitalize on the incredible growth opportunities and stay relevant with today's social, always-connected customer.

## Key Areas of Social Media Risk

Social Business cuts across nearly every department, business unit, and region, and extends from employees to customers to partners to the public, creating many different possible areas of concern spanning reputational, regulatory, legal, and market risk. The first step in mitigating risk is identifying and evaluating key risk areas. Here are 10 to consider[2]:

- **Information leaks.** Given the large amount of sharing that occurs on social networking sites, confidential information, trade secrets, and intellectual property may be disclosed (often accidentally) by employees. For example, a well-intentioned manager might update her LinkedIn profile to be more appealing to prospective hires, but in so doing accidentally spill the beans about a secret product that is currently being developed.

  *Recommended strategy:* Provide continuous employee training and reminders, as well as clear guidelines on what employees may publicly share about their job and projects.

- **Fraud.** Due to social media's instant global, viral reach, account hacking by malicious third parties or disgruntled current or former employees can do a lot of damage in a very small amount of time. Consider what happened in the public markets a few years ago, when hackers took over the Associated Press account on Twitter and posted a false story about a bombing at the White House. This fake "news" caused the Dow Jones Industrial Average to fall 150 points over the course of several minutes.

  *Recommended strategy:* The U.S. Commodity Futures Trading Commission has called for fines to be imposed on companies that don't address basic vulnerabilities that would allow social media accounts to be hacked in ways that could manipulate the public markets. Regardless, companies should protect their social media accounts with safeguards such as complex passwords that must be changed frequently, monitoring tools (such as Viralheat and Salesforce Radian6) to detect rumors or compromised accounts, and ready-to-implement crisis management plans.

---

2. "Top 10 Legal Issues in Social Media," Neal & McDevitt Intellectual Property and Marketing Attorneys, accessed October 28, 2015. http://www.nealmcdevitt.com/assets/news/Top_10_Social_Media_Legal_Issues_FINAL.PDF; "A Comprehensive Approach to Managing Social Media Risk and Compliance," Accenture, accessed October 28, 2015. https://www.accenture.com/t20150715T045906__w__/us-en/_acnmedia/Accenture/Conversion-Assets/DotCom/Documents/Global/PDF/Dualpub_1/accenture-comprehensive-approach-managing-social-media-risk-compliance.pdf

- **Brand reputation.** As we explored in Chapter 8, sometimes the bad news that has gone viral is not fraudulent. Deleting negative reviews and comments is not a good idea. Not only may it constitute false advertising, but doing so typically causes a backlash and even outrage versus owning up to the mistake, apologizing, and articulating the way forward.

  *Recommended strategy:* Publish readily accessible "Terms of Use" for the company's social media accounts for those instances when you want to remove objectionable material. Utilize account monitoring tools and establish ready-to-implement crisis management plans. Provide employee training to reduce the likelihood that your employees will inadvertently trigger a negative viral campaign.

- **Trademark or copyright violations.** Unauthorized use of third-party content, trademarks, or copyright-protected works, such as images, video, and source code, could lead to issues with infringement liability.

  *Recommended strategy:* Most social networking sites now have built-in infringement reporting mechanisms that allow trademark owners to take action. For company-owned sites and blogs, the "safe harbor" provision in copyright law protects the company from liability if the infringing content is taken down upon receiving notice.

- **Records retention and electronic discovery.** Regulatory bodies including the SEC, FINRA, IIROC, and FCA now treat social media content, including Facebook posts and messages, tweets, and LinkedIn profiles, messaging, and updates, as "discoverable" information to the same extent as emails; thus they may be subpoenaed in the context of litigation.

  *Recommended strategy:* Organizations with electronic records retention policies must ensure that social media communications are explicitly included. Periodically conduct internal spot checks to ensure the technology and procedures are functioning properly.

- **Securities law.** Thanks to the actions of Netflix, the SEC now allows companies to use social media outlets such as Facebook and Twitter to disclose key information in compliance with Regulation Fair Disclosure (Regulation FD), as long as investors have been alerted ahead of time about which social media sites and accounts will be used for this purpose. But there is still plenty of securities risk when it comes to social media, as the then-CFO of Houston-based clothing retailer Francesca's learned a few years ago, when he tweeted, "Board meeting. Good numbers=Happy Board" (Figure 11.1). Subsequently, Francesca's stock price surged 15% during the week preceding its earnings announcement, prompting an SEC investigation and dismissal of the CFO.

  *Recommended strategy:* Train company officers and others privy to inside information on disclosure do's and don'ts. Although disclosure rules have been broadened for social media, there are still limitations. CFOs can just as easily email similar statements or mention them to a friend during a casual encounter such as a round of golf. Look up social media accounts of prospective executive hires to see if they have a history of good judgment. Put training and technology safeguards in place.

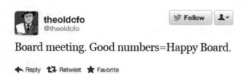

**theoldcfo**
@theoldcfo

Follow  ⬇

Board meeting. Good numbers=Happy Board.

↩ Reply   ⟲ Retweet   ★ Favorite

**Figure 11.1**
*Tweet posted on March 2012 by Gene Morphis (@theoldcfo), former CFO of specialty retailer Francesca's Holdings Corporation. This message was found to violate the Securities and Exchange Commission's Regulation Fair Disclosure* (Source: Twitter)

- **Privacy and publicity.** Just as promoting user-generated content may infringe on someone else's copyright, so it may also violate the privacy or publicity rights of these individuals. Your marketing team, for instance, may stumble upon a great user-generated video about how wonderful your brand is and be tempted to feature it on the company website. A great example is specialty eyewear retailer Warby Parker. Its marketing team frequently features photos of customers wearing their eyeglasses (shared by those customers via social media), as doing so fits with the authentic, customer-friendly nature of the brand, but they make sure to first obtain permission and the proper releases.

In industries with specific privacy regulations, such as financial services (e.g., protection of personally identifiable information), law (e.g., attorney–client privilege), and health care (e.g., Health Insurance Portability and Accountability Act [HIPAA]), firms and employees must take extra precautions and ensure they do not disclose client or patient confidential information. Industries with these regulatory requirements are often subject to increased scrutiny and risk.

In the world of debt collections, while the US Fair Debt Collection Practices Act allows collection agencies to utilize social networking for research purposes (tracking down consumers who have unlisted phone numbers or changes of address, and ascertaining whether the consumer is still making unneeded purchases despite unpaid debt), most state laws stipulate that debt collectors cannot publicly talk about a debt or even tell a debtor's family, friends, or coworkers about a debt.[3]

*Recommended strategy:* For user-generated content such as photos or video, ask for permission. Often, the customer who tweeted or posted a photo to Instagram will appreciate the publicity opportunity and say yes. Establish clear policies and procedures about using or sharing client information, and then train employees on those policies and procedures. If your organization deals with information concerning minors, make sure to comply with the Children's Online Privacy Protection Act of 1998 (COPPA), which details what should be included in privacy policies and when to seek verifiable consent from a parent or legal guardian.

---

3. "Woman Sues Debt Collectors for MySpace Posting," *Wired.* March 31, 2009. http://www.wired.com/2009/03/woman-sues-debt/

- **Disparagement and defamation.** Social media can become a forum for defamatory statements about individuals and disparaging remarks about companies. Overzealous employees, for example, may post disparaging remarks about a competitor's offerings that may not be entirely true or accurate and open the possibility of liability and legal action.

  *Recommended strategy:* Establish employee guidelines, policies, and training.

- **Advertising law and disclosure of paid endorsements.** The Federal Trade Commission (FTC) has issued "Guides Concerning the Use of Endorsements and Testimonials in Advertising," which require bloggers and other social media users to disclose when they have been paid (in cash or in kind) to publicly endorse a product or service. The classic example is "mommy bloggers" who received free diapers and other baby supplies, and then wrote blog posts about how great those products were. These rules apply to sweepstakes and contests, too. Companies that incentivize social media posts by offering entry into contests in exchange for 'likes' or posts must ensure participants disclose their participation, such as with a #sweepstakes or #contest hashtag. Celebrities who endorse products must also somehow disclose that they are paid to endorse in every tweet or Pin or post.

  Along the same lines, employees who promote their company's offerings should disclose they are employed by that company. Employees who "rate up" the products of their employer may violate advertising laws.

  *Recommended strategy:* Companies, especially those that offer free products to influencers, should have clearly stated policies reminding recipients to disclose their relationship. If you are considering running sweepstakes and contests, be sure to reference both state and federal laws requiring disclaimers and notices as well as the guidelines established by Facebook, Twitter, and Pinterest. Finally, employee guidelines and training are key to risk mitigation.

- **Employment law.** The specifics around HR use of social media as it pertains to prospective, current, and former employees are nuanced and vary by state. There are several important considerations, as summarized in a recent report by InfoLawGroup LLP.[4] First, as a growing number of recruiting teams and hiring managers look at prospective candidates' social media profiles to vet these candidates, more conservative legal teams may view information obtained from social media as constituting a "consumer report" under the Fair Credit Reporting Act. This interpretation would require employers to obtain the candidate's consent before accessing this information or may prohibit them from using this kind of information altogether in making hiring decisions.

  Another hot topic is the extent to which employees may have privacy rights concerning use of social media while at work and the extent to which employers may monitor their activities (even going so far as asking for account passwords and asserting ownership of

---

4. "The Legal Implications of Social Networking," InfoLawGroup LLP. Accessed October 28, 2015. http://www.infolawgroup.com/2011/06/articles/social-networking/the-legal-implications-of-social-networking-the-basics-part-one

employee accounts) or ask employees to post about company matters to their personal accounts. For example, the National Labor Relations Board has asserted the freedom of speech right of both union and non-union workers to discuss working conditions without fear of retaliation, including doing so on social media.

Financial services may be an exception when it comes to monitoring employee social media accounts. From a FINRA/SEC vantage point, a growing chorus is insisting that state laws that prohibit employers from monitoring ought not be applicable given regulatory and supervisory obligations.

Finally, there is an ongoing debate around social media account ownership when an employee establishes an account for the purpose of conducting business at a specific employer but then leaves the firm.

*Recommended strategy:* These topics regarding current and prospective employees are not new. Convene your HR and legal teams to review how the laws and your organization's policies should be adapted or extended to social media.

Technically, any communication on social media could be viewed as an advertisement when it is done on behalf of a company, so laws governing appropriate advertising apply. It's important for business leaders to understand these new opportunities and new risks for everything from sales and marketing to employment practices liability, crisis management, brand reputation, and cybersecurity. Social media posts can also intersect with bullying and harassment concerns—anything that can happen in a workplace can now happen online.

The lightning speed at which content spreads on social networks means that everything must be monitored continuously, and every key player in a company needs to be trained on the risks inherent in utilizing social media. Once something gets posted, it is instantly publicly available, and potentially viral. You can't retrieve any mistakes made on social media, so you must have safeguards in place to prevent and mitigate these dangers through a combination of a well-thought-out social media policy and extensive employee training (more on this later).

## Considerations for Highly Regulated Industries

Industries that operate under the scrutiny of strict laws and regulations, such as financial services and pharmaceuticals, face additional challenges when it comes to adopting social media. Every post, tweet, 'like,' 'favorite,' or DM that has to do with the business coming from any employee is subject to certain rules and must be retained.

A tweet sent by an employee that fails to get captured can land the firm in hot water, even if the contents of the tweet were completely innocuous. A pharmaceutical firm 'liking' a consumer's comment on a Facebook product page related to its drug could similarly face repercussions. These unpleasant possibilities can have a chilling effect on an organization, making it less enticing to jump into social media. Unfortunately, these extra rules might also lead companies to behave too conservatively, so that they miss out on the myriad benefits of joining social networks. It is therefore imperative for heads of business to collaborate closely and on an ongoing basis with their legal and risk counterparts to first make a business case for social media, then decide together which level of risk is acceptable (acknowledging that "zero" is rarely the optimal level of risk), and implement steps toward risk mitigation.

Though still evolving (as the social networks themselves continually evolve), social media guidelines and regulations in financial services, pharmaceuticals, and health care have been issued and are being successfully navigated by companies. While it's beyond the scope of this book to review in detail the specific social media regulations for every industry in every country, the following examples are illustrative of the intent and requirements that appear or will appear in other regulatory rules.

## Financial Services on Social Media

Despite being heavily regulated, financial institutions were among some of the first to enter into Social Business. Their leap into social media was primarily driven by their clients, who turn to friends on social media for advisor referrals, and then research and reach out to those advisors via social media.

Regulatory bodies of the financial services industry—including the Financial Industry Regulatory Authority (FINRA), Federal Financial Institutions Examination Council (FFIEC), and Securities and Exchange Commission (SEC) in the United States; the Canadian Securities Administrators, Investment Industry Regulatory Organization of Canada (IIROC), and Mutual Fund Dealers Association (MFDA) in Canada; the Financial Conduct Authority (FCA) in the United Kingdom; and L'Autorité des marchés financiers (AMF) in France—have each issued social-media-specific regulations, guidelines, and sanctions for nonadherence. Fortunately, the rules developed by these organizations are similar, focusing on many of the same tenets.

In the US broker-dealer world, FINRA has been vocal for some time regarding the use of social media by registered representatives. As early as 1999 and 2003, respectively, FINRA issued guidance on participation in electronic chat rooms and interactive message forums. In 2010, it issued Regulatory Notice 10-06, "Guidance on Blogs and Social Networking Web Sites"; in 2011, it issued follow-on guidelines, Regulatory Notice 11-39, "Social Media Websites and the Use of Personal Devices for Business Communications."

In Canada, IIROC has issued notice 11-0349, "Guidelines for the Review, Supervision and Retention of Advertisements, Sales Literature and Correspondence." This document specifically provides guidance on IIROC's expectations for Canadian investment dealers regarding the use of social media sites in communicating with clients.

Looking broadly across the social media regulatory landscape, there are essentially four compliance pillars for financial advisors in the United States, Canada, and the United Kingdom:

- **Recordkeeping responsibilities.** Firms are required to retain records of communications related to the broker-dealer's business conducted through social media sites.[5] Firms are responsible for records retention regardless of "the type of device or technology used to transmit the communication," or "whether it is a firm-issued or [the] personal device of the individual."

*Recommended strategy:* Using a third-party technology vendor such as Actiance, Smarsh, or my firm Hearsay Social, broker-dealers can ensure all social media communications are retained, generally in a universal archive such as Symantec Enterprise Vault, Autonomy Enterprise Archive Solution, or ZL Technologies. The regulations require the preservation of the records for a period of not less than three years, with the records being stored in an easily accessible place during the first two years.

- **Supervision.** Interactive posts on Twitter and Facebook must be supervised after the fact in accordance with FINRA Rules 2210 and 3110. This can be done using sampling and lexicon-based searches with common infraction keywords. Similarly, IIROC Rule 29.7(2) requires dealer members to establish policies and procedures that allow them to comply with their supervisory obligations ex post facto for interactive or dynamic content, which include real-time discussions, tweets, comments, and @replies.

In contrast, online banner advertisements, website copy, and social media profiles are considered static content, which must be reviewed and preapproved by a registered principal prior to use.

*Recommended strategy:* Have a system in place to log when static content is preapproved and by whom and when. This sort of logging is required by regulation and is an important part of documenting policies and procedures and having an audit trail.

- **Content.** First, firms and registered representatives must adhere to regulatory standards requiring each recommendation be suitable for every investor to whom it is made (FINRA Rule 2111). Second, firms must put out only content that is fair, balanced, and not misleading (FINRA Rule 2210). Firms may not link to any third-party site they know or suspect contains false or misleading content. A third-party post such as a Yelp review is not generally considered firm communication with the public subject to Rule 2210 (and therefore do not require the principal preapproval, content, and filing requirements). The exceptions are if the firm has been involved in the preparation of the content, or explicitly or implicitly endorsed or approved the content (say, by 'liking' or commenting on the post).

In Canada, IIROC Rule 29.7 requires that marketing and advertising communications must not be misleading or contain an unjustified promise of specific results. The IIROC notice also warns dealers to exercise extreme caution when engaging in third-party communications (e.g., providing links on the dealer's website to third-party sites).

*Recommended strategy:* Because social media posts are generally "one-to-many" (viewable by many people), the implication for firms and advisors is to not issue

---

5. As required by Rules 17a-3 and 17a-4 of the Securities Exchange Act of 1934, FINRA Rule 4511, and FINRA Rule 2210(b).

any product recommendations via social media. Recommendations are best made during one-to-one or one-to-few channels such as email, phone, and in-person meetings.

- **Policy and training.** Firms must set and document a policy as well as conduct appropriate training and education concerning their social media policies. They must also follow up on signs of potential noncompliance.

  *Recommended strategy:* Though not required, a best practice is to require registered representatives to certify at least annually that they are knowledgeable of, and in compliance with, the firm's social media policies.

The SEC has issued similar guidance for registered investment advisers, who are subject to the Investment Advisers Act of 1940. In 2014, the SEC actually softened its stance on advisors' use of recommendations and other public commentary when those messages appear on an independent, third-party social media site (such as Yelp or Angie's List), the advisor was not directly or indirectly involved in authoring the commentary, and the advisor publishes all of the unedited comments appearing on the independent social media site regarding the advisor, including both positive and negative comments.[6]

The Canadian Securities Administrators (CSA) has issued guidance on social media for portfolio managers (who are subject to provincial securities legislation). In CSA Staff Notice 31-325, "Marketing Practices of Portfolio Managers," the CSA specifically identifies potential concerns and compliance challenges for firms to consider when using social media sites as a means of communicating with the general public and clients.

In the United Kingdom, the FCA has issued guidance for advisors that is largely consistent with that provided by the SEC, FINRA, IIROC, and MFDA:

- **Recordkeeping responsibilities.** Firms must keep adequate records and have their own archive, rather than rely on social networking sites to maintain records.[7]

- **Supervision.** Firms must have adequate systems in place to approve digital media communications as well as monitor noncompliant language. Approval should be done by an "appropriate person" in the firm.

- **Content.** Financial messages should be easily identifiable and not misleading. Companies should add the hashtag #ad on Twitter to identify any promotions, and they should target messages to the appropriate audiences to avoid confusion. Finally, firms should include risk warnings, disclosures, and other required statements—use of links and graphics for these disclosures is fine if they are character-limited.

---

6. "U.S. SEC Issues New Social Media Guidance for Financial Advisers," *Reuters.* April 1, 2014. http://www.reuters.com/article/2014/04/01/sec-socialmedia-idUSL1N0MT19T20140401

7. Conduct of Business Sourcebook 4.11; MCOB 3.10; ICOBS 2.4.

## Ways Financial Advisors Can Stay Compliant

Avoid third-party endorsements you are entangled with and avoid all recommendations (you can disable these for your LinkedIn profile under "Account Settings"). Add a disclaimer to your profile saying you do not accept write-in endorsements or recommendations.

Do not tweet about or otherwise endorse specific stocks or mutual funds, as this could be a violation of FINRA's suitability rule. Do not give investment advice, recommend products, promise performance results, or represent opinions as facts on social media.

Third-party content you post or link to may be considered your content, so promote such content with care and self-scrutiny.

Do not retweet a third party, such as an equities research analyst or client, who provides a testimonial about your performance or a product or service offered by your firm. Doing so would constitute an advertisement.

Be careful what and how a post is 'liked' or 'favorited' on your social media page. Under the current SEC guidance, a third-party 'like' may simply indicate that a visitor enjoyed an article you shared, whereas a 'like' solicited by you as an indication of a client's experience with you or your firm may be construed as a testimonial, which is a regulatory infraction. As a best practice, prominently display language on your LinkedIn profile and Facebook business page indicating you (and your firm) are not responsible for and do not encourage third parties to post anything on your behalf.

Looking more broadly across the financial services, in 2013 FFIEC published social media guidance for banks, savings associations, and credit unions, as well as for nonbank entities that are supervised by the Consumer Financial Protection Bureau (CFPB), focusing on six key issues:[8]

- **Risk management.** Financial institutions should include social media in their overall risk management programs and are expected to establish a governance structure, including the implementation of controls and policies and procedures, as well as ongoing risk assessments.

- **Third-party social media vendor management.** Financial institutions are expected to conduct evaluations of risks posed by third-party social media providers such as Facebook or Twitter, even if there is no commercial relationship.

---

8. "Social Media: Consumer Compliance Risk Management Guidance," Federal Financial Institutions Examination Council (FFIEC). December 11, 2013. http://files.consumerfinance.gov/f/201309_cfpb_social_media_guidance.pdf

- **Employee training.** Financial institutions should provide training and guidance on social media compliance for official work-related use to all employees who officially communicate on behalf of the financial institution.

- **Complaint submission and processing.** Financial institutions are expected to monitor all communications posted to social media pages administered by the institution or authorized third party (such as a bank or brokerage's official Facebook Page). Financial institutions can use their discretion to evaluate which negative comments should be considered as complaints or inquiries and therefore warrant a response.

- **Regulatory requirements.** All legal and regulatory requirements otherwise applicable to financial institutions' deposit, lending, payment services, marketing, advertising, and other activities remain applicable on social media channels. For example, the following consumer data privacy requirements still apply: GLBA Privacy Rules and Interagency Data Security Guidelines, CAN-SPAM Act and Telephone Consumer Protection Act, Children's Online Privacy Protection Act (COPPA), and Fair Credit Reporting Act (FCRA).

- **Other privacy issues.** Financial institutions are encouraged to have procedures in place to monitor and take down sensitive content, such as when customers inadvertently post confidential or sensitive information such as an account number or Social Security number on the institution's social media page.

## Note

Just as marketing and customer service teams are staffing up and/or reallocating team members to focus on social media, so compliance and supervision teams need to do the same. In practice, the increase in time and staff required has been incremental or marginal, not an order of magnitude, and as the program grows, we observe clear economy-of-scale efficiencies. The vast majority of advisors never have any compliance infractions.

Each organization is unique, but here are some general guidelines on supervision resourcing based on a survey of several dozen Hearsay Social brokerage customers:

- New supervisors should start with 300 or fewer advisors.

- Experienced supervisors with established approval processes in place and familiarity with the workflow software can support up to 500 advisors.

- Scale efficiencies start to appear at 1000 advisors or more. On average, the equivalent of 3.5 supervisors can oversee 2000 advisors, 4 to 5 supervisors can easily support 3000 advisors, and so on.

## Pharmaceutical Companies on Social Media

A growing number of pharmaceutical companies are using social media to learn more about the patient experience (side effects, consumer perceptions of medications, how patients are managing disease) and uncover trends and new product ideas.

The most recent guidance from the US Food and Drug Administration (FDA), entitled "Internet/Social Media Platforms with Character Space Limitations: Presenting Risk and Benefit Information for Prescription Drugs and Medical Devices," focuses on the use of "online microblogging platforms" such as Twitter, as well as online paid search advertisements.[9] Here is a summary of the FDA guidelines:

- Social media posts should have a comparable balance of risk and benefit, regardless of character space constraints. The benefit should be accurate, factual, and not misleading. The risk should be part of each communication and should include the most serious risk, along with a direct hyperlink to a comprehensive set of risk information. If balanced content cannot be achieved, that may be a good reason to not utilize the social media platform for a particular drug.

- Drug companies are not permitted to respond in public to any public inquiries about off-label drug use posted to social media sites. Any communication about off-label drug use must be done on a private, one-to-one basis.

- The first (or only) link included must be to a page containing more complete information about risk. Inclusion of an additional link or links is fine. Links should be named to clearly indicate the topic (for example, www.drugname.com/risk). The destination page should clearly display the brand and established name (according to the logo lock up) together with information on dosage, form, and ingredient information.

- Symbols (such as &), punctuation marks, and scientific abbreviations can be used to address character space constraints.

- The message must include the full FDA-approved product name.

Given these restrictive rules, most pharmaceutical companies are not tweeting very much these days about the drugs. Instead, they mostly talk about diseases, community and philanthropic initiatives, and scientific findings.

## Healthcare Providers on Social Media

In the adjacent field of health care, hospitals, clinics, and medical service providers are using social media to launch innovative marketing campaigns, connect with patients and families to offer information, and showcase their involvement in the community. As shown in Figure 11.2, Brigham and Women's Hospital in Boston, Massachusetts, has an active and vibrant Facebook Page. This hospital also has robust presences on Twitter, LinkedIn, Pinterest, Instagram, and YouTube.

---

9. "FDA Issues Draft Guidances for Industry on Social Media and Internet Communications About Medical Products: Designed with Patients in Mind," FDA Blog. June 17, 2014. http://www.fda.gov/downloads/drugs/guidancecomplianceregulatoryinformation/guidances/ucm401087.pdf

**Figure 11.2**
*The Facebook Page of Brigham and Women's Hospital* (Source: Facebook)

The major social media legal and risk considerations for healthcare organizations can be summarized as follows:

- **Privacy and confidentiality of patient information.** Providers must safeguard protected patient information, including name, address, and email address, per HIPAA and state laws. Posting on social media does not violate privacy laws so long as providers don't post patient information without proper authorization.

- **Laws governing the practice of medicine.** All of the same responsibilities and issues regarding licensure, reporting address changes, malpractice, prohibited referrals, and boundary issues extend into the realm of social media. Many doctors, nurses, and medical staff will choose to use a pseudonym or their initials instead of a full name so that patients can't find them on Facebook or Twitter, for example.

- **Disclosures.** Given the informal nature of social media and the fact that not all patients may be social-media savvy, providers should include a disclaimer reminding site visitors that their posts are public. For example, consider including text like this: *"This is a public site. Please do not post personal information about yourself or others, including medical information, address, phone, date of birth, or Social Security number."*

Although the pharmaceutical and healthcare industries currently have fewer stated rules relative to financial services when it comes to social media, that doesn't mean they face less risk. Especially in regulated industries, legal and risk professionals need to be at the forefront of this evolving landscape to put the right strategies in place. Rather than hinder innovation, they have a duty—and tremendous opportunity—to make valuable contributions to the strategic direction of their organizations by enabling Social Business. Their role isn't to stifle innovation or grassroots organizing, but rather to make it possible for these organizations to adapt to today's social and always-connected customer while staying in compliance with industry regulation.

## The Risk Mitigation Playbook

Amidst this milieu of rules and regulations, risk mitigation ultimately comes down to maintaining a balanced strategy and execution encompassing four key areas: governance, process, system, and culture (as summarized in Figure 11.3). Balance is key. Take culture, for example. On the one hand, it's a good idea to promote a risk-aware culture so that your employees take necessary precautions before acting. On the other hand, it's all too easy for the cultural pendulum to swing too far toward risk aversion, paralyzing the organization so that it isn't able to embrace change and capitalize on new opportunities. It's important to identify key risks and put processes and systems in place to address them while remaining sufficiently aware to avoid over-engineering. Too much process is stifling, needlessly hindering business growth.

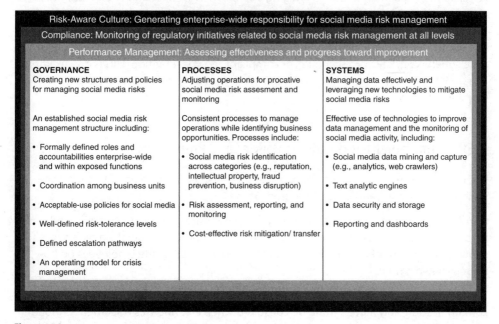

**Figure 11.3**
*Successful risk mitigation comes down to establishing the right governance, processes, systems, and culture* (Source: Accenture, 2014)

The most successful organizations keep it simple (well, as simple as possible) and focus on four pillars of action: (1) identify key risks and establish procedures to address them; (2) implement social media policies and procedures; (3) develop employee training, empowerment, and safeguards; and (4) implement IT systems.

## STEP #1. Identify Key Risks and Establish Procedures to Address Them

As with anything else, organizations have to pick their battles and determine which risk areas related to social media are showstoppers versus which are acceptable risks justified by the potential business returns. Some organizations may choose to be more or less conservative in their approach—but without question, the optimal level of risk is not zero.

Once key risk areas are identified, each area should be assigned to a clear owner who is responsible for establishing risk tolerance levels, policies and procedures designed to mitigate the risks based on levels of acceptable risk, and systems to enforce the policies. For each risk category within each Social Business use case, you should define edge cases, escalation paths, and an operating model for crisis management, while being mindful not to establish policies that can't realistically work.

Legal and risk teams must keep up with how social media and other technologies are evolving, and periodically reassess risk and procedures based on this changing landscape. For example, consumer mobile messaging apps such as WeChat and WhatsApp, which were nonexistent just a few years ago, are now everywhere. Surely there are people in your organizations using them this very moment to communicate with customers and one another—yet there are no technology integration APIs that would allow compliance supervision, keyword scanning, or compliant records retention. This is one example of a gap that must be addressed with regulators, with technology providers, and via employee policies.

## STEP #2. Implement Social Media Policies and Procedures

The next step is to establish internal policies that reflect and support the governance structures, principles, and procedures from Step #1.

As mentioned in the previous section, regulated firms are required to establish and document an employee social media policy. For most other firms, it generally makes sense to stipulate what's out of bounds and optionally to proactively guide employees on how to do social media right.

Everyone from legal and risk management, to human resources, to marketing, sales, communication, and more should be consulted when creating this document—though ultimately it's a best practice for the Social Business project owner to own the overall policies and procedures to ensure they are communicated and enforced. Sometimes there isn't a good one-size-fits-all policy for an entire organization, and individual departments or supervisors need to craft their own policies or addenda. In such a case, it is important to maintain a central point of governance to maintain consistency across the enterprise.

Once adopted, the social media policy should be frequently analyzed and revised, at least annually. It's a living document that must respond to changing circumstances, regulations, and new technological developments. Supervisors—or in financial services, compliance officers—need to be designated to assume responsibility for training and enforcement of the policy through spot-checking or certification.

Most policies govern the types of accounts that can be created (e.g., Facebook Business Pages might be permissible, but not Facebook personal profiles), who is permitted to create them, and which content is appropriate to publish, including guidance about copyright law. They also specify when to use disclaimers, how to manage and close these accounts, and which records need to be maintained. The policy may also cover the life cycle of an account to address what happens when an employee joins the company with his or her own social media account and subsequently leaves.

Account ownership can be contentious, so establishing rules in this area from the outset is very beneficial. Some companies choose to keep social media accounts purely professional, for the benefit of the business. Others operate more in a gray area, where employees can mix personal and professional contacts and mingle their activity in different contexts.

Policies should be clear about enforcement mechanisms, oversight and supervision, and the consequences for professionals if they violate the terms. Clearly state what are grounds for employee termination versus which behaviors are more adequately addressed through probation (e.g., profanity or inappropriate behavior in social media posts representing the company).

Relating to questions of decorum, social media discussion moderators should communicate a clear statement of which type of post demands deletion. As discussed in Chapter 4, some organizations such as Smucker's have faced consumer backlash for deleting negative social media comments, so it's important for the ground rules to be established up front. In addition to standard conduct codes that address issues such as profanity, hate speech, harassment, and bullying speech, some policies take on more social media–specific issues, including best practices and etiquette for each site (e.g., appropriate numbers of posts per day, protocol for friending/following, and conventions like #TBT on Facebook), transparency and openness in interactions, and keeping a respectful attitude.

Medical nonprofit Mayo Clinic has done an excellent job of crafting a short and simple social media policy incorporating many of these best practices, shown in the following sidebar.

### Mayo Clinic's Social Media Guidelines for Employees

*Source: http://sharing.mayoclinic.org/guidelines/for-mayo-clinic-employees/*

The following are guidelines for Mayo Clinic employees and students who participate in social media. Social media includes personal blogs and other websites, including Facebook, LinkedIn, Twitter, YouTube, or others. These guidelines apply whether employees and students are posting to their own sites or commenting on other sites:

- Follow all applicable Mayo Clinic policies. For example, you must not share confidential or proprietary information about Mayo Clinic and you must maintain patient privacy. Among the policies most pertinent to this discussion are those concerning patient confidentiality, government affairs, mutual respect, political activity, computer, email, & Internet use, the Mayo Clinic Integrity Program, photography and video, and release of patient information to media.

- Write in the first person. Where your connection to Mayo Clinic is apparent, make it clear that you are speaking for yourself and not on behalf of Mayo Clinic. In those circumstances, you should include this disclaimer: "The views expressed on this [blog; website] are my own and do not reflect the views of my employer." Consider adding this language in an "About me" section of your blog or social media profile.

- If you identify your affiliation to Mayo Clinic, your social media activities should be consistent with Mayo's high standards of professional conduct.

- If you communicate in the public internet about Mayo Clinic or Mayo Clinic–related matters, you must disclose your connection with Mayo Clinic and your role at Mayo.

- Be professional, use good judgment, and be accurate and honest in your communications; errors, omissions, or unprofessional language or behavior reflect poorly on Mayo, and may result in liability for you or Mayo Clinic. Be respectful and professional to fellow employees, business partners, competitors, and patients.

- Ensure that your social media activity does not interfere with your work commitments.

- Mayo Clinic strongly discourages "friending" of patients on social media websites. Staff in patient care roles generally should not initiate or accept "friend" requests except in unusual circumstances such as the situation where an in-person friendship predates the treatment relationship.

- Mayo Clinic discourages staff in management/supervisory roles from initiating "friend" requests with employees they manage. Managers/supervisors may accept "friend" requests if initiated by the employee, and if the manager/supervisor does not believe it will negatively impact the work relationship.

- Mayo Clinic does not endorse people, products, services, and organizations. Official Mayo Clinic accounts should not be used to provide such endorsements. For personal social media accounts where your connection to Mayo Clinic is apparent, you should be careful to avoid implying that an endorsement of a person or product is on behalf of Mayo Clinic, rather than a personal endorsement. As an example, LinkedIn users may endorse individuals or companies, but may not use Mayo Clinic's name in connection with the endorsement, state or imply that the endorsement is on behalf of Mayo Clinic, or state specifically that the endorsement is based on work done at Mayo Clinic.

- Unless approved by the Center for Social Media, your social media name, handle, and URL should not include Mayo Clinic's name or logo.

If you have any questions about what is appropriate to include in your social media profile(s), contact socialmediacenter@mayo.edu.

Like Mayo Clinic, many other organizations have decided to share their social media policies on their public websites, perhaps to help others and to make them easily accessible for staff as well as interested customers and partners. Social Media Governance has created a helpful index to many of these, spanning public and private sectors, various industries, and geographic regions; you can find it at http://www.socialmediagovernance.com/policies.

## STEP #3. Develop Ongoing Employee Training, Empowerment, and Safeguards

After your policies and procedures are established and have full cross-functional buy-in, training and educating employees on them is a critical next step. Include social media training in your new-hire onboarding and provide annual updates. In regulated industries, it's helpful to document training when it takes place, and to require every company employee to review the policy each year, perhaps asking that all employees sign a declaration of renewed understanding. This should apply broadly, not just to personnel using social media for business. Many companies focused on enabling the subset of employees participating in Social Business forget the importance of training everyone else—in the Facebook era, any employee or associate that identifies himself or herself as affiliated with your company instantly becomes a digital brand ambassador.

Knowing that some employees may be reluctant to adopt social media at all, it's a good idea to start any training with an overview of *why* Social Business is worth the investment of time and effort it requires. From there, employees at all levels must be informed about which content to share, with whom they can share it, and what they shouldn't be sharing.

Employees should be reminded about best practices for keeping their personal and professional lives separate on social media. They should also be warned not to establish relationships with working groups or other collectives online that could inadvertently lead them to reveal sensitive information about their job or about the brand.

## STEP #4. Implement IT Systems

Digital communication on social networks requires close coordination and partnership between the legal/compliance and IT functions. Especially for larger organizations with more than a few employees and multiple Social Business use cases, use of technology systems is critical to efficiently scale governance and compliance.

As we'll discuss in Chapter 12, the enforcement of company social media policies, from supervision (pre- and post-review) and recordkeeping to e-discovery, monitoring, and data-leak prevention, should be fully or largely automated through the use of technology. Otherwise, the staffing requirements can quickly become insupportable.

## Summary

Today's legal, risk, and compliance teams must mobilize to help their organizations navigate the challenges and opportunities in the Social Business era. In times like these of seismic change, doing nothing is not an option.

For many businesses, the greatest challenges may be cultural. Especially in highly regulated industries, organizational norms and policies established decades ago for a much slower-moving and offline world do not obviously translate into a social, always-connected world. But forge ahead we must. Chief legal and risk officers must proactively educate themselves and their staff on the latest technologies—as is true for other functional leaders, traditional roles and mindsets must evolve to adapt to today's reality of constant disruptive innovation. Though the optimal level of risk is rarely zero, general counsels and heads of risk must strive to lead their organizations in mitigating strategic, legal, market, reputation, regulatory, and network threats and risk.

Even regulators have come to embrace Social Business and are doing their part to update rules and laws accordingly. Nevertheless, the constantly evolving nature of the technology landscape creates a moving target, as evidenced by the sudden rise of mobile messaging apps such as WhatsApp, Facebook Messenger, and Snapchat, for which the integration capabilities for supervision and archiving didn't exist as of the writing of this manuscript.

The winners of tomorrow will be those who view these disruptive technological changes as a call to action; the losers will be those who are unable to see—or refuse to see—a way forward.

## 12

*"Information technology and business are becoming inextricably interwoven. I don't think anybody can talk meaningfully about one without talking about the other."*
—Bill Gates

# The Changing IT and Information Security Landscape

Every sector in every region around the world is being transformed by the onslaught of disruptive consumer technologies. Pushed by their customers, general managers, heads of sales and service, chief marketing officers, and VPs of recruiting know that they face a Social Business Imperative—that every company today must become a high-technology company, and that every leader must master innovation as part of his or her role. They and their teams are rushing to keep up with today's social, always-connected customer, and they need IT's help.

Unfortunately, in some companies, IT is viewed as the keeper of legacy systems rather than as a partner in innovation. This perception and often reality both must change. In a world where social, mobile, and digital technologies permeate every aspect of life and work, IT has a critical leadership role to play in helping CEOs re-architect their business models and business practices around today's social, always-connected customer and take full advantage of the tremendous data opportunity.

Before they can blossom in this role, IT departments need to shift their culture and mindset from command and control to more agile, from defense only to also playing offense, from infrastructure only to also fostering innovation. This change must start at the top, with the chief information officer (CIO). To once again become the ones others look to for technology guidance on Social Business and other strategic initiatives, IT departments must do three things.

First, they must streamline their legacy systems and infrastructure, so that "keeping the lights on" doesn't consume the entirety of their resources, attention, and focus.

As Ron Kifer, now retired VP of Global IT at HP, says, "It is tough to be strategic when your pants are on fire." It's beyond the scope of this chapter and book to discuss all the ways this can and should happen, but I will say that cloud computing is providing CIOs with a great opportunity to outsource while upgrading much of their legacy infrastructure.

Second, although many IT staffs are already well versed in the risks of social media, they must also become experts in the business growth opportunities on social media. This is not easy to do. Just as salespeople and marketers today are confronted with a newly empowered customer who can and prefers to do her own product research online and make her own buying decisions, so too are IT departments confronted with newly empowered business leaders and employees who can research technologies and vendors online and want to drive their own enterprise software buying decisions. IT leaders must develop a deep understanding of both the business and the range of technology solutions on the market, and then be able to bring new knowledge, partners, and thinking to their conversations with their business counterparts that those business leaders wouldn't be able to find on their own from Google or talking with a vendor.

Finally, CIOs, in partnership with information security (InfoSec), legal, compliance, and HR leaders, must address the risks and threats of these digital initiatives, including the ramifications of employees bringing their own devices and applications to work. Today's constantly connected consumers are also your employees, and they— rather than your IT department—are now in full control of their own technology. Employees have their personal Facebook, LinkedIn, and Twitter accounts, which they could (*and in many cases should*) be checking during work hours on work devices. They can download software applications from the cloud or use a web-based tool that hasn't been reviewed or approved by the IT department. They own their own smartphones and laptops, making it possible for them to transfer data back and forth between their corporate and personal machines, or even access corporate data remotely. The new reality is that consumerized IT is dispersed and decentralized, creating fresh challenges—and opportunities—for businesses.

No doubt today's IT departments must up their defensive game to address these new realities, yet playing defense alone is not enough. The new possibilities stemming from digital, social, and mobile technologies create opportunities to redefine nearly every business process and to create completely new products and services—and CIOs must rise to the occasion to facilitate the company's exploitation of these opportunities.

## The Age of the Chief Innovation Officer

The demands on CIOs have never been greater—but then the opportunities to have a profound impact on the organization have never been greater, either. As we have detailed throughout the course of this book, social media in particular is full of business opportunity—in fact, it has become a business *imperative* by virtue of improving customer relevancy, accelerating growth, and enabling new business models.

So where should CIOs begin? They should sit down with their business partners to review and prioritize their various technology initiatives, including Social Business. Chances are good there are already numerous Social Business projects under way. IT's job is to determine which ones offer the greatest opportunities and which ones pose the greatest threats, and then focus resources and attention there.

Here are some questions that may help in determining priorities and fit in areas where IT can play the most important and impactful role:

- Which current Social Business initiatives are currently under way across the organization? Are there areas where IT could add value versus slowing things down?

- How is Social Business potentially disruptive to your core business model? Which new adjacent or completely new technology-enabled businesses or business practices should you be thinking about and testing?

- What technologies should you build and which vendors could you partner with to enable your organization to better adapt to and serve the needs of today's digital customer (and employee)?

- How do emerging business priorities rank against the previously set IT agenda? How agile does the IT organization need to be to keep up with the rapid pace of change in consumer technology?

- What is the right operating model for IT involvement that accelerates and bolsters our efforts while still ensuring our business feels ownership and accountability for doing its part to drive innovation?

- How does IT make the current effort more effective and strategic, perhaps by integrating with existing systems or helping to spread best practices to other regions and business units?

## Consumerization of IT

In the past, IT organizations dictated the technology used by employees. Employees had little choice but to fall in line to get their jobs done. Google, smartphones, LinkedIn, and Dropbox have changed all of this. Except in perhaps very highly regulated organizations, gone are the days of corporate IT-issued, totally locked-down BlackBerry devices. Employees won't have it.

Employees want to check their work email and also watch a YouTube video without having to carry two devices. They want the ever-advancing features offered by consumer gadgets, such as Apple watches and tablets. They want to access a slew of mobile apps, including productivity apps that could help them work faster and more efficiently. They want to "multiscreen"—that is, depending on where they happen to be and what they happen to be doing, they want to use a device of their choosing that is best suited for the task at hand.

From the perspective of many business leaders, the consumerization of IT has been a boon, increasing productivity, streamlining expenses, keeping employees happy, and even helping to recruit new ones, especially millennials. But IT consumerization also poses significant risks to organizations. For instance, losing the device or having your account hacked could potentially compromise sensitive company-owned information. IT and InfoSec teams must manage the delicate balance of empowering while protecting the business and employees, of enabling the tremendous productivity gains from these devices and apps while mitigating the most serious threats they introduce. As part of this balancing act, two primary aspects need to be managed: bring your own device and bring your own apps.

From iPhones and iPads to Android devices and laptops, "bring your own device" (BYOD) is firmly entrenched across most organizations, whether or not it's the official policy. Just as today's consumers value ease and convenience, so too do employees.

For most IT departments, it's not merely that they have lost control—they often don't even have visibility. Thirty percent or more of BYOD is invisible to IT departments, according to a recent report by Ovum. More than half of the staff interviewed in this report said they used a personal smartphone or tablet to access corporate data, but 62% did not have a corporate IT policy (at least that they're aware of) guiding what they should and should not do. IT organizations must come up with strategies to manage the trend in BYOD, embracing its possibilities rather than fighting or ignoring it.

These same BYOD rules and considerations extend beyond hardware devices to social media accounts and other apps. "Bring your own application" (BYOA)—sometimes known as "shadow IT"—describes the practice of employees and departments other than the IT department deploying or utilizing applications without approval or even knowledge from the IT department. BYOA can range from using Gmail, GoToMeeting, or TripIt for work purposes to responding to customers on Twitter and LinkedIn. Less than a decade ago, organizations were able to dictate and limit the software that was downloaded onto corporate devices, and employees had little choice but to use it to get their work done. Nowadays employees don't even need to download the software they want to use; often they can access it from their BYOD smartphone or tablet, totally undetected by the IT department.

BYOD and cloud apps have enabled the rise of shadow IT. Any employee can access and sign up through any device, including his or her personal phone. This proposition has been too enticing for most employees to resist. In a survey conducted by Stratecast, 80% of employees admitted to using non-approved software as service applications in their jobs. The survey estimated that upwards of 35% of "software as a service" applications are purchased and used without corporate IT oversight. And chances are, while the application in question may not have been approved by the IT department, it was likely given the green light by the head of the employee's own department, sanctioning its use. In one case, a big tech company audited itself a few years ago and discovered that at least 67 different internal groups were using Salesforce.com. The company's IT department did not know about *any* of them.

It's not a matter of employees going rogue. Facing mounting pressure, most employees just want to get their jobs done. Nearly half of the respondents in the Stratecast survey said that they opted for a particular application because they were familiar with it and could avoid a steep learning curve. Employees also realize the risk involved, with one-third or more acknowledging that they have a high level of concern for potential problems such as theft of sensitive corporate data, compromised accounts, lost or deleted data, viruses and malware, failure to comply with regulations, or data breaches.

# Social Media Policies and Training

IT departments need to address the risks of BYOD, BYOA, and shadow IT head-on. This means establishing a clear InfoSec policy that aligns with business objectives and, most importantly, that is owned and enforced by business leaders, and integrated with employees' overall social media policy as described in Chapter 11. An overly heavy-handed policy, however, will most likely backfire. Today's employees expect the freedom to pick the devices and applications that work best for them without having to jump through hoops to get their jobs done.

IT teams can further safeguard the organization by installing antivirus and security software to protect the organization as a whole (and employees from themselves). They can also incorporate tighter controls for the most sensitive data, such as encrypting any database containing personally identifiable customer data.

With the changing demographics of employees—particularly the arrival of millennials and Generation Z, digital natives who are always connected—organizations need to incorporate social media as part of their new-hire onboarding and ongoing training. Employees must be reminded that the small bits of personal information that they share on social media might seem insignificant on their own but could be pieced together and used as part of a social engineering attack. Business leaders should understand that the cost of a data breach is not just the data itself but the loss of customer trust in the brand.

One common InfoSec strategy these days is to draw the line on company information. Organizations need to help their staff understand how their data is classified. What is deemed sensitive? What can be freely and openly shared—or is even encouraged to be shared? What can employees disclose about the company on social networks, including personal and more private networks? Employees need to recognize that when they identify themselves as an employee of the company, they become a representative of the company in the digital world (even if they disclose that "all thoughts are mine").

Today's leading IT and information security organizations are always evaluating emerging social and cloud apps likely to be used within their organizations, prioritizing the top threats, translating these into simple and easy-to-understand guidelines, and then working with business leaders to require periodic training to be conducted in ways that make employees feel self-motivated to take extra precautions on behalf of the company. For example, to drive home the potential threats, one InfoSec leader divided employees into different teams, had them simulate how a scam operates and how quickly it can infiltrate an organization, and then encouraged the employees to come up with ways to prevent such a threat from happening for real.

## Summary

Today, every company faces the Social Business Imperative. Customers and employees alike are constantly connected, and social media is where they spend the most time while connected. As social network sites and mobile messaging apps become much more than 'liking' and messages, expanding into realms as far and wide as wearables, connected cars, on-demand services, and payments, social media will truly permeate every part of an organization internally and externally. The implications for businesses are enormous, but business leaders need IT's partnership in ideas and in action to manage these threats and opportunities.

In parallel, the fact that employees' personal online activities and apps can have a deep impact on companies presents a double-edged sword for today's businesses and IT organizations. On the one hand, it is a boon for productivity and employee engagement. On the other hand, it exposes the organization and employees themselves to a host of new risks, such as social engineering scams, security vulnerabilities, and data breaches.

IT departments are in an unprecedented position. Although they don't have the monopoly over the organization's technology that they once did, IT leaders and staff are playing a more critical role now than ever before in both innovating and protecting the organization and its core assets. Education, training, policies, security software—all of that is easy. Much harder is making the shift in culture and mindset from rigid to nimble, from complete to prioritized, from static to moving target, from infrastructure to innovation. It won't be easy, but organizations have no choice: Today's social, always-connected customer and employee demands information technology leadership.

# Closing Remarks

*"Everything changes and nothing stands still."*
—Heraclitus of Ephesus (535–475 BC)

We are today in the midst of a consumer revolution, started by but no longer limited to millennials. Traditional institutions, from brands to governments to employers, no longer dictate the terms of engagement. Marketers, advertisers, PR, HR, and IT professionals no longer control brand reputation, messaging, or even the enterprise technologies used at a company. Social media hasn't just created yet another channel in which to do business; it has launched an entirely new way of doing business based on responsive engagement, transparency, and community—the Social Business Imperative. In an era when every 60 seconds sees 100,000 new tweets, 6 million additional Facebook views, and more than 100 new LinkedIn accounts, content, influence, and authenticity have become king.

We know that the economic promise of Social Business is enormous. As we shared in the Introduction, McKinsey estimates as much as $1.3 trillion of economic value could be created by adopting social media across all business sectors.[1] In my own and my colleagues' work at Hearsay Social, we regularly see Social Business programs driving double-digit percentage lifts in new client acquisition, loyalty and upselling, and NPS, *controlling for all else.*

Yet many organizations have yet to fully embrace and actualize the gains from Social Business.

Why this reluctance? The primary reason is that Social Business requires change management—serious, integrated, sustained investment of resources, time, and commitment across multiple stakeholders. This can be daunting, as suggested by the focus of Part III of this book. A second reason for the failure to implement a sustainable social media strategy is that success metrics are sometimes nonobvious, complex, or long-term oriented, making it all too easy for busy and risk-averse leaders to dismiss the opportunity as "unproven."

---

1. http://www.mckinsey.com/insights/high_tech_telecoms_internet/the_social_economy

My friend Chris Heuer, founder of Social Media Club, describes the conundrum perfectly: "Most businesses are not going to be early adopters of massive transformations."[2] Yet massive transformations all around us are already disrupting and destroying many traditional business models, and the accelerated pace of disruption means that anyone who isn't an early adopter may be too late.

The cost of missing out on the Social Business Imperative now far outweighs the cost of getting and staying on this digital frontier. Customers, prospects, employees, and future recruits are all spending countless hours each day on social media, and its popularity is only increasing. Your business *must* engage on social media with those users, or it won't survive.

The coming years will see customer engagement on social networks continue to multiply. In addition, sharing and connectivity will extend beyond the PCs, smartphones, and tablets of today to appliances, cars, and everyday objects—the Internet of Things. The data created, captured, and analyzed across all current and future connected nodes will enable unprecedented efficiency, personalization, and convenience—but will also engender a host of new legal, regulatory, and cybersecurity concerns that must be addressed. More than at any other time in history, the future is full of unfathomable opportunity and possibility.

As Ralph Waldo Emerson once said, "This time, like all times, is a very good one, if we but know what to do with it." We have entered a brave new world, and there's no turning back now, so let us embrace it.

Thank you for reading and best of luck on your Social Business journey!

@clarashih

---

2. http://oursocialtimes.com/what-is-social-business/

# Index

## Numbers

# REGISTER YOUR PRODUCT at informit.com/register

## Access Additional Benefits and SAVE 35% on Your Next Purchase

- Download available product updates.
- Access bonus material when applicable.
- Receive exclusive offers on new editions and related products.
  (Just check the box to hear from us when setting up your account.)
- Get a coupon for 35% for your next purchase, valid for 30 days. Your code will be available in your InformIT cart. (You will also find it in the Manage Codes section of your account page.)

Registration benefits vary by product. Benefits will be listed on your account page under Registered Products.

---

**InformIT.com—The Trusted Technology Learning Source**
InformIT is the online home of information technology brands at Pearson, the world's foremost education company. At InformIT.com you can
- Shop our books, eBooks, software, and video training.
- Take advantage of our special offers and promotions (informit.com/promotions).
- Sign up for special offers and content newsletters (informit.com/newsletters).
- Read free articles and blogs by information technology experts.
- Access thousands of free chapters and video lessons.

**Connect with InformIT—Visit informit.com/community**
Learn about InformIT community events and programs.

# informIT.com
the trusted technology learning source

Addison-Wesley · Cisco Press · IBM Press · Microsoft Press · Pearson IT Certification · Prentice Hall · Que · Sams · VMware Press

ALWAYS LEARNING                                                                 PEARSON

Social media is now the dominant online activity and drives more website traffic than online search. The implications for businesses are as profound as the rise of Google fifteen years ago. Delegating this opportunity to a social media team is not enough—today's leaders must *personally* grasp the tectonic changes arising from today's social, always-connected customer, and must re-architect business practices and models accordingly.

In *The Social Business Imperative,* Silicon Valley entrepreneur and renowned thought leader Clara Shih identifies powerful new opportunities created by social media across the entire customer lifecycle. The functional breadth of this book is critical for today's leaders, who must deliver a consistent experience across every brand touchpoint, from marketing to sales to customer service, online to offline, because that is what the customer expects.

This guide is a must-read for all professionals—from boards of directors to front-line sales managers, and from chief marketing officers to recruiting, IT, and compliance directors—who need to understand the digital transformation taking place not only in their own department but in all departments. Only with this broader understanding can functional leaders effectively collaborate on delivering a cohesive customer experience spanning previous organizational silos.

Going far beyond her global best-seller *The Facebook Era,* Clara offers unprecedented insights into why and how traditional organizations must re-imagine their existing business processes to capture "the digital last mile" across social media, mobile messaging apps, the Internet of Everything, and the collaborative economy. Drawing on her immense experience helping Fortune 500 companies operationalize digital transformation to drive measurable uplift in sales and loyalty, Shih also presents powerful new case studies spanning multiple industries and ... by Parker.

**CLARA SHIH** is founder and CEO of Hearsay Social, an enterprise software company whose predictive, omnichannel marketing platform helps financial advisors engage clients across all social media while complying with industry regulations. Clara has been named one of *Fortune*'s "Most Powerful Women Entrepreneurs," *Fast Company*'s "Most Influential People in Technology," *BusinessWeek*'s "Top Young Entrepreneurs," and both *Fortune*'s and *Ad Age*'s "40 Under 40." She was also named a "Young Global Leader" by the World Economic Forum. Clara is a member of the Starbucks board of directors and has served in a variety of roles at Google, Microsoft, and Salesforce.com. She holds a B.S. and an M.S. in computer science from Stanford, as well as an M.S. in Internet studies from Oxford.

informit.com/ph
socialbizimperative.com
facebook.com/socialbizimperative
linkedin.com/in/clarashih
twitter.com/clarashih

Cover photograph by Gonzalo Aragon, ShutterSto...
Cover design by Chuti Prasertsith

♻ Text printed on recycled paper

COMMUNITY
THRIFT STORE
$ 1.75
01-08

**BUSINESS AND MANAGEMENT**

ISBN-13: 978-0-13-426343-4
ISBN-10:    0-13-426343-X

5 2 4 9 9

9 780134 263434

**$24.99 USA** / $30.99 CANADA

PRENTICE HALL

ALWAYS LEARNING

PEARSON